RUPERT RED TWO

RUPERT RED TWO

A Fighter Pilot's Life
from Thunderbolts to Thunderchiefs

JACK BROUGHTON

ZENITH PRESS

First published in 2007 by Zenith Press, an imprint of MBI Publishing Company LLC, Galtier Plaza, Suite 200, 380 Jackson Street, St. Paul, MN 55101 USA

Zenith Press titles are also available at discounts in bulk quantity for industrial or sales-promotional use. For details write to Special Sales Manager at MBI Publishing Company, Galtier Plaza, Suite 200, 380 Jackson Street, St. Paul, MN 55101 USA.

To find out more about our books, join us online at www.zenithpress.com.

Designer: Jennifer Maass

Printed in the United States of America

Library of Congress Cataloging-in-Publication Data

Broughton, Jack, 1926-
  Rupert red two : a fighter pilot's life from Thunderbolts to Thunderchiefs / by Jack Broughton.
     p. cm.
  ISBN-13: 978-0-7603-3217-7 (hardbound w/ jacket)
  1. Broughton, Jack, 1926- 2. Air pilots, Military—United States—Biography. I. Title.
UG626.2.B76A3 2008
358.4092—dc22
[B]
                          2007021896

On the cover: Painting by Jerry Roth

All photographs from the author's collection

CONTENTS

A FIGHTER PILOT'S FIGHTERS

P-47 Thunderbolt
Germany. I thought the Jug was as large as a fighter could be, but after nine hundred hours flying time, it was like sitting in an easy chair.

P-51 Mustang
Germany, Nellis AFB, and Luke AFB. Truly a classic, no matter what the mission.

F-80C Shooting Star
Nellis AFB, Korea, and Luke AFB. Our first combat jet was highly maneuverable and an excellent weapons platform.

F-84E Thunderjet
Nellis AFB, Korea, and Luke AFB. The E got its combat baptism testing the Oerlikon rocket in Korea, and the G gained fame with the Thunderbirds.

F-84F Thunderjet
Luke AFB. We won the Bendix trans-continental race with this fighter, then put it to work as the Thunderbird's first swept-wing aircraft.

F-86A Saber
Nellis AFB. The A was the first in a highly successful series of swept-wing fighters.

F-86D Saber
Vincent AFB. This air defense version (D and L) flew sort of like an 86 should, but it was often tough to get its rockets on target.

F-100C Super Saber
Nellis AFB. The 100C took the Thunderbirds supersonic.

F-101B Voodoo
Tyndall AFB. It felt like trying to balance on the point of a pencil, wondering if I was going to pitch up or the canopy was going to fly off

F-102 Delta Dagger
Tyndall AFB. The dependable deuce did its air defense mission well, but you could also rack it around the sky in style.

F-104 Starfighter
Tyndall AFB. The sleek, futuristic Starfighter was a ball to fly, and you could go from takeoff to way up there in nothing flat—but then you had to head for home before you ran out of fuel.

F-105D Thunderchief
Southeast Asia. The Thud shed its mantle of a low-level, high-speed nuclear fighter-bomber to become the conventional-weapons workhorse striking Hanoi and North Vietnam.

F-106A Delta Dart
Minot AFB. The six shined as a fighter-interceptor, claimed all sorts of records, and she is the one I would like to have parked in my garage.

FOREWORD

Dr. Richard P. Hallion
United States Air Force Historian, 1991–2002

History records that the name Jack Broughton is a proud one, associated with two great and legendary fighters. One was an eighteenth-century boxer, the first to give rules to pugilism, a profound and gifted student of the ring who was determined to impart as much expertise as he could to those who would follow. The other was a twentieth-century fighter pilot who, with equal skill, courage, and dedication, fought in a far more lethal arena, one of four dimensions: height, reach, breadth, and speed. Likewise known for his bare-knuckles approach to combat, he was at least equally committed to his men and their welfare. This book is about him, is by him. But before discussing it, some introductory words are in order.

Flying in a jet fighter is difficult to describe. To those who have experienced it, no explanation is necessary. To those who have not, no explanation can really suffice. Describing the *piloting* experience is more challenging yet. No one has ever done it better than Jack Broughton, who has that airman's rarest combination of talents: a record of uncommon aerial skill and valor crossed with proven skills of insight and narration, and thus the ability to impart the experience of seeing the world through the cockpit of some F-numbered brute.

One of the very best to have ever strapped into a fighter and taken off into harm's way, Col. Jacksel "Jack" Broughton first burst upon the public scene in 1969 with publication of *Thud Ridge*, a remarkable memoir that, nearly forty years after its publication, is still the best Vietnam combat memoir ever written. Of him another legendary airman, Leo Thorsness—Medal of Honor recipient, MiG and SAM killer, and unconquered prisoner of war—said, "Jack Broughton expected a lot from every pilot in the gaggle, but no more than he gave." As the spare, blunt language of *Thud Ridge* revealed, he gave a lot. A personal chronicle presenting the staggeringly frustrating, costly, and challenging air war that Lyndon Johnson and Robert McNamara forced upon the American military, it had, and still has, no equal. Written from a fighter pilot's perspective, it viewed the war through the cockpit glass of the massive Republic F-105D Thunderchief, the "Thud" of the title, as flak, surface-to-air missiles, and MiGs did their worst. (The "Ridge" was self-explanatory: a spiny range of jagged, brutal terrain over which too many of Jack Broughton's comrades were shot down.) It was an angry book; as its reviewer in the Air Force's own *Air University Review* noted somewhat uncomfortably in 1970, "Detachment is not Colonel Broughton's forte." Of course not! Nor did it *need* to be: his book was an angry challenge to America's political and military leaders to do better by their air warriors, for they had already done their worst.

I first read *Thud Ridge* (and first became aware of Jack Broughton) as a college student in 1969. At the time Jane Fonda was railing against the war, and good men betrayed by Washington politicians were languishing in the Hanoi Hilton. Pseudointellectuals on

American campuses were preaching that Stalinist totalitarians represented the wave of the future. Furthermore, largely self-styled "military thinkers," most of whom had never been closer to a cockpit than their first-class seat in an airliner, enunciated "the limits of air power" with that easy veneer of authoritativeness possessed by all too many among the university, think-tank, and war-college set. It is one of only two books I read every year (the other is Herman Wouk's *The Caine Mutiny*), and it is not too much to state that it gave voice to a pervasive discontent within the joint-service fighter community, one that played a pivotal and shaping role in transforming training, doctrine, policy, and even the acquisition of future combat systems. In the Gulf War of 1991, the apotheosis of American airpower, we can see the logical outcome of the transformation in American airpower first called for by the legions of airmen Jack Broughton gave voice to in *Thud Ridge*. He followed that book with another passionate account of the Vietnam air war, *Going Downtown*, which, more broadly written and detached, might have been subtitled *The Rest of the Story*. It, too, is a page-turner, a necessary waypoint for anyone attempting to understand America's air war in Southeast Asia. After several civilian ventures, he had moved on to Edwards Air Force Base, to join the Rockwell Aircraft team shepherding the B-1 program through resumed flight testing following the dreadful, hollow-force stringencies of the Carter years, where military airmen could not even get new flight suits to replace their worn ones.

Thud Ridge and *Going Downtown* offered hints to the reader that their author had an extensive fighter background. That background is the subject of this book, altogether a happier, more pleasant, and more evocative look at fighter life—specifically U.S. Air Force fighter life—than its predecessors. It is about what is, undoubtedly, the Golden Age of the American fighter, that period from the late Second World War through the buildup to Vietnam that coincided with three great and transforming revolutions in aeronautics. The first was the invention of the jet engine, which took airplanes beyond five hundred miles per hour. The second was the revolution in high-speed aerodynamics, typified by the introduction of the swept wing , the delta wing, and the Coke-bottle or wasp-waisted fuselages resulting from the use of the area rule developed by Richard Whitcomb of NASA. Less obviously, this revolution included the introduction of the very thin wing (largely unseen since the early 1920s) and the all-moving tail (likewise, largely unseen since the time of World War I). The third was the gradual development of sophisticated airborne electronics, the path to the "weapons systems airplane" typified by interceptors such as the F-106, missile-armed fighters like the F-4, and attack aircraft such as the F-111.

Between 1945 and the early 1960s, the United States acquired over twenty thousand fighter aircraft. While its first—aircraft like the F-80 and F-84—were straight-wing, low-powered aircraft largely combining the aerodynamics of propeller-driven airplanes like the P-47 Thunderbolt and P-51 Mustang, with the new miracle of the jet engine, its last were Mach-2.0-plus machines like the F-106 Delta Dart, capable of operating up to sixty thousand feet and zoom-climbing well beyond that, armed with atomic-warhead-equipped missiles. These were airplanes that defined aeronautics, and the roster of their names, to this day, brings forth an evocative series of images to anyone who ever saw—and especially those who flew—them: Shooting Star, Thunderjet, Sabre, Thunderstreak, Scorpion, Starfire, Super Sabre, Voodoo, Delta Dagger, Starfighter, Thunderchief, Delta Dart. The latter six were the 5,525 proud birds of the "Century Series," the F-100, F-101, F-102, F-104, F-105, and F-106. All of these were flown by men who spoke a new routine language of flight: G-suit, Machmeter, ejection seat, gas turbine, speed of sound, afterburner, inertial coupling, adverse yaw, slab-tail, aerial refueling.

The USAF fighter force of the 1940s through early 1960s was a force in constant transition, from the last propeller-driven days of the army air forces to the young, jet-powered adulthood of the independent air force. It had been born of an occupation air arm in the late 1940s, with Thunderbolts in Germany, Mustangs in the Far East, and the new jets at home. Aces abounded, together with gifted youngsters such as Jack Broughton (West Point, Class of 1945). It was a time of risk: somewhere, every day, an air force fighter crashed. To a generation of airmen schooled in the hard world of combat against the Luftwaffe or Japanese airmen in the Second World War, the loss rates and challenges of peacetime flying were acceptable. But it was a hard and unforgiving school that shaped a tough mindset and made one either very professional, or very dead, very quickly.

Jack Broughton went through that crucible, and not only survived, but thrived. Having started his air force career flying the last of the service's propeller-driven fighters, the P-47 Thunderbolt and the P-51 Mustang, in Europe, he came back to America, joined the jet age, and went off to Korea, flying back-to-back fighter-bomber tours in America's first jet, the F-80 Shooting Star and its slightly later stablemate, the Republic F-84 Thunderjet. It was a hard war, far more than is commonly realized, with unforgiving weather, mountainous terrain, a merciless foe, and underpowered and sometimes inadequate airplanes. But they made a difference, as North Korean leader Kim Il-Sung frantically informed the Soviet Union's "Deeply Respected Josef Vissarionovich Stalin":

> The enemy's air force numbering about a thousand airplanes of various types, facing no rebuff from our side, totally dominate the air space and perform air raids at the fronts and in the rear day and night. At the fronts, under the air cover of hundreds of airplanes, the motorized units of the enemy engage us in combat at their free will and inflict great losses to our manpower and destroy our armaments. Moreover, by

> freely destroying railroads and highways, telegraph
> and telephone communications lines, means of trans-
> portation and other facilities, the enemy's air force
> impedes the provision of supplies to our combat
> units and bars maneuvers by our troops, thereby
> making their timely redeployments impossible. We
> experience this difficulty on all fronts.

Jack Broughton's part of that was 114 combat missions in the thick of flak and MiGs. These missions seasoned him and then made of him a gifted fighter leader, one who would need all that skill and experience for what he would experience over a decade hence in another Asian air war, flying another Republic product, the Thud. From Korea he moved into the supersonic, taking over the Thunderbirds flying demonstration team in 1954 and transitioning them from the firmly subsonic straight-wing Thunderjet to the tran-sonic sweptwing Thunderstreak, and on to the supersonic Super Sabre, first of the Century Series. Few could have met the challenge of performing back-to-back transitions in three very different airplanes presenting three very different abilities to maneuver, and thus requir-ing three very different shows. But Broughton did, and though he left the Thunderbirds for ground tours and duty as a military advisor in Turkey, the air force had marked him out for further command.

That command came as an air defender. By now the air force was at the end of the supersonic revolution, and as a service it had experi-enced major transformation as well. In 1949, the Soviet Union had exploded its first atomic bomb, four years after the United States. In the early 1950s it had matched the United States in introducing a supersonic jet fighter, the MiG-19, into service, and testing a hydrogen bomb. And in 1957 Soviet rocket scientists orbited Sputnik. For the United States Air Force, the future looked to be one of nuclear war-fare. Thus, its fighter force increasingly became a force of nuclear-

bomb-equipped fighter-bombers, such as the F-100 and F-105 (ironically, they would go to war as conventional iron-bomb droppers in Southeast Asia), or missile-armed fighters such as the F-101 and F-106, intended to defend the skies of the United States from Soviet nuclear-armed bombers. Pundits might scoff at a Soviet bomber threat, but it was there, in the form of Tupolev's Badger and turboprop Bear. And so, for three winters, Jack Broughton flew as a commander of an F-106 squadron based at Minot, North Dakota, the famed (or infamous) "Northern Tier," patrolling the skies against, quite literally, the Soviet Bear.

From there, it was off to the National War College, two tours in Southeast Asia, and a fateful rendezvous with the Soviet freighter *Turkestan* (but for all that, read *Thud Ridge* and *Going Downtown*). Until then, sit back and strap in—tight. You're joining the U.S. Army Air Force at the end of the Big One. You'll be passing from the era of the propeller-driven airplane to the era of the supersonic jet, flying with an author of impeccable credentials: four Distinguished Flying Crosses, two Silver Stars, the Air Force Cross, over two hundred combat missions deep into enemy territory in three different kinds of fighters in two wars. You'll love it!

CHAPTER 1

STAND UP AND
BE COUNTED

Why does one want to walk on wings? Why force one's body from a plane to make a parachute jump? Why should man want to fly at all? People often ask these questions. But what civilization was not founded on adventure, and how long could one exist without it? Some answer the attainment of knowledge. Some say wealth, or power, is sufficient cause. I believe the risks I take are justified by the sheer love of the life I lead.

—Charles Lindbergh

It seemed like only a few seconds ago that I was sitting on the take-off end of the runway at our air force base just north of Minot, North Dakota, aligning the sophisticated navigation system on my single-seat, sleek and powerful delta-winged F-106 fighter interceptor.

It was the best of its kind in the world, with the speed, range, and time-to-climb records to prove it. I went to full throttle, released the brakes, and plugged in the jolting afterburner and she jumped like a thoroughbred breaking from the starting gate. As l broke ground, I still had a mile of that big, long runway in front of me, so I held her on the deck, sucked up the gear, and accelerated. I stood her on her tail and leveled off at forty thousand feet. Actually, it had taken about two minutes. What a kick.

On that August morning in 1963, the sky was clear blue as far as the eye could see. It was visual flight rules all the way to Malmstrom Air Force Base in Montana, home base of my boss, the commander of our air defense sector. My flight plan called for me to be under my own control; I didn't have to talk to any air-traffic controllers, and I was clear to enjoy zipping along at close to the speed of sound.

I put her on autopilot and gazed comfortably at the portion of America and Canada we were assigned to patrol and defend. Canada was just a few miles off my right wing, and the Rocky Mountains were still a few hundred miles ahead. Wherever you looked it was flat, and everything sort of blended together with very few distinguishing features. It looked the same way when you were on the ground. Off to the right, at my two o'clock position, there was a vast expanse of absolutely nothing, and if my eyes could have seen far enough along that line, they would have seen the North Pole. That was the route that attacking Russian bombers would prefer, over the Pole and straight into the American heartland. Our job was to prevent them from doing that, day or night, in any weather, and we did have tough weather in Minot most of the time.

I was on my way to a monthly meeting with my boss. One of the things I wanted to talk about was Project Red Glow, which directed me to cycle my aircraft through an air force–run, civilian-oriented repair depot that was supposed to update the birds with the latest modifications. When our usually dependable Delta Darts returned from those modifications, they were prone to doing strange things, which was very hazardous in our type of work. If you were chasing an unknown bogie at supersonic speed, at night and in severe weather with your nose pointed straight up or straight down and an armed nuclear rocket in your belly, you sure didn't need a crippling aircraft malfunction. In fact, the bird I was flying had only been back a few weeks, but we figured we had already corrected and flight-tested any problems she might have developed.

Suddenly my radarscope gave a quick, lightning-bolt *pfzfft*, and all went silent. The aircraft rolled hard right, and the nose went straight down. Then the stick slammed back between my legs into the front of the ejection seat, and my nose went straight up, with my right hand still on the stick but my right elbow pinned back between the side of the seat and the right cockpit wall. I could not move my right arm, nor would any amount of pressure move the locked stick. The pressure against my right hip was intense.

Punching out was not an option. The success rate of the F-106 ejection seat was zero. Twelve guys had already tried it. None got out. All twelve had augured in and been instantly killed. The seat had never fired. In the spot I was in, pinned against the cockpit wall, even if the seat did fire, the locked stick would have gutted me and amputated my right side from the lower rib cage down.

While still going straight up and rapidly running out of air speed, in what amounted to a vertical stall, I found that by reducing throttle and using my left foot to feed in a little left rudder, I could get the nose to fall off to the left side and down. But as soon as I headed down and my air speed increased past 320 knots, I was snapped straight up again. I repeated the reduced throttle and left-rudder exercise and got the nose down once more, and this time extended the speed brake, which swung the nose slightly above the horizon. That left me with my wings sort of level, stalled out and falling through the sky at a few thousand feet per minute.

The limited controls that I had were pretty squishy, so I tried for a bit more air speed. I passed through 320 knots and did it all over again. I was running out of options, but by using the rudders to skid sideways, I managed to work my way around to a spot about thirty miles north of the Minot runway at thirty thousand feet. I got the landing gear down with only a small pitch-up of the nose that left me in a nose-high position, almost in F-106 landing attitude.

No radio of course meant no contact with Minot tower. They had no idea that I was about to try to pay them a surprise visit in a giant, descending, rudder-exercise stall at 320 knots. Luckily, nobody got in the way, and nothing changed until the tires screeched onto the runway and I established a local land-speed record. The drag chute held, and the brakes did their job.

The fire trucks raced toward the end of the runway to meet me. I got the canopy open, popped my oxygen mask loose, and gave them the thumbs-up signal, so they just followed me as I taxied in. But as I coasted into the squadron parking area, our maintenance crew frantically signaled me to cut the engine and waved the fire guys in. I stop-cocked the throttle and stuffed the safety pins into the ejection seat as one of our crew chiefs ran toward me as fast as he could, carrying an access ladder which he slammed over the canopy rail. By the time I hit the bottom rung of the ladder, I could see the smoke billowing from the aircraft's burning rear end.

When we got the fire out, we discovered that during the depot modification a heat exchanger junction had been improperly reconnected in a manner that would have been almost impossible to detect. That resulted in superheated air from the engine destroying the wire bundles, switches, and other components that usually allowed the pilot to control the aircraft. We could check all our birds for similar discrepancies, make the necessary corrections, and hope it wouldn't happen again. Not so easily correctable, though, was that lethal F-106 ejection seat. I knew immediately that it was my job, as the man running the

5th Fighter Interceptor Squadron, to pursue every possible approach to removing the depot-installed time bombs from our machines and to raise all the hell I could to get a new ejection seat in all 106s.

I couldn't make things happen fast enough. We lost two more pilots just in my squadron, and came close to losing a third. That was it. I contacted my sector and division commanders, and received their concurrence in grounding my entire squadron of twenty-six F-106s. I stipulated that I would always maintain our four hot, five-minute-alert birds, and in case of national emergency my grounding order would be cancelled.

We began systematically disassembling our aircraft to be certain that all systems were functional, properly rigged, and free of FOD (foreign-object damage). We repeated every possible rigging and ballistic check on the ejection seats, but we knew that the real answer to the seat problem was a completely new ejection seat for the F-106.

My inspection program took more time and effort than expected, which did not please Air Defense Command (ADC). More accurately, I think, it was an embarrassment to them. ADC's commanding general, Herbert Thatcher, summoned me to Colorado Springs for an explanation.

The general sat at the head of the table in the conference room, flanked by his staff chiefs, who ranged in rank from two-star general to senior colonel. As a lieutenant colonel, I was the lowest-ranking officer in the room and sat at the opposite end of the general's conference table. I presented what I believed was a highly convincing briefing. I finished with a summation of our inspection results to date, and a recommendation that all F-106 squadrons undergo similar inspections. And I stressed the absolute necessity for a new F-106 ejection seat.

General Thatcher asked me to leave the room while he and his staff conferred. When he called me back in, he came straight to the point. "We appreciate your intentions in this matter, Colonel, but we feel that the interests of the command would be better served by other approaches. My staff will form an inspection team to evaluate the situation and will recommend what, if any, command-wide actions should be pursued. Therefore, I am suggesting that you unground your F-106 aircraft immediately."

I had known General Thatcher for quite awhile. I admired him for his accomplishments and his position. I liked him, and he had given every indication that the feeling was mutual. It was obvious during the ongoing meeting that his staff, especially his deputy commander for maintenance, was pushing him to overrule me. It was also certain that justifying the current situation to Washington had generated high-level pressure on him. But I was also experiencing pressures. I was now the point man, the only spokesman for my dead fellow fighter pilots who had pulled those ejection seat firing handles in vain. I represented all the enlisted airmen, the crew chiefs, and system specialists who were freezing their butts off, day and night, to make our aircraft acceptably safe. A lot of people were betting on me.

For a moment I didn't know how to reply to General Thatcher, and then I knew there was only one thing I could say. "General, if you give me a direct order to unground my aircraft, I'll do it immediately. But if you give me that direct order, sir, the next good guy we kill in a 106 is on you, personally."

The room was dead silent. I had hit the nerve I had aimed for in a very senior fellow aviator. General Thatcher placed his hands on the edge of the table, stood, and paused as he stared directly at me. Then, in a quiet, cold voice, he said, "God damn you Jack Broughton." And with that, and without another glance at me or anybody else, he strode from the room. The meeting was over, and everybody left. Nobody said hello, goodbye, or kiss my ass to me.

I fired up my 106 and flew back to Minot, wondering where I'd be working next week. In spite of all the good lessons I'd learned in the twenty-one years since the day in 1942 that I entered West Point, I still had a lot more to learn. As the hundreds of miles of frozen, snow-covered emptiness coasted by far below, the silence of my cramped cockpit was jammed with my thoughts. Sometimes, when you're cruising in that exclusive fighter-pilot configuration, your thoughts can fly even faster than your aircraft.

I thought I had this routine of being a career-oriented regular air force officer all figured out, but at the moment I wasn't so sure about that. Why was I in the middle of the massive task of trying to make the world's latest and most complex fighter interceptor aircraft safe enough for my pilots and me to accomplish our mission? "They," whoever they were, were supposed to provide us with efficient, combat-ready aircraft. Could one lieutenant colonel and his dedicated squadron correct the deadly inefficiency of the massive air force depot maintenance system? Why was I taking on America's aerospace design and production empires, the Fortune 500 companies who have certified their F-106 ejection seat as completely operational, and who have convinced the top levels of air force management that they know what they're talking about? All I knew was that the F-106 ejection seat did not work and had killed every pilot who had tried to use it. And why had I been stubborn enough to lock horns with the high-ranking general officer who ran the vast Air Defense Command? Face it—a bottle top colonel versus a four star general is bad odds.

Swiveling my head and taking in the vastness of the temporarily friendly sky in front of me seemed to elicit an easy answer. I had accepted command of the 5th Fighter Interceptor Squadron, and every facet of that squadron was my responsibility. Slipshod maintenance and modification practices by a faraway, predominantly civilian organization had made my aircraft unsafe, and while no corrective action was apparent at higher levels of command, my pilots and I were expected to press on as usual. It was implicit in the oath that I had taken in acceptance of a commission as an officer that a situation such as this demanded that I do all in my power to make things right. As an aside, I will not deny that my mother told me that I sometimes reminded her of her rough, tough Irish immigrant father "Bunt" McGinley, who was "always ready for a fight or a frolic."

Being in the middle of such a confrontation is not what I envisioned when I first considered the merits of becoming a military officer. Then, in the early 1940s, as I approached the end of high school, nobody in Rochester, New York, knew very much of anything about the military. Each Armistice Day we bought our Buddy Poppies, and at the eleventh hour of the eleventh day of the eleventh month, the moment the armistice was signed ending World War I, all of America stopped for two minutes as we bowed our heads and remembered those who had died for us in that "war to end all wars." I do not remember any other military-related activities or any participation of real, live veterans. Those of us approaching high school graduation and contemplating college knew that there were military academies called West Point and Annapolis, whose football teams played the annual Army-Navy Game, but nobody thought much, if anything, about going there. It was close to impossible to get accepted at either place. You had to be appointed by a congressman, and everybody knew that those appointments only went to sons of very rich people with strong political connections or to sons of big generals and admirals in Washington, D.C. Besides, you had to be a genius because the academic requirements were so tough. Another consideration was that we had all lived through the Great Depression and knew the value of even a nickel. We knew that you didn't make much money in the military, and I knew from Cliff, an older high school fraternity friend who was in the National Guard, that I made more money a month with my two newspaper delivery routes than the twenty-one dollars a month they paid army privates. Things had started changing quite rapidly as 1940 rolled towards 1941. We all read our newspapers more carefully. There were more and more good war movies to see, and preceding the movies were the all-important newsreel, the only live, moving picture we had of action around the globe. The newsreels always showed some of the latest European war action, some of it only a couple of weeks old. Sunday nights we gathered around the one family radio we owned to hear Walter Winchell's opening words, "Good evening, Mr. and Mrs. America and all the ships at sea." Each week he gave us fifteen minutes of the real story from New York, as Hitler moved in Europe and Japan threatened in the Pacific. He even suggested that the U.S. military might be far from being combat ready. The U.S. Army tried to counter such allegations and hoped to generate the image of strength by conducting a highly publicized military exercise in Louisiana between ill-trained red and blue forces. Our troops had neither equipment nor ammunition. One of the unwanted outcomes was a story that received broad attention. It concerned a GI from the red forces raising the broomstick he carried to simulate a rifle, pointing it at a blue GI, and shouting, "Bang. You're dead!" The blue GI's reply was, "No, I'm not. I'm a tank." That didn't sound too good to us, but anyway, most everybody figured we weren't going to get mixed up in other people's wars.

Seems strange how two small things from those days influenced my life, without my recognizing it, and painted lasting pictures that never went away. Every weekend we got the Sunday edition of the *New York Herald Tribune*. Like Winchell's broadcasts, the *Herald Tribune* was the unchallenged word from New York. A highlight for me was the sepia-tone, eight-page rotogravure section with current pictures of worldwide action. One Sunday, on the right side of the first page was a picture of a single-engine, two-place, open-cockpit navy dive bomber high above the ocean with fluffy clouds below and the sun on the horizon in the background. The pilot, with his cloth helmet and goggles, was at the controls, while the gunner in the rear cockpit manned his turret-mounted machine gun and searched the sky for enemy aircraft. That was the hottest picture I had ever seen. I could easily visualize myself in that front cockpit, and every detail of that picture is still crystal clear to me. I knew I wanted to be a military pilot.

Rochester can get about as cold and snowbound as anyplace, and since car ownership was not a consideration for most of us, foot treks could be long, cold, and snow covered, but we didn't know anything different. I was dating a gal who lived on what was then the outskirts of town. After a downtown movie, we could take the bus to the last stop on the line, which was a short walk to her house. However, the five miles from her house to my house was pretty wide open and strictly a shank's mare stretch for me. During one of those completely solitary and silent walks I got another, unexpected mental shove that moved me toward the military. Somewhere around midnight on that very cold night, about four miles along the way, the sky was clear, the moon was bright, and as usual there was not a soul or a light in sight. It was an easy walk that night, since it was not snowing and the hard-packed snow was crunching under my feet. My National Guard friend Cliff had been activated and was somewhere far away in the infantry, and I was thinking how proud he must be to be serving our nation. I was wearing my wool high school fraternity jacket, which was bright red and bright blue, with my red, white, and blue Theta Phi patch on my chest. Without conscious thought command I was marching crisply along, with precisely timed strides, wondering if a guy could get into a distinctive military outfit that wore special sharp uniforms and had a very special mission. Like the rotogravure picture, it is still crystal clear in my memory, and if I listen, I can still hear the snow crunching underfoot. Subconsciously, that may have pushed me along my way, but I never specifically thought of it again after that night, until fourteen years later, when I became the leader of the air force acrobatic team, the Thunderbirds.

The Japanese sneak attack on Pearl Harbor obviously changed America and the world forever. It crystallized my plans and confirmed my decision that I wanted to be a regular air force flying officer. Here's how it unfolded for me.

For a kid from Rochester, becoming a military aviator had been strictly the stuff of dreams. But all of a sudden, at sixteen, maybe it wasn't such a dream. Not with America at war. The morning after Pearl Harbor, I rushed downtown to the navy recruiting office—the navy, only because that was the only recruiting office I knew how to get to. And the navy had airplanes, didn't they?

We drove there in my buddy Cozy's car, the "Guano Wagon," a 1927 Chevy two-door sedan Cozy had bought for nine dollars. It was in good mechanical condition, and we cleaned it up and got it running pretty well. The Guano Wagon was great for dates and cruising, and in those days, with gasoline eleven cents a gallon and a buddy who worked at the Mobile station selling us used oil for a nickel a fill up, it was well within a high school kid's budget. But that morning, the Guano Wagon was for serious business, the United States Navy.

The navy wasn't messing with formalities. Medics gave you a cursory check, and if you could fill out a few simple forms, touch your toes and your nose, clear the basic health checks, and carry on an understandable conversation with the chief petty officer, you received a reporting date only a few days in the future.

The chief petty officer looked me up and down and said, "How old are you, kid?"

I puffed my chest up and said, "Sixteen, but I'll be seventeen next month. I'm a senior in high school, and I'm in great shape to fight for my country. I want to fly."

The CPO nodded almost fondly and said, "G'wan back and finish school, kid. There'll be plenty time to get your ass shot at later."

I was crushed. My country was at war, and they wouldn't take me. Well, the navy wouldn't, which left me with my first choice anyway, the army. But sixteen was also too young for the army. So was seventeen. But I didn't want to wait a whole year, and I had already decided to pass up an offer of a college football scholarship. I wanted to serve my country. I wanted to fly. I wanted a regular commission in the army air corps and a career as a military flying officer. I wanted my silver pilot wings pinned on the tunic of my pinks and greens—the best looking uniform the military ever had—and a discretely floppy-brimmed officer's hat to top it off. But not only was my age an obstacle, I lacked the two years of college required to go directly into the army flying training program. But I did know, at seventeen, one way to get there: West Point.

I also knew that an appointment to West Point or Annapolis required a congressional appointment. If you were the son of a West Point graduate or a descendant of a high-ranking military figure, you had a head start. If you were the son of a wealthy man with proper political affiliations, that also helped. None of the above applied to me. My Dad was a drapery hardware salesman who worked hard to get us through the depression and provide us with a decent lifestyle. My only military ancestry consisted of two great uncles who had fought on opposite sides in the Civil War. Dad's sole connection to the local Republican Party was that he and my mom voted regularly.

We had a family friend, Cary Brown, a retired army colonel, a West Point graduate. He and his wife were influential in our church, and his two sons were now West Point cadets. I asked Colonel Brown for help and advice, and got both. He and two other men from church wrote letters for me to Representative O'Brien of the Thirty-Eighth Congressional District of the State of New York.

I was carrying both morning and evening paper routes, which you could do with good legs and a good bike. I got a friend to take the routes for a couple of days and took a night train to Washington. Early the next morning, I was in Representative O'Brien's office. His secretary was an impressive lady who greeted me warmly. When I told her I wanted to go to West Point, this year, she said that Mr. O'Brien had already made his academy appointments for the year. I must have looked mighty disappointed, because she leaned back in her chair, studied me a moment, and then said, "Exactly why do you want to go to West Point?"

I blurted out something that I think sounded like, "I want to fight for my country."

Whatever I said, she seemed to like it. She told me that now, with the war, there was a possibility of a second echelon of appointments, and asked where I was staying. When I said I didn't know, she picked up the phone and called a nearby YMCA and made a reservation for me. Then she motioned me to wait and left the office. When she returned she said Congressman O'Brien would meet me at the office at eight in the morning, and after he and I had talked, I could tag along with him for most of the day. Okay? You bet.

They booked me into a double room at the YMCA, and my roommate was a husky army master sergeant with three rows of ribbons on his chest. Just being near this seasoned veteran pumped me up a bit more. That evening, when he left to meet friends, I slipped into his GI overcoat. I stood in front of the mirror, my eyes fixed on the chevrons and hash marks on the arms and sleeves, and decided I looked good in a uniform.

In the morning, meeting a real live congressman was another thrill. To my surprise and relief, it was an easy conversation. We parted with a good handshake, a reminder that I was asking for a pretty big order, and the promise that he would do the best he could for me. I knew he was sincere.

Back in Rochester, things seemed to go either super fast or super slow. Graduation was approaching, but then what? Then I got lucky. Congressman O'Brien's secretary was right: there would be a second echelon of new cadets, doubling the inbound West Point class from 800 to 1,600. Congressman O'Brien could issue new primary, first-alternate, and second-alternate appointments. I got the second-alternate appointment.

And another lucky break: I scored well enough on my New York State Scholastic Aptitude Tests so that West Point waived their academic entrance examinations, and it was on to New York City for a super physical. I had already been to New York a few times before and thought that for a seventeen-year-old from upstate, I was pretty hot stuff in the Big Apple. But the night before that physical I was a scared kid. When I got off the train at Grand Central Terminal I went upstairs in the terminal to the adjoining Commodore Hotel, checked in, and went straight to my room.

Not knowing which dreaded disease the army medics would find in me in the morning, I limited my big-city actions to a sandwich in the hotel drugstore and early bed. I wanted to be well rested, but spent the whole night listening to my irregular heartbeat, feeling the pains in my chest, and counting my racing pulse.

The next morning I joined a couple of hundred other bare-ass potential cadets wandering around a cold, poorly lighted, cavernous concrete barn, where numbers of white-jacketed individuals of unknown credentials poked, probed, punctured, and analyzed every orifice of our bodies. I thought it was nothing short of miraculous that after a couple of hours of that, everybody seemed to wind up at the end of the line with his own tee shirt and shorts.

A few days after I graduated from high school, my dad answered the doorbell, signed for a telegram, and handed it to me. I had been accepted and had two days to get to West Point to be sworn in. I gave my mom a big hug and kiss, embraced my dad, and prepared to leave the next day to become a warrior.

West Point is a place you can't wait to get into, and then can't wait to get out of, especially if there is a war going on and you are anxious to get into combat. But even when you didn't like it, you loved it and were proud to be part of it. To an unsuspecting new plebe, though, with no knowledge of what to expect, the academy experience can be traumatic. Hazing was real and painful and the academic routine terrifying to a seventeen-year-old just out of high school. Compounding the pressure was the announcement that the four-year course would be crammed into three years. It ratcheted up another notch with the option of flight training, still within the three years, for those who volunteered and qualified academically. The struggle to get through that first year and a half was almost overwhelming.

My battles with the Tactical Department and the Academic Department more than once sent me reeling into the ropes. When that happened I would go to my favorite "thinking place," across Thayer Road to the hundred-year-old stone railing along the edge of the cliff overlooking the Hudson River. And I would cool off, simmer down, and remember my goal: to graduate from West Point.

And if it was a dark winter night, I would look up at the sky and think that it was only ten years ago that army air corps pilots were flying the airmail up and down this same gorge in the same bad weather in their open-cockpit airplanes. I desperately wanted those silver wings and now, in the spring of 1944, I would have my chance. In another few weeks, we'd be off to flying training.

CHAPTER 2

HANGAR SIX

The train from San Antonio was hot, but the noon sun in Uvalde, Texas, felt hotter as sixty-four temporarily liberated West Point classmates boarded buses for our civilian primary flying school called Hangar Six. United States Vice President John Nance Garner owned Hangar Six, located on Garner Field, along with most of the rest of Uvalde. Everybody from Uvalde knew that John Nance could do no wrong.

We moved into the barracks, met our aviation cadet counterparts, and anticipated getting our hands on the sleek, low-wing, open-cockpit Fairchild PT-19 monoplanes that we were to fly. Our flight of four, two aviation cadets and two pointers, had orders to report to the main hangar and look for our instructor, whose name was George Ensley. We were pumped up, and it seemed like nothing could go wrong—until we met our instructor.

I expected that my instructor would remind me of Roscoe Turner, or Wiley Post, or Jimmy Matern or Captain Midnight, but it didn't work that way. George Ensley was frail and unkempt looking. He would not look any of us in the eye, preferring to keep his eyes on his absolutely scruffy brown loafers, which he had obviously never cleaned or shined and were splitting apart at the seams. He smoked incessantly. Our fellow cadets from the academy came from all corners of the nation, and we were certainly used to and comfortable with southern accents. Ensley's speech had little in common with a southern accent. He mumbled, slurred his words, and generally spoke very softly from a head-drooped position. We were very intent on his every word, but his mutterings were extremely difficult to comprehend.

We obediently followed Ensley as he shuffled out to the flight line for an introduction to the PT-19. He explained that we would sit in the front cockpit, and when he was flying with us he would sit in back. We took brief turns sitting in the cockpit, exploring the controls and trying to understand what Ensley was saying.

Airborne communications between PT-19 seats would be either hand signals or one-way talk from the instructor to us using a simple system called a "gosport" (named after the airfield in England where they were developed during World War I). We were to connect rubber hoses to ports on each earpiece of our cloth helmets, and our instructor would speak into a funnel-shaped mouthpiece on the other end of the tubes. It was sort of like a tin-can-and-string phone kids played with, but it worked.

Then Ensley abruptly switched gears and shook us up. He looked up at us for the first time, and his thin face looked mean and his voice came out the same way. He had a vicious streak. In a louder and still garbled voice, he barked, "Now you mistuhs listen up good! Sometimes dodos like you get sick and puke. Ah gotta ride in that back seat, 'nif any you bastards puke on me, ah'll guarantee yo ass is washed out. Ya heah?"

Getting sick was the last thing we were thinking about, but we nodded agreement as Ensley continued, "Now, ya gonna puke, stick up ya right hand—high, like this, then lean over the right side and puke at ya armpit, like ugghahhh." We stood in silent amazement. "Yur puking right 'n' ah'm leaning left, 'n' ya furget it 'n' yur washed out."

Ensley looked nervously at his watch as we exchanged insecure glances, wondering what kind of character we had drawn for an instructor. You could tell he was uptight, and my classmate Harry Drake and I seemed to make him more nervous as we automatically answered him with West Point crisp "Yes, sirs."

He looked at his loafers for a few seconds then said, "Ah got 'pointment, but y'all git a hour sitting in a cockpit. Names and times'll be on a flight schedule board for mo'nin' by then." As he shuffled off toward the group of female clerks emerging from the administration building, we felt shortchanged, since the other instructors were still busily helping their students become comfortable with their new machinery.

I drew the first dual instruction flight with Ensley the next morning. The thrill of being airborne was overriding, and initially Ensley's mannerisms seemed only part of the game. We flew around the local area, and Ensley demonstrated some of the control functions and aircraft responses, then gave me a chance to feel the aircraft out. I was excited and I overcontrolled, but loved every sensation of flight. As I was plowing through my first-ever try at a thirty-degree bank, Ensley suddenly shook the stick from side to side, indicating he had control, and yelled through the gosport, "Damn, mistuh, yur rough 'n' tight. Put yur hands 'n' feet onna controls while I set up this turn 'n' see ya can getta feel fer it."

Ensley put us in a forty-five–degree bank to the left, the most unusual flight attitude I had experienced to date. I attempted to assimilate the feel of back pressure and aileron and rudder pressure that combined to accomplish the banked turn while keeping the nose on the horizon. "Ya got it," he barked through the gosport, and I lunged to grasp the controls.

I grabbed too hard, and the nose went up, then I pushed too hard, and the nose of the small, sensitive aircraft dived the other way. Ensley knew what to expect from the surprised neophyte who had never experienced such a spatial orientation, and he let the porpoise action go for another cycle before thrusting his speaker end of the gosport out into the slipstream and violently shaking the stick from side to side to reassume control. The slipstream's scream through the earpieces of my helmet added to the bouncing confusion, and I knew that things were not going well.

My ears were hurting by the time Ensley leveled the Fairchild and pulled his end of the gosport back into the rear cockpit. I certainly had not expected this kind of an opening act as the gosport announced, "Mistuh, ya remind me some monkey screwing a football. Ah say be smuth, be smuth. Now, heahs one mo chance 'fore we go back. Ah say again: be smuuuth, 'n' ah'm gonna set up this turn, 'n' yur gonna hold the nose level."

Ensley set up another turn, a bit tighter than the preceding one, but offered no advice on technique. The results were quite similar to the earlier attempt. Ensley took over, flew us back to Garner Field, and told me to watch how he got into the traffic pattern and landed. When we parked the PT-19 and got out, Ensley was half smiling. He had established his authority.

The next few flights were more of the same, with Ensley continuing to criticize me for being too stiff, but offering little or no instruction. I got better just from repetition of the drills, lots of hangar flying with classmates, and sheer determination.

Ensley was madly chasing a young lady who worked in Hangar Six operations. Cornering her before work, on every coffee break she had, and the minute she left work was his main focus. Teaching us to fly was of little concern to him. Suddenly, Ensley just seemed to quit even pretending to instruct us and put the three of us up for our solo flights. I can clearly remember singing "Swinging on a Star" at the top of my lungs as I soared through the sky under my own control.

It was great to have a bit of freedom after breaking out of the Point during gloom period, that time of the year when it seems like the New York winter will never end. At Uvalde, on weekends, we could even go off base! Catching the bus to the intersection of the two streets that formed downtown Uvalde and walking to the town beer parlor to hangar fly and have a couple of cool ones with your buddies on Saturday afternoon was heady stuff. There were also some local folks who tried to enhance our social life. The Ramsey family had a good-sized ranch outside town, and every once in a while, if you were lucky enough to spot the list within two minutes of when it was posted, you could sign up for one of the afternoon parties they graciously hosted. My classmate Walt Dabney got on one of those lists, and it changed his life. The hospitality, real people food, horses to ride, and a swimming hole were enough to make any cadet happy. But the Ramseys had two beautiful daughters, and Walt fell madly in love with Charlotte. West Point graduation and marriage were far from the minds of most of us at the moment, but that turned out to be the direction in which Walt and Charlotte were headed.

Ensley's romance, on the other hand, was apparently not going so well, and that meant more bad news for his students in general and me in particular. Somewhere along the line he had learned that not only did I play football with what was then the awesome army team, I was also a weightlifter, and he chipped at me constantly for being a musclebound jockstrap.

When Ensley entered the briefing room on the next Monday morning, he looked like he had been up all night and had not even bothered to wash his face or comb his hair. We looked apprehensively at each other, then all eyes shifted to Ensley as he slouched up to me with a cigarette drooping limply from the corner of his mouth, blew smoke in my face, and snarled, "OK, Broughton, you're first. Lessee if you can show me some pylon eights without tearin' a stick outta the cockpit."

I felt good about the way I got set up in the first pylon eight—a training maneuver where you pick a center point, a point on the left of center, and one to the right, then rotate around them while you trace a figure eight in the sky. Ensley hadn't said a word. That didn't last long. "Steepen up the bank, and don't be so damn stiff," Ensley shouted from the back seat.

I winced and banked the wings of the PT-19 steeper, even though I thought that it would goof up the pylon eight I was flying. I had set this one up just like it says in the book, and it looked good to me. I had picked two dirt roads that intersected at ninety degrees for the junction of the top and bottom loops of the figure eight I would trace from six hundred feet up. The westerly wind was lined up with one of the roads, and I had two perfect pylons to mark my turns. One was a farmhouse about one football field south of the intersection, and the other was a water trough at the east end of a plowed field about another football field to the north of the intersection. It should have been a piece of cake, but Ensley wasn't about to let that happen. As I expected, the steeper bank made it look like the farmhouse was creeping up ahead of the left wingtip, and the smooth, round bottom of the "8" was turning into a lopsided egg.

"Yur off," Ensley shouted. "Try 'gin."

I swore to myself, if the little wimp would keep quiet I could do it. I pulled hard into an even tighter bank to the left, flew past the house, and continued west, into the wind for a full minute. Then I started a smooth turn back to the right and rolled out, straight and level, just in time to bisect the road intersection and roll back up into a left bank calculated to trace the top of an eight around the water trough. It looked great.

"Yur too steep," Ensley shouted.

I gritted my teeth and fought my temper. The wingtip was glued to the trough, I was downwind, and there was no need to shallow out the bank.

"Flatten it out, mistuh," Ensley shouted again.

Reluctantly, I released some pressure and watched the wind take over and slide the trough back behind my wingtip.

"Yur all over the sky, ya musclebound jockstrap!" the voice screeched again. "Put ya head on ya left knee, 'n' ah'll see ah can loosen ya up." As I assumed the position, Ensley whacked the stick hard left three times, with my head taking the blows. It stung, but more than that it infuriated.

Even with the wind whipping past the cockpit, I was now sweating heavily. Cursing to myself again, I tried to salvage the maneuver. With a steep bank I managed to get the wingtip back on the trough, but I had over-controlled, and the smooth arcs had become a jagged mess.

"Do it again, mistuh," Ensley shouted viciously, " 'n' quit trying make me puke by yanking 'round alla square corners."

I rolled out, took a deep breath, gave myself a two-second attitude lecture, and surveyed the situation. I was in surprisingly good position, with the southbound road just off my left wingtip. I picked up the eight from the top and rolled around the course like I was on tracks. And this time Ensley was silent, probably looking at his watch, thinking that it was getting close to break time for the girls of the records section. The maneuver was about as close to perfect as a primary cadet could get.

Time seemed to be standing still, and I felt like I could almost smell Ensley's frustration and gall. I imagined that it seemed logical to him that the stuffy West Pointer in the other cockpit was fair game. No way was he going to waste his time teaching me to be smooth. I could visualize him clucking his tongue, nodding, and thinking, "To hell wi' 'im. Ah just say 'e's tight 'n' erratic onnis coordination maneuvers—prob'ly musclebound from playin' big-deal f'tball. Even he beats the check ride, least ah'll be ridda 'im. Yeah, washout check ride for you, Mistuh West Point."

Ensley yanked back on the throttle and barked, "Forced landing," I guess hoping that I would screw it up in some way. I glanced in the mirror, and he seemed immersed in thought, only half watching as I set up an approach to the open field surrounding the water trough. As soon as Ensley could see that I was all lined up for what was a no-brainer, all he said was, "Take us home." I parked, and as he climbed down to the ramp and turned towards the canteen where the girls were gathering, he said, "Ah'm puttin' ya up fo' a army check ride M'nday marn," and walked away.

The army check ride, which was a pass-it-or-you're-all-done affair, was indeed scheduled for Monday morning, and I knew that my chances of beating that ride and avoiding being washed out were not great. I also believed that it could be done. I convinced myself that, God willing, and if I wanted to beat that ride badly enough, and if I prepared properly, I could do it.

The tactical officer had given me some stuff to do on Saturday, but the duties were not overly demanding. Thus, I had time to study and practically memorize the student handbook and all the daily notes on past flights that I had written to myself in the handbook. I flew maneuvers in my mind and with my hands, and by Saturday night I was so tied up in knots I would have been lucky to remember how to get a Fairchild PT-19 started and airborne. I vowed to get a good night's sleep, but I mostly tossed and turned and sweated and listened to other guys laughing and making random Saturday night piss calls. When I got up in the morning, I realized that I was on a course that was leading me straight toward what I dreaded most in life—washing out.

I was scheduled to lead the Sunday barracks scrub-and-polish detail from eight until noon, and the sweat and physical effort seemed to loosen me up and make me feel better and more aggressive. My mind would try to relax, and I found I could even maintain a positive attitude for a few minutes, but a remark, a sight, or a sound would throw me back into the sheer terror of the last-chance check ride scheduled for Monday morning, and my muscles would knot and the sweat would flow. After one of these Jekyll-and-Hyde sessions, my mind abruptly cleared, and I knew exactly what I had to do.

I showered, put on a fresh, crisp, short-sleeved khaki uniform, and rode silently on the two o'clock liberty bus to Uvalde. I paid little attention to the conversations going on among my classmates around me, some of whom sort of ignored me anyway. They considered me practically gone and didn't want to get any bad luck on themselves. They didn't know of anyone who had beaten an army check ride.

When the bus stopped at the corner of Main and Garner in Uvalde, I got off and quietly split from the gang of cadets that was standing in the normal places, trying to figure out what to do in the completely shut-down Texas town on a Sunday afternoon. I walked east along Main Street with nobody else around. The few stores near the corner of Garner were closed, and beyond them all the houses were closed up. The only sound or movement came from my shoes on the sidewalk.

Four blocks down the street, I came to a small, gray wooden church trimmed in white with a petite wooden cross atop a short steeple. The hand-painted wooden sign said St. Vincent's Episcopal Church, and it looked almost like a doll church when compared to the Cadet Chapel at the Point, St. Patrick's Cathedral in New York City, or St. Paul's in Rochester, but I knew that was not of import at the moment.

It was uncomfortably hot as I tentatively stepped up the single wood-plank step that led to the church door and tried the handle. It was unlocked, and the door squeaked open.

Once inside, with the door closed, St. Vincent's looked even smaller and very empty. There were ten rows of plain wooden pews, split by a narrow aisle that led to a simple altar topped by a hand-carved cross, and there was a plain wooden pulpit angled off on the right side of the pews. I raised my eyes to the cross, bowed the typical, casual, Episcopalian nod of reverence, and the floorboards squeaked as I walked forward toward the front pew. It was at least ten degrees hotter inside the noninsulated church than it was under the blistering sun outside. The windows were shut, and not a breath of air moved inside. The only sounds were the sounds I created. Sweat was already trickling down my collar and turning my khaki uniform black as I sighed with inner relief, settled to my knees, raised my eyes above the altar and crossed myself. I knew I was where I wanted and needed to be.

The 1928 prayer book of the Episcopal Church was the same everyplace, and I found comfort in roaming through fields of word and verse that I knew and loved. Then, with no conscious inner direction, my prayers left the book and turned into a simple two-way conversation that very comfortably examined and probed my desire, strength, coordination, and relaxation, my love of country and flying, my duty to family and friends, and determination to do it right—to somehow do it relaxed, smoothly, but to make it!

For the first time in a long while, time had meant nothing, and when I stepped outside and softly closed the door to St. Vincent's, I was surprised to see that more than two hours had passed. I was physically and emotionally drained, my khaki uniform was sweat blackened and limp, but I was ready to go and bite 'em in the ass and do good work. I walked back to the bus stop with my chest high and a smile on my face. That night, I slept great, just great.

When I reported to operations on Monday morning, I learned that First Lieutenant Brown would be my check pilot and that he was in a meeting but would be along shortly. I was told to wait at aircraft number 033, parked on spot 05. I felt very determined and purposeful as I picked up my chute and hit the ramp. The lieutenant was still not in sight after I had completed a walk-around inspection of 033, so I paced for a few minutes, then had another conversation with the really big check pilot.

An approaching figure interrupted me. He turned out to be a West Point classmate named Ralph Ford, whom I had always considered to be a cold bottle of piss. Ralph was headed for a solo flight, with his chute over his shoulder, looking quite disinterested as usual. Pausing, he said, "Hear you're going for an army check ride." As I nodded yes, Ford continued, without emotion, "You'll probably flunk it; guess everybody does. But don't feel bad about it. Lotsa luck."

Out of the corner of my eye I saw a lieutenant starting across the ramp, with a chute slung over his shoulder. I still had time to look after the departing classmate and mutter, "Screw you Ralph. If guys like that can make it, I sure as hell can make it."

As Lieutenant Brown approached the aircraft, I popped to my best attention, snapped a sharp salute, and said, "Cadet Broughton, reporting to Lieutenant Brown, as ordered, sir." Brown returned the salute, and I hoped he might think that I was not some wimp kid, going through the elimination formalities and ready to be kicked out and sent back home.

Lieutenant Brown was sharp looking, and though he maintained the noncommittal attitude expected of a washout check pilot, he was pleasant enough as he introduced himself and briefed me on what he expected. I thought, "This guy is sure a ton above Ensley," and I was not one bit afraid.

Lieutenant Brown was obviously not a softie, and he had sent his fair share of cadets packing. However, he just looked like he took his responsibilities seriously, and he had to know how his evaluations could affect the lives of the young studs he rode with. I assumed that he had checked my records and grade slips, and I figured they were probably in about the same shape as Ensley's loafers. All of this made absolutely no difference to him, and he would have to see for himself, which was what the army was paying him for.

Initially things went well. I was relaxed and smooth. Then part way through a pylon eight, we hit a persistent series of dandy thermals, and as I fought to maintain my cool, my mind unconsciously flashed to the pylon-eight episode with Ensley, and I felt that cool slipping and my muscles tensing.

Lieutenant Brown appeared to be satisfied with my flying for the first twenty minutes of the flight. Then, as we bounced around and I tightened up on the controls, he rocked the stick and spoke into the gosport, "Let me have the controls." I felt nothing but utter panic.

Brown did a couple of clearing turns as he continued to talk. "Mister Broughton, why don't you just hang your hands over the edge of the cockpit for a minute." As I draped my hands over the cockpit rail, I enjoyed the feel of the rushing slipstream, and Brown asked, "Anyone ever show you how smoothly this little machine can do a barrel roll?" I shook my head no.

As Brown dived to pick up some air speed, he said, "You can follow me through on the controls if you want."

I eagerly placed my hands and feet lightly on the controls and was amazed at the grace of a barrel roll that kept my butt on the seat at a constant one G, even when inverted. The control motions seemed almost effortless. I had a glimmer of hope, maybe even understanding, that needed only to be translated into a feel for it.

As we bottomed, Brown spoke again, "See how easy it is?" I nodded eagerly as Brown continued, "Sort of like the birds. You don't see them fighting and thrashing around, but they sure fly good. OK, you got it, and let's do that pylon eight again." He shook the stick and I was ready. The calm determination had returned.

The rest of the check ride went OK until we got back to the field and I saw that the windsock was pointing a good thirty degrees off the desired landing heading and I was going to have to make a crosswind landing. I set it up poorly, because nobody had told me or showed me how to set it up properly. I fought it all the way down the approach to what would surely have been a rotten touchdown if Brown had not ordered me to go around. "Anyone ever tell you or show you how to make a crosswind landing?" Brown asked as we worked our way around the traffic pattern. When I again shook my head in the negative, I glanced in the mirror and saw Brown nodding to himself in understanding.

He talked me all the way through the next crosswind approach, explaining how to crab into the wind, hold pressure on the rudder, dip the wing into the wind, and kick it out just before touchdown. The result was a decent touchdown. Brown didn't say a word on my next crosswind landing, and I greased it in.

When we parked and climbed down to the ground, I was more apprehensive than I had ever been in my life. Lieutenant Brown looked like he was thinking as he climbed down, which did nothing to reduce my stress level. Brown looked me in the eyes, smiled, and said, "Relax, Mister Broughton, that was a good ride. You're a good learner, and I'm passing you on the check ride. I'll take care of the flight forms and direct that you get moved to a new flight, with a new instructor, so you can get on with the business of learning to fly. OK? You're on your way."

I was so elated I almost jumped into the air as I saluted with, "Yes, sir! Thank you, sir, thanks for showing me those things." When Brown returned his salute and turned to leave, I was so excited I could hardly get out of my chute.

Passing the wingtip, on his way back to the Army Flight Office, Brown looked back, pleased that Junior Birdman Broughton was happy, and added, "I want to hear lots of good things about you, Mister Broughton."

George Chambers made arrangements for his new student, Cadet Broughton, to report an hour early the next morning. George was a much older man, by cadet standards, and must have been in his thirties. For that first hour all he and I did was shoot the breeze. We sat on a bench outside the hangar and talked about flying. There wasn't any engine noise yet, so George had me watch the Mexican eagles floating and gently riding the early morning updrafts. Back where I came from we called them crows, but regardless of what you called them, they were smooth and graceful. I got the message.

An hour later, George and I were airborne. With each bit of real instruction, my proficiency, confidence, and morale climbed. The next Sunday, I was back at St. Vincent's, but it seemed a lot cooler, and I didn't even break into a sweat.

Before the first flight in the acrobatics phase, George explained how to do a loop properly. He also explained some don'ts: don't pull the plane straight up and make an oblong loop, and don't release all of your back pressure going over the top of the loop and stall-out upside down.

In the acrobatic area, George flew a demonstration loop just like he had briefed it, smooth as silk. He shook the stick from side to side, held his hands aloft, and it was time for me to try a loop.

I rolled the PT-19 into my clearing turns and dropped the nose as my air speed climbed and the wind whistled ever louder past the wing wires. I pulled in a healthy chunk of back pressure as gravity pushed me deeper into the seat. I loved it!

Almost instantly the little Fairchild was pointing straight up at the brilliant blue sky and the cotton balls of cumulus cloud. Thrilled, almost hypnotized, I held the stick and rudders steady as the base of the clouds seemed to slide into formation alongside my wingtip. The sights and sensations were fascinating, and everything seemed to momentarily stand still for me to enjoy. Then suddenly I realized that things were getting awfully quiet and that the wing wires were barely whistling at me. I was no longer being pushed down into the seat but was instead floating up into the seatbelt, as things rapidly became very, very silent. "Damn," I fussed aloud. "Back pressure, you idiot!"

But the PT-19, hanging on its prop, was not about to forgive the first-time looper for his lack of attention. She bucked a couple of times, as if to chastise me for sightseeing when I should have kept hauling back on the stick. The engine coughed hoarsely, and with a gentle buffet the tail washed up and back while the nose fell through the horizon and stared at the ground below. I knew enough not to touch anything while she fell and flew herself back into controllable condition.

As we fell, the wings regained their lost lift, and the prop started gulping meaningful bites of air, and the controls came to life again. I was fascinated with the onrush of the ground and the sensation that I once again had control. I knew I could return to level flight at the altitude we had entered the loop. I also knew that I was about to get my ass chewed.

Instead, Chambers' voice almost had a laugh in it as he shook the stick and the gosport filled my ears with, "Well that was an OK entry, and the recovery from unusual positions was fine, but I can't say much for that topside maneuver. Here, I've got it, and follow me through on the controls."

I raised my hands to acknowledge the command and nodded yes to nobody in particular, since the prop and engine were the only things in front of me. I moved my hands ever so close to the stick and throttle and held my feet so they barely touched the rudder pedals. Chambers again performed a flawless maneuver as I absorbed the control pressure and the timing. As we approached the vertical, George said, "Look out the side. As the horizon comes square to your shoulders, you're going straight up. Now you just keep feeding in some back pressure . . . and over the top . . . nice and easy."

I knew I had the feel down pretty pat now, and I showed it on the next three, increasingly symmetrical loops. As we bottomed from the third one, Chambers said through the gosport, "OK, let's head over to the right and pick up that southbound road and S across the road back to the base. Then I want some power on landings to the X."

As I casually turned right, George pulled the throttle all the way back, and I instinctively set up a forced landing approach to an open Texas field, thinking, "Old George sure keeps you hopping, but now it's fun." The man and the machinery were getting on the same frequency.

Tom Catron and I were buddies from back at the point, and we spent a lot of time hangar flying together. One afternoon, as we walked back from the flight line to the barracks, Tom reached into his flying suit pocket and pulled out a pack of Bull Durham chewing tobacco. He pushed it toward me with, "Chewin' crap?"

I pulled a few shreds from the pack and stuck them back between my cheek and teeth and almost immediately began to spit as the bitter juice flowed. I wasn't really wild about the stuff, but I had bought a package. Since some of the country boys had touted "chewin' " as the in thing for big-time aviators like us, I was learning to tolerate it, but I spit almost incessantly. I was surprised that Tom had carried it in his flying suit and asked, "You use that crap while you're flying?"

"Just when I'm solo," replied Tom. "Can't very well spit in the instructor's face back there."

Puzzled, I asked, "How the hell do you spit when you're flying without getting it all over everything?"

"Easy," replied Tom, "just do a roll and spit when you're upside down." That seemed simple enough, and I immediately knew that I had a new challenge to master. Actually, neither George Chambers nor I had been fully satisfied with the quality of my slow rolls earlier that afternoon, and I was scheduled for some solo practice the next day.

By my third practice roll I was proud of myself: big man had just done what felt like a perfect slow roll. I reached into my flight suit pocket, pulled out the chewin' crap, popped a small wad into my mouth, and dropped the nose for another roll. The entry was smooth, but I was hurrying a bit, and already I wished I could spit. As I rolled over the top, wings level, I had to spit—or swallow, which was unthinkable. As I puckered and tried to figure the proper "ptui" angle, I put too much forward pressure on the stick as I spit. The inverted nose went up, and my head went back. Some of the crap went into my locked throat, gagging me. Some covered my upside-down face and goggles, blinding me. And the bird fell out of the roll like a dead duck as the choking, half-sick junior birdman fought to gain control of himself and his machine.

Back on the ground, I managed to avoid George and duck into the latrine. After washing my face, neck, goggles and helmet as best I could hurriedly do, I looked into the mirror, shook my head, and admonished, "Big deal, you got a lot more to learn." I reached for the Bull Durham package and tossed the chewin' crap into the waste can as I trotted off for debriefing.

The acrobatic phase wound down, and primary graduation approached. Final check rides were scheduled to last just long enough so that each cadet graduated with sixty hours and ten minutes, exactly, since that was what Hangar Six was paid for. It was all fun at the moment, since we were quite comfortable with the PT-19 and nobody was going to get washed out at that stage of the game.

The West Point air cadets approached the end of primary with mixed emotions. The life of the past few months had been full of good flying and freedom from the smothering West Point system, and we had loved it. We did not look forward to rejoining our mole classmates who were preparing for careers as ground officers, and we knew the army and the superintendent of the U.S. Military Academy and the commandant of cadets would make sure that the Tactical Department reminded us of our status as soon as we got back. But to hell with that; we had eight days' leave before worrying about that stuff.

CHAPTER 3

TRANSITION

S tewart Field, located along the Hudson River outside Newburgh, New York, was the new training base for the West Point junior birdmen. With the opening of Stewart Field, the Academy, thirty miles away, could rein them in, bring them back under Academy control, get them back in the academic program, and, if the army air force insisted, allow them to get on with learning to fly. As for us, we were anxious to get airborne again.

Our training was going to be experimental in nature, since we were bypassing the normal basic flying in the BT-13 Vultee Vibrator and were going directly into the more powerful, more sophisticated North American AT-6 Texan that was far more advanced than anything basic cadets had seen before.

The welcome at Stewart was about what we had expected. Colonel Schlater, a pilot, was the overall commander, but it was easy to see that the ground-pounders who ran the Point also called the shots at Stewart. In his opening speech he introduced the nonrated lieutenant colonel who represented the West Point Tactical Department. The game plan was clear, and all of us sort of sank in our seats. He announced that he was there to help us get reacclimated and reoriented and had arranged for a four-day refamiliarization period before we needed to worry about things like flying. For our convenience he had arranged for our M1 rifles to be shipped from the Point.

We felt like we were plebes again. The days opened with a one-mile double-time from the barracks to the athletic area, followed by one hour of tumbling, fumbling, and doing sit-ups, before a return double-time back to the barracks and a hurried breakfast. The rest of the four days were filled with lectures on barracks standards for inspections, arrangement of trunk lockers, which were called foot lockers every place in the military except at West Point, and rifle inspections. Can you imagine how enthusiastic a junior birdman can get about swabbing down an M1 Garand grunt's rifle?

Saturday morning inspection, still unaffectionately known as Sami, would be followed by a parade. Sunday morning's inspection would offer the opportunity to verify correction of irregularities noted on Saturday, and would be followed by a lecture on the policy for awarding demerits, the walking of penalty tours for excess demerits, and the restrictions covering once-a-month off-base weekends for those fortunate enough not to have excessive demerits. Whew, boy! We were back.

Finally, on Monday we got to the flight line and met our instructors. It would have been difficult to find a more eager crew as we launched in our new, sophisticated steeds. The airplane was fun from the start, but it was demanding.

The course was a blur of transition, lots of basic instruments, acrobatics, navigation, hurdle landing stages, pats on the back, and ass chewings. And there were checklists, never to be forgotten or ignored. Before takeoff it was "cigarettes for the poor Russians" (controls, instruments, gas, flaps, trim, pitch, and run-up). Before landing it was the wobble pump, to be sure the hydraulic pressure was up, and "gump" (gas, undercarriage, mixture, and pitch). I didn't know it then, but those checklists were to serve me well, with bits of adaptation, for another forty years.

There were the never-ending horrors of the Link trainer, often at night, and the pain of passing ground school courses like Morse code, with a telegraph key yet! But we mucked through it, even with extra instruction at night. The tactical department was always there just to be sure we always had a little bit more to accomplish than we could be comfortable with.

We wound up doing a lot of our instrument practicing on buddy rides, with one of us observing and the other one under the hood. It could become very boring staring at the instruments and droning over set courses time after time, so one day two of us decided to see how high we could get the AT-6 while checking out this hypoxia stuff we had been hearing about. We got our Texan up to 19,600 feet, sans oxygen. Just like they told us, we didn't know it, but we were both drunk as skunks from lack of oxygen, and closer than our young minds realized to passing out and creating a big hole in the ground below. Fortunately, our bird would climb no higher, and while we were wandering back from goofyland, we discovered we were supporting bad headaches.

Halfway through basic, the master of the sword, a colonel directing athletics and physical fitness at the Point, decided that we needed some hands-on parachute experience, since the army had learned that the paratroopers often got hurt when landing from a jump. My flight was scheduled for the first day of his crazy drill, and I was appropriately roughed up. It took four people and one AT-6 to adequately bruise one cadet. I was strapped into an already opened parachute and positioned with my rear end facing the rear end of a tied down AT-6 whose engine was running at idle. Two enlisted men held me around

the waist while the third signaled the pilot to advance the T-6 throttle
and create a seventy-mile an hour wind. When they released me, I took
off horizontally, behind the inflated chute, about three feet above the
ground. My flight was short and painful and proved beyond a doubt
that crashing into the ground in an uncontrolled mode hurt. Colonel
Schlater, after viewing one of the early wild rides, called the drill off
over the protests of the representatives of the master of the sword and
the Tactical Department. We were told that those gentlemen grum-
bled that tough soldiers should be able to take that sort of training in
stride and wear their bandages proudly.

At the end of basic we should have gone into advanced training in
the same T-6, followed by pinning on our wings. But the army insisted
that we go back to the Point for six months of academics, with only
occasional proficiency flying, then complete advanced flying training
and graduate with our mole classmates. Finishing basic was a definite
milestone in our aviation careers, but for us it amounted to getting on
GI buses and riding thirty miles down Storm King highway to reenter
West Point. It was good to see some of our mole buddies again, but
there was no whooping it up.

Our flying proficiency dropped dangerously low during the academic
interim. When you, as an aviator in training, went a month or more
without getting off the ground, you were nervous, all thumbs, and
very susceptible to busting your ass. To generate some flying time for
the cadets, our army air force instructors set up a weekend cross-country program. If you could get on the schedule, and if the weather happened to be acceptable, an instructor would take four cadets on a
weekend round robin to build confidence and flying time. It was a
good idea, but unfortunately it didn't always work well. During one of
those flights, a lack of proficiency killed Bobby Clark while his flight
was returning from a weekend cross-country to his hometown in
Nebraska. While returning to Stewart on Sunday evening, they were

forced to fly night-weather formation, down low in the Catskill Mountains, in a snow storm, fuel warning lights glowing, trying to maintain visual flight on an instrument-flight clearance. Bobby was flying number four in the flight, and the accident board concluded that the snow was so heavy that all Bobby could see was the little green position light on his element leader's wing. The instructor was leading, and even though he was doing his best to be extra smooth, the wind whistling down the river and through the mountains made for a bumpy flight.

Bobby's low-fuel warning light was probably giving him vertigo as its red flashes bounced off the canopy, onto the windscreen, and then onto the white mist of snow and cloud outside. Things were probably all crooked as he tried to focus on that little green wingtip light and fly formation on it. It's doubtful that the tricks of shaking his head or yelling made the vertigo go away. Maybe he glanced quickly into the cockpit and reached unsuccessfully toward the fuel warning light in hopes of dimming it. Even if his eyes were only gone from the green light on the wingtip for a millisecond, the green light could have faded to nothing. He probably rammed the throttle full forward, but there was nothing to see but white and black, and he didn't know if he was upside down or right side up. If he swung his attention to the gauges, it would have been hard to believe them if they told him he was in a nose-low, left-hand bank. He probably experienced full terror and full disorientation, but he would have known that he had to believe the gauges. He rolled right and he pulled back on the stick—too late.

A frozen funeral march to the West Point cemetery, in death step, for two miles, by two thousand young men in miserable winter uniforms was absolute hell. During the painful march, I determined that no matter how long it took me I needed to master the most demanding requirements of flying under night weather situations.

On the way back from the historic West Point Cemetery, one of my heroes, the enlisted cymbal player in the West Point band, was in view directly in front of my company, as we double-timed the return two miles to a blaring "When the Saints Go Marching In." I was always fascinated by the cymbal player as he bounced smartly forward on the double, never missing a beat and crashing the cymbals together, flinging the right one high above his head and catching it in stride as it fell back into his hand. For three years, he, whoever he was, always made me feel that he was playing especially for me at parades. Just watching him that frozen afternoon strengthened my desire to be super proficient and prepared to complete any maneuver I started. Funny what you remember.

Counting down the days until we finished up academics and got back to Stewart was a lot like counting down the days until graduation. You couldn't make it happen soon enough. We finally finished our finals and formalities, got signed off by the academic department, packed up and headed back to Stewart Field. Since we were flying the same AT-6s, there was no new aircraft transition to go through, and we dived into the serious business of polishing our skills to earn our wings.

The Tactical Department would not quit until graduation day, but we were close enough and had survived the system long enough that it didn't bother us much. Most of us were able to take our authorized weekend a month, and New York City was the main target. Some of the guys were true-loving it with June-brides-to-be, but most of us were more into great parties in a Big Apple that was then a gloriously fun city, open, friendly, and safe to roam at any hour of the day or night. We were in our third year in the area, and most of us had solid social contacts and knew the town. But, if you were at loose ends and looking for a date, not to worry. In a crisp cadet uniform you only needed to hang around under the clock in the Waldorf Hotel lobby for the appearance of the sweet young thing who would invariably wander by. She would keep looking at her watch, and if you introduced yourself, she would be unable to understand how she could have been stood up by an unknown somebody else, but she would be ready to lead you to where the party was.

The wildest night of advanced training came when the weatherman completely blew the wind-direction forecast by 180 degrees. My section was scheduled for the longest night round-robin cross-country to date, and we needed to be sharp on our fuel management and navigation. We did our flight planning very carefully, using the forecast winds that were relatively stiff, and off we went on a night that was clear but very black. A couple of hours later there were AT-6s temporarily parked at airports all over the countryside of New York, Connecticut, and Pennsylvania, and one was even parked in some surprised people's house.

The navigation aids available to us, as we entered black airspace that was completely new to us, were not all that sophisticated, and the coffee-grinder radios we had were great at picking up static and not too much else. We thought that the mass of lighted cities, bridges, and airfields surrounding New York would make navigating a snap, but everything sort of ran together. Since we were using the wrong wind factor with a preplanned throttle setting, nothing turned up where it was supposed to be. I got completely lost, was hurting for fuel, and got my first real case of vertigo when the lights of the East Coast and the stars got all mixed up. I worked through the vertigo by yelling at nobody, shaking my head, and bouncing around a bit, and spotted a rotating beacon, not a split, double-flashing beacon that would indicate a military airfield, but a single-flashing beacon telling me there was some sort of an air patch down there. I buzzed the beacon with my landing gear down and my landing lights on and saw that it was on an open grass polo field, complete with white fences and goal wickets. It had no lights whatsoever and was probably used by light civilian aircraft. It wasn't very long, but I didn't have too much choice. I started a 360-degree turn, remembering all I had learned when we practiced hurdle stage landings. I set up a power-on stall over an imaginary ten-foot clothesline strung along that white picket fence, just like they taught me in basic. I touched down solidly on the grass and stopped with room to spare. A guy drove across the grass in a '36 Ford pickup, climbed up on the wing, and wanted to know what was going on. I asked him which way to the Hudson River and West Point. He pointed about forty-five degrees off the far goal wicket. I thanked him, taxied back to the white fence, went through my pretakeoff routine, and cobbed it while holding the brakes until the tail started to come up off the ground. I was real light on fuel, and as I released the brakes, I zipped across the black grass and was out of there, airborne and sweating the fumes. Once I spotted the Hudson River and identified the mass of New York lights, the rest was routine. Back at Stewart, nobody even asked why I was late. When I got to the air cadet locker room, my instructor arrived, and it was clear that he had been waiting for my return at the officers' club bar. I told him what had transpired, and he got a good chuckle out of that as he clapped me on the back, said, "Good show," and headed back to the club.

While I had been exploring polo fields, my friend "Horrible" Horowitz had been exploring railroad bridges disguised as runways, and he didn't make out too well. Horrible, while running out of fuel, mistook a bridge for a runway and tried to land on it. Recognizing his error at the last minute, he rammed the throttle forward. However, there wasn't enough fuel to allow his engine to accelerate, and he was headed toward a house at the end of the bridge. The house belonged to a Polish family having a family party to celebrate the safe return of a young sergeant from overseas combat duty. The sergeant, having heard the sound of failed aircraft engines before, led the charge of the party people out the front door to see what was happening. Horrible, with no engine and a windmilling propeller, was going no place but down. The sergeant's grandmother, not quite up to the festivities, was sitting at the kitchen table, next to the refrigerator, munching crackers and cheese, when Horrible flew in through the kitchen door and split the ice box with his prop. All the good folks helped him out of the cockpit and into the party while the sergeant made sure the switches were all shut off. Air Cadet Horowitz, despite regulations, was bombed out of his gourd by the time the closest military authorities arrived, but that fact was never documented in any investigative records.

I was once again overwhelmed with mixed emotions as victory in Europe became a fact on May 7, 1945. Thank God for that, but I had missed out on combat in Europe. Our schedule went on without interruption or celebrations.

As the course wound down, "Boots" Blesse and I were scheduled as a two-ship flight to alternate chasing each other while practicing solo hooded instruments. I know of nobody in our class who wanted to fly combat as sincerely as Boots and myself. We were on our own for the flight and didn't even go through the motions of the instrument ride. Instead, we went straight to some relatively isolated farm country, where we split and came back at each other and went at it dogfighting as hard as we could. We started from a reasonably safe altitude but were so into our mock combat that we were soon down on the deck, still trying to outdo each other. It was late on a hazy day, and the lowering sun made the sky at fifty feet look yellow. We wound up barely over the housetops of a small town, both in vertical banks, looking at each other through a very imposing set of electrical high lines. I don't remember either one of us calling it quits, but it didn't take too many smarts to figure that avoiding those high lines was the most important task at hand. We broke it off, and each went home on his own. We were each to get our combat chances, but we didn't know it at that time.

With final check rides out of the way, we packed and prepared to leave Stewart for the few remaining days at the Point. We lined up in front of our T-6s to receive our wings on June 2, and nobody minded the bus ride back to the Point that day. Pinning those silver wings on my West Point dress tunic while pulling the grommet out of my West Point dress hat has to be an all-time memory highlight.

June Week and graduation was fun time, with friends and family helping us realize that we were moving on. On June 5, Gen. Omar Bradley made the big speech, and our cadet hats went flying into the air. Those of us in the army air force had a mandatory duty at Stewart before we were free to leave the area. Although we were now commissioned officers, rated as pilots, and therefore authorized to draw flying pay, we could not actually draw that flying pay until we got airborne at least one time. Some of us got on those damned buses one more time and headed for Stewart, where the AT-6s were waiting to allow each of us to get airborne for five minutes, but Tom Catron and I had a better idea.

My date for a couple of the functions during June Week had been a lanky blond gal from New York City named Sally, who had a year-old son. Her girlfriend, who also had a year-old son, had offered to drive her to the Point and back, and to take care of Sally's son in the interim. On graduation afternoon she learned that Tom and I were headed for Darien, Connecticut, to participate in a wedding and offered to take us there. We accepted and also talked her into driving us to Stewart for our mandatory flight. We beat the buses, and Tom and I were first in line for what was our first commissioned flight, and almost our last flight.

We were pretty suave as we strode out to our T-6 with our wings, second lieutenant's gold bars, and brand new fifty-mission crush hats. I took the front seat first, cranked up and at the end of the runway went through my cigarettes-for-the-poor-Russians checklist. Each of us was to make one circuit of the airstrip, one landing, and log a total of ten minutes' flying time between us. After my landing, I taxied back to takeoff position, and Tom and I switched seats.

Tom popped the throttle, and we raced down the runway. Approaching takeoff speed, we abruptly found ourselves airborne, with the nose heading straight up, approaching a stall a few feet above the strip. Tom had ignored cigarettes for the poor Russians, and the elevator trim tab was still rolled full back from my landing. Both of us leaned on the stick and spun the round aluminum trim wheel, and the trusty Texan hung on the prop long enough to save our butts. It was a very quiet trip around the traffic pattern as each of us figured out that maybe we were not such cool cats after all.

We were cool again by the time we got back to the Point, picked up our bags, and rode to the Thayer Hotel, the staunch bastion of West Point regular army society, located next to the main gate. Booze had been off limits while we were cadets, and booze in the Thayer cocktail lounge had been unthinkable, but Tom and I had long ago decided that we would have a highball in the Thayer before we cleared the post.

Midafternoon on graduation day found the Thayer busy with celebrating senior officers and their wives, and lots of those senior heads spun when two silver-winged second balloons entered the lounge with two striking women and two babies. We ordered highballs, and as the waiter gushed over his lavish tip, Tom and I bounced the children and savored the highballs and the moment. As we stood to leave, a distinguished army matron approached, extended her hand, and offered congratulations. Chucking each child under the chin, she added, "My, you young people of today never cease to amaze me." It was the perfect exit from the Point and good for laughs en route to the freedom of graduation leave.

Most of us covered a lot of ground on graduation leave, working our way across country to that first assignment as a second lieutenant. We were headed for replacement training units (RTUs). The personnel ouija board spoke, and despite any personal desires, I was on my way to an operational B-25 RTU in Enid, Oklahoma. I learned that they had plenty of aircraft and lots of flying time and were turning out combat-ready pilots. That was OK with me, for the moment.

The B-25 was big, and its two huge engines were noisy. It was more like a truck than a sporty car, but it was a combat aircraft. Enid was hot and dusty, and the billowing clouds of the thunder bumpers were huge. Nonetheless, we were better airmen after some eighty hours' more flying experience, and we were finally certified as combat ready in something.

Even though we were qualified to fight in the B-25, there was no requirement for our services in the Pacific at the moment. Then, as flying at Enid closed down, Archie Patterson and I received orders to report to the B-17 RTU at Lockbourne Field in Columbus, Ohio. Four-engine bombers? Hey, it was more flying time and more experience. We packed our few gypsy belongings in our B4 bags and were on a train from Florida to Columbus the next day. Our train route was through Baltimore, Maryland, where we had an overnight layover before our connection to Columbus. By the time we had checked into the hotel on August fifteenth, the news broke: VJ day! The war was over! Again, thank God that it was over, but again we had missed the action. But at the moment we didn't even care. Arch and I poured out on the streets with everybody else and whooped it up with thousands of our fellow Americans we had never seen before. Being in uniform, we couldn't spend a penny, and we kissed girls, drank all we could use, ate more crab than I had ever seen before, danced in the streets, and didn't worry a bit about going to B-17 training in the morning.

Fortunately, we had made a reservation at a downtown Columbus hotel that was only a short walk from the train station, since Columbus was in the same state of celebration that Baltimore had been in the night before. We jumped right in to join the festivities. There were only a few people on duty when we checked in at Lockbourne the next morning. All they did was tell us that the B-17 program was cancelled, and the base was closing, and we were to report to the surviving B-17 RTU in Sebring, Florida.

Sebring was sort of like Enid in some ways, except it was sticky and hot. When we checked in at the personnel office, we received a very unusual offer. They told us that we and our other West Point classmates had been ordered to report to a new institution called the Junior Officers Staff Course, which was to be initiated in Orlando, Florida. However, we weren't due there until right after the first of the year. Nobody knew what the new school was all about, but they did know that Sebring was also in the process of closing down. But the kicker was that we had a choice of what we could do between September and January. We could take off on our own and do as we wished, reporting in once a month for the next five months to collect our pay, or we could put our names on the list for the fading opportunity to get combat-ready in what was probably the last B-17 class. Naturally, we signed up for the B-17 and started training again.

We used to think the B-25 was big until we started crawling around the B-17 with its four engines. We also used to think the B-25 was a load to fly until we started hauling the Fortress around the traffic pattern in the heat and humidity of Florida. Since the entire B-17 training program and the base at Sebring were both shutting down, our course boiled down to three elements. A bunch of officers who were either getting out of the army or moving elsewhere helped us learn to take off and land the B-17. Then they showed us how to practice instrument navigation around the radio ranges that dotted Florida. Finally, they told us to bore holes in the sky to get a total of 150 hours of B-17 time so they could give us a flight check and sign us off as combat ready.

Winter was approaching, though you couldn't notice it, and the medics at Sebring were selected to be one of the nation's first test facilities for a new, highly touted anti-flu vaccine. The initial trials were to be on small groups of healthy young males, and our post–West Point group won that prize. One morning as we finished physical training, we were ordered, not requested, to report to the base dispensary right after lunch for flu shots. After taking the shots and sweating all afternoon in our non–air conditioned, wooden, ground-school building, Al Blue, my well-over-six-foot-tall classmate and I headed for the equally humid stuffy officers' club. We each gulped down two ice-cold draft beers and left for our equally hot barracks, where we could at least take our shirts off. We walked through the screened veranda at the club entrance and onto three rickety wooden steps that led down to the wooden walkway that ran out to the street. Al made the first step down, whereupon his legs quit working, but his head kept descending. He looked like a tree being chopped down as he collapsed, motionless, face down on the walkway. By the time I got an ambulance and got him to the dispensary, it looked like a mini–West Point reunion, and the last of the beds were filling up as lieutenants were being dragged and carried in from all directions. All I wanted to do was get out of there and get away from all those sick people. I made it back to the barracks before it got me. We were out of it for a week, and learned that the vaccine had been withdrawn pending further research.

Orlando was a complete boondoggle, but that's where we got the break we had been waiting for. We were on our way overseas. All of us were on orders to all corners of the globe, and I was part of a small group headed for Europe. Some of us were going to the Twelfth Tactical Air Force, not to push around those big bombers, but to fly fighters. Hooray! Four of us were to report to the 366th Fighter Group, which was equipped with P-47 Thunderbolts; the "Jug." Hooray again. Next stop was the port of New York.

Walt Dabney, Wilbur Pugh, Robert E. Pine (better known as "Root" or "Robert E. Rooster"), and I all drew identical port call instructions. As the port of embarkation personnel people processed our orders and we were transported to the dock berthing the USS *Rushville Victory*, we already knew we were in for quite a ride crossing the North Atlantic during the fierce March storms. It was cold as I walked up the gang-plank, and I eagerly accepted a cup of black coffee from a Red Cross lady. I also accepted a sturdy black wool scarf that carried a small label indicating that it had been knit by a Red Cross volunteer from the Fayette County Chapter in Uniontown, Pennsylvania. I wrapped that scarf around my neck a few hours later when I first stuck my nose out on deck, and I continued to use it all over the world for many years. It never seemed to wear out, and I still have it sixty years later. I wrote a fifty-year thank you to the Fayette County chapter ten years ago.

We got quite a surprise as we boarded. We tossed our B4 bags in what was labeled as an officers section, where the canvas cots were stacked four high along the walls. We were immediately drawn aside and briefed that each one of us would be in temporary command of a group of enlisted men in a particular compartment of the ship. I won the duty of commanding five hundred black construction engineer troops getting their first look at the ocean. The detachment consisted of one super-sharp master sergeant named James Johnson and 499 young, thoroughly terrified privates on their first experience away from home. Segregation was a fact of life at that time, and it was obvi-ous that the army was not going out of its way to make my young, frightened troops comfortable. They were crammed into the bottom front hold. We cast off at three o'clock, and half of my charges got sick before we got out of the harbor, the rest shortly thereafter.

We were in heavy seas before dark. The bow would climb high on a monstrous wave, then seem to hang, suspended and shivering like a fish on a hook, before dropping vertically to crash back onto the water and shake everyone on board to the bones, especially the five hundred and one of us in the bottom front hold.

By the end of the second day out, with no respite from the pound-ing, things were bad in that bottom front hold. Only Sergeant Johnson and I had avoided being sick. I was on duty around midnight when the drains in our one and only common latrine plugged up and the water started to rise in the closed-in steel box of urinals, toilets, and nonoperational sinks. A phone call to the bridge accomplished nothing, and within thirty minutes the water was a foot deep, topped by a layer of floating vomit and excrement. Johnson and I rescued one private who had entered the latrine, taken one look, and passed out, face down, and was in the process of drowning in a foot of water.

Then, about two thirty in the morning, that black engineer company that I had inherited showed its stuff. The various compartments of the ship were separated by huge emergency fire and flood-control doors that were mounted on rollers and normally secured open. During a particularly rough series of crashes back to the sea, one of the doors on the second deck broke free and rolled to a slamming-shut position that rocked the entire ship like a torpedo hit. All emergency alarms immediately screeched and clanged at full volume, signaling strap on your orange life jacket and climb for the deck.

Instantaneously, 499 very sick, very scared youngsters swept past Johnson and me like a tidal wave of orange heading up. They started from last place, but they climbed over, under, and through those on the higher decks that were in front of them and were among the first on the frozen, windswept deck.

Every time I would get a break from the bottom front hold, I'd head topside for some much needed gulps of fresh air. It was an awesome place, since I usually got there at night and when there was not another soul in sight. You had to watch your step, since everything was coated with ice, and grotesque icicle shapes clung tenuously to the ship's hardware above you. I always wore my gloves and made sure I had something firm to hang onto. At night the wildly pitching, frothing sea seemed to provide itself with an eerie light gray backlighting that stretched forever, in all directions, as the white foam reached for the deck and your feet. The ship's wild pitching and rolling into the biting, frigid wind made it like the best thrill ride ever. It was a show that no man could duplicate, and it always left me both humbled and refreshed.

It got a bit better as we plowed eastward. Johnson and I came up with an old record player and some V disks, and some boxing gloves, and the troops began dancing around to "Hey ba-ba-re-bop" or punching each other around a hastily improvised boxing ring. Most of the time the ring wouldn't stay still or level long enough for anyone to get hurt by a punch, and one contestant, who was hit by his opponent as the ship was on a down-slide, bounced on the deck and slid under the bottom rope for fifty feet before crashing into a wall. As referee, I ruled it a TKO, to a mixed chorus of boos and cheers. Eventually people began to eat a bit, but it was not a very fun cruise.

Eleven days after leaving New York, we docked at the sprawling logistical empire of the port of Le Havre, France. The troops were whisked away by endless convoys of six-by-six trucks. Our little group of officers had a day to waste before we were to head for Frankfurt, Germany, and we quickly found straw sacks in a huge tent that was big enough to house hundreds. There was an officers' beer tent close by, but it was a half-mile walk to the closest slit-trench latrine. Bock beer was in season and available in unlimited quantities, and we made up for the dry days on the ship. We had no idea of the potency of the European dark spring brew we were gulping, and we were all smashed in no time. We spent most of the night trotting back and forth on the obstacle course to the latrine.

CHAPTER 4

THE JUG

Itold myself that riding in the back end of the four-wheel-drive steel box known as a radio van was not all that bad, since it was taking four of us to our first combat unit. In fact, it was a horrible ride over dark, rutted roads, and after six hours in search of the village of Fritzlar, Germany, we were lost.

Finally, well after midnight, a faded, arrow-shaped sign said Bad Wildungen one way and Fritzlar another. The driver swung the lurching, springless vehicle left and finally found the dimly lit gate of the old Luftwaffe base that was the current home of the 366th Fighter Group.

It was 3:30 a.m. when the radio van squealed to a stop in front of a building with a sign that said officers' club. We pulled our B4 bags from the van, swung our stiff butts and legs down to the pavement, stared into the darkness, and wondered what would happen next.

Headlights and flying gravel announced the high-speed approach of a military police jeep. An MP sergeant braked to a skidding stop, leaned past the steering wheel, and popped a smart highball to our group. We returned the salute and turned our attention to the sleepy-eyed lieutenant riding in the jeep's right seat.

The officer of the day climbed down to introduce himself and shake hands. "Mattie Matthews, 390th Squadron. They expected you guys about eight last night. Personnel guy gave up and asked me to meet you if you got in before morning. No place to put you this time of night but upstairs in the big storage room in the club. You'll find a couple of cots up there, and a few chairs and some rugs, so I guess that'll have to do for a couple of hours."

We followed as the OD pushed open the big, ornate wooden door of the club and climbed toward another large door on the second floor. Matthews pushed the door open, motioned us in, and turned back down the stairs. I got the distinct impression that he knew what was inside and wanted no part of it. "See ya later," Matthews said from the base of the stairs, and he was gone.

I was the first to enter, and it was like running into a wall—a wall of stink. The dim light from the stairway reached into a long, rectangular room and barely touched a small, unlighted lamp on a table like the tables in the bar below. The windows at the front of the building were closed and shuttered, and the place reeked of stale booze, stale cigarette smoke, sweat, and not-so-long-forgotten sex.

I fumbled to light the table lamp, as Walt and Wilbur forced the window bolts open to let in the air that was already turning gray with the approach of dawn. The feeble lamp revealed a pair of GI canvas cots, a few more tables and some chairs, some crumpled towels, several empty booze bottles strewn about, and three large, partially rolled up rugs. The fresh air helped a bit, and since Root and Wilbur were already on the canvas cots, Walt and I tried to convert the loose ends of two of the rug rolls into a place to stretch out. I managed to log about ninety minutes of half sleep.

After crawling into the crumpled uniforms, we stood close to the front door, trying to look casual, but we must have looked like friggin' new guys (FNGs), because almost immediately a stiff-looking captain walked up and said, "You must be the friggin' new guys."

We all stood very straight and answered, "Yes, sir," as he just kept on talking.

Before he offered his hand, we heard, "Woodruff, Roscoe B., Captain, Class of June '43. I'm commander of the 389th Fighter Squadron, and I'm here to claim Second Lieutenants Broughton, Jacksel M.; Dabney, Walter D.; and Pugh, Wilbur R." As we stepped forward, we shook hands and he added, "Heh, heh, can't wait to see if the West Point Corps of Cadets has really gone to hell like they say, heh, heh."

I hoped I didn't exhale too loudly as I thought, "Whew, boy."

Roscoe was quick to let us know that while we were assigned as pilots, he was mainly interested in us as three regular army officers and fellow military academy graduates who would help him put some order into this ragamuffin organization through the performance of our additional duties. By the time Roscoe had led us through an abbreviated check-in at his orderly room I was squadron technical supply officer, Walt was the squadron supply officer, and Wilbur was the squadron adjutant.

He finally took us to the flight line and turned us over to the squadron operations (ops) officer. All the other pilots were delighted to see us, because many of them were just waiting to go home, and the arrival of the three of us meant that three of the old heads would be hitting the road back to the States. Most of the buck pilots had come through the aviation cadet training program and were reserve lieutenants or captains. Some of them just wanted to get back to civilian life and were counting the days until they could go home and get out. Others were submitting all sorts of forms and documentation in hopes of being selected to stay in the service and obtain regular commissions. Most of them had flown some combat, and they were, to say the least, a loose bunch. They considered checking-out the FNGs in the Jug as a game rather than a procedure.

I drew a first lieutenant named Tom Mansil to check me out, and Tom just wanted to go home and had absolutely no desire to ever get airborne under his own control again. The duty of checking me out was a bad deal for him, since he would be required to fire up a Jug and chase me as safety observer on my first flight. He gave me a flight manual and some air speeds for takeoff and landing, then we went out to a Jug so I could get some cockpit time. As I walked up to that Jug and looked up at that huge round R-2800 engine and that four-bladed, ten-foot-diameter paddle prop, I felt very small. I climbed what seemed like a long way up to the wing and stepped into the cockpit as Tom made some nose- and wing-attitude gestures with his hands, then pointed out the various switches and gauges. We had only been there a few minutes, and I was way behind the power curve trying to figure out what did what when Tom casually said, "OK, get whatever cockpit time you want. Work call in ops is 0730 in the morning and we're scheduled for 0800 takeoff." He sort of half chuckled as he added, "Got to go build up my courage."

My classmate Bob Spragins had gone through a different RTU, had checked in with the 389th Fighter Squadron a couple of months before me, and was a big deal, with almost twenty hours in the Jug. He had inherited a two-bedroom apartment, barracks style, and since his old head roommate had rotated to the States, he asked me to move in with him. I told him about my brief flight orientation, and he allowed that he had received about the same treatment. The attitude of the old heads seemed to be that anyone with wings should be able to step in and fly a Jug, despite the fact that the old heads had enjoyed the benefits of a three-month RTU during their learning process. Sprag suggested that I wear long johns under my flight suit the next morning in anticipation of a cold cockpit and a cockpit heater that probably wouldn't work.

The next morning, the squadron mounted a max effort, considering the deplorable condition our maintenance was in, and had six jugs ready before 8:00 a.m., three for FNGs and three for chase pilots. All the other pilots and most of the enlisted troops from the squadron were gathered on the balcony of operations or in front of the maintenance hangar. The very first replacements were about to launch. They had never flown a Jug before, and they were West Pointers just like that prick, Captain Woodruff.

In any chase flight, the FNG normally went first, and the old head followed to observe and advise as required. Tom wasn't having any of that, and as we walked out to our aircraft, he told me that he would launch first, then watch my takeoff, whereupon I could look for him to be circling directly off the end of the runway. That just didn't ring true, but I thought, "What's a FNG to do?"

After we cranked up, Tom called Fritzlar tower, and we were the first to taxi along the bumpy, pierced-plank taxiway to the end of the runway. Tom got takeoff clearance. Off he went down the runway, not interested in flying but forced to fly, full throttle plus water injection on to insure a fast takeoff. He disappeared, going as fast as he could go. I went through my cigarettes-for-the-poor-Russians checklist and rolled as briefed, with the new sensation of pierced plank rumbling and whining under the wheels. The takeoff was smooth in the eyes of the observers, and spectacular and thrilling for me. I was airborne in a world-class fighter.

I was pretty sure that I had Tom figured out, but I gave the pre-briefed call that I was airborne, and as expected, got no reply. I learned later that Tom had made a big circle and a long, straight-in approach to land, claiming radio problems. Tom never flew again at Fritzlar, but when someone like him dropped out, more of the scarce flying hours were available for the FNGs.

I didn't do anything wild on that first, unescorted Jug ride. I checked the new landscape rather closely but didn't wander too far out of sight of the airstrip. Actually, it felt great to be up there all by myself, with nobody to bother me; just me and my Jug. I felt the machine out and pushed, pulled, turned, stalled, and did all the things I thought I needed to do to make my first ride a good one. It didn't take long to find that the cockpit was hot as hell, and it was the cooling system, not the heater, that didn't work. My long johns were soaking wet with sweat as I thought, "Robert Elias Spragins, I owe you one."

An hour later I called for landing instructions and entered the traffic pattern, to find that with gear and flaps down the Jug turned and approached the pierced plank strip very differently than my most recent mount, the B-17. I horsed her into an acceptable alignment with the five thousand–foot-long pierced plank strip and could have landed safely, but I cobbed it as I shoved the throttle full forward, and went around because I was having fun. I had plenty of fuel, and I made another go-around because I knew I could do it better, and because for the first time in my life I was savoring the quest for perfection that could be shared by a man and a combat fighter.

My go-around did not please some of the assembled spectator pilots, now including my erstwhile chase pilot, back from his five-minute flight, who were betting on which one of the FNGs would get his machine down smoothly on the first try. Getting it down out of the first traffic pattern on my checkout ride had never entered my mind as a criterion of success. I wanted to learn the aircraft. My second pattern was good, and I touched down smoothly. Great; let's do it again, and I went around, feeling I was learning by the second. My third pattern looked the same as the second but felt better, and I rolled out to a comfortable full stop. As I taxied back, the bumpy, pierced plank almost felt familiar, and I knew I was in my element, at last.

The rush to get people back to the United States had about cleaned us out of enlisted maintenance troops, and our squadron was down to one crew chief per four P-47s. Each flight within the squadron had four aircraft, and if you wanted to fly, you worked on your own aircraft, with that one crew chief supervising the pilot's do-it-yourself maintenance. Sprag and I made a strange but real friendship with our most unusual crew chief, Staff Sgt. Ben Harr. A burly giant in cowboy boots who spoke in a loud, gravely voice, his favorite task was driving the refueling truck. When the war started, he had been in prison for manslaughter. He was from Chicago, and he had been an auto mechanic by day and a professional wrestler at night. One night, during a wrestling match, his opponent failed to follow the script and kicked Harr in the balls. Harr picked him up by the ankles, rammed his head into the mat, broke his neck, and his opponent died on the spot. Under his awesome appearance, Harr was a gentle soul, and his prison record had been clean. With the start of the war, he qualified for a program allowing parole and direct entry into the military. His military record was outstanding, and he enjoyed teaching the dumb lieutenants the rudiments of flight-line maintenance. We had fun working for him.

Once we FNGs proved that we could get a Jug up and down, we were accepted and invited to the periodic visits to the pilots' rest camp. It was located on the shores of the Edersee and had been inherited from the German Luftwaffe. The Edersee was a huge lake, backing up into a valley behind a formidable dam that had been a major part of Hitler's hydroelectric program. Many Allied aircraft went down trying to bust that dam before the Brits came up with a unique night-aiming device that did the job. The rest camp resembled a vacation house and was under what would have been the flight path of the attacking British aircraft. The first time I walked off our GI bus and looked at it, I just stared, visualizing the skip bombers and the flak and the historical electricity of the place. We shot liberated Luger pistols at tin cans, took pictures while trying to figure out how to operate liberated or bartered Leica cameras, and listened to V disk records and told war stories. Two of our squadron pilots had been pulled out of the squadron to fill base positions that aligned with their previous civilian occupations. One ran the officers' club, while the other ran the base exchange. Thus, the food and booze at the Edersee were exceptional and plentiful.

Captain Roscoe B. Woodruff was definitely not one of the guys. He didn't spend much time on the flight line, but he had to fly once in a while to collect his flying pay. The old heads warned us that he was a lousy pilot and that a flight scheduled on Roscoe's wing was a cause for fear and personal precaution. I was soon to find out how true that was.

I was scheduled as Roscoe's number four in a flight of four. The flight briefing was long and boring, as we once again went through the basics of flying combat spread formation while observing radio silence. When we got airborne, he kicked the rudders, signaling spread formation, and we started combat maneuvering. We crossed over and under and went north and south and high and low and east and west, never getting more than twenty degrees off of straight and level. We wound up over the wooded mountain country, and Roscoe wiggled his wings to pull us back into finger-four formation as he started about a twenty-degree descent that, after fifty miles, had us down to about a thousand feet in a valley surrounded by mountains. Then he signaled that he was pushing the power up, and we started to climb up the side of a long range of ascending hills that eventually got quite high.

When your leader selects a throttle setting, he knows that number two and three who are sitting close on his wing will be using a bit more power than he is, as they jockey the throttle to stay in position. Number four, flying off of three's wing, will need even more power as he works a bit harder to maintain position, a la snap the whip. As he climbed, Roscoe sank ever closer to the rising line of the rock incline, and he kept pushing his throttle forward. By the time he was about 90 percent of the way to the top of the crests, Roscoe was almost at full power, and I remember him looking from side to side to see if we were maintaining proper position. Two and three were working hard, as we were now skimming the tree tops, and this proud second lieutenant was approaching a stall, hanging on to save his ass. In such a situation, up to a point, you can break formation and slide gently to the side, reversing course to fall back down the slope and regain air speed and stability. We had passed that point, and if I wiggled I was dead. I was trying to push the prop and throttle through the firewall, while Roscoe, now sensing that his aircraft was close to stalling, was hunched over, looking at his instrument panel. If my gallant beast had put out a half inch less manifold pressure, that would have been all she wrote. We fell over the crest, and as we fell down the back side, Roscoe broke radio silence with, "Well, let's head for home." From that day on, any time Roscoe was on the schedule, I was very busy with my additional duty.

My additional duty as the squadron tech supply officer made me responsible for the evils of this particular squadron's flight line supply procedures of past years. It was no secret that whatever Uncle Sam had sent overseas was for the troops, and the troops had used it as they saw fit. You name it, sunglasses, leather jackets, gasoline, booze—if it was there, it had been put there to be used, and accountability was an unknown. Suddenly, Washington demanded a detailed accounting of what had been expended, by whom, and when and where. The requirement was impossible to satisfy legally, since equipment had been used, lost, thrown away, stolen, sold on the black market, or taken home over the past several years. There simply was no accountability, and it was a giant bureaucratic farce to pretend that self-righteous audits could change the situation.

Along with the job, I inherited Tech Sergeant Adderholt as a helper or perhaps as a responsibility. He was a good ol' country boy who was vitally interested in booze and sex and was up to his ass in frauleins and the black market. He presented me with a funny little book of army air forces property cards that indicated that we needed to justify the staggering sum of 385,000 1946 U.S. dollars' worth of government property. Adderholt said no sweat, and would the lieutenant like a neat sixteen-year-old *schatzi*, who can keep him real warm at night and also cook and do laundry? I politely declined and was far more interested in how we were going to clean up the accountability mess.

Adderholt was right: it was a no-sweat situation. Surplus disposal was a big program at that time, and Adderholt had a buddy who was the ranking master sergeant in the surplus program at Fritzlar.

The dollar amount of my account was minuscule in the big picture of those days. As an example, there were over four hundred brand-new surplus fighters, parked in rows on the far side of the field at Fritzlar, waiting to be destroyed. There were Jugs and P-51s and P-38s with maybe two or three flying hours on them, and the demolition teams would break them into three pieces. Cletrac bulldozers would then rumble over them with their tank-like treads and squish them flat. Finally, crews stacked the flattened aircraft on rail cars and sent them to the Volkswagen plant. Sprag and I, in uniform and armed with screwdrivers, climbed the fence one evening and tried to scrounge the cockpit clocks out of a couple of the Mustangs waiting to be destroyed. We figured they would be neat desk clocks. While we were unscrewing them, an army MP spotted us and sounded the alarm. Sirens blared, lights flashed, and a platoon of MPs descended on us with M1 rifles drawn and bayonets fixed. After being spread-eagled in the spring mud and searched, we were cuffed, interrogated, and finally allowed to climb back over the fence to our side of the field, with a formal report to follow. We checked with our binoculars the next day and watched as they blew up that row of shiny Mustangs.

Regardless of the big picture, I had an account to clear. We needed some transportation, but the base motor pool was not responsive to our requirements. One of the departing old heads had cornered a surplus jeep that he had painted purple, and I took it off his hands for fifty bucks. It became the prime vehicle in the Broughton-Adderholt Surplus Disposition business.

For no particular reason we started with flashlights. Everyone really needed to have a flashlight, and that demand had reduced our balance from the 325 flashlights we were supposed to have on the shelves to a total on hand of zero. We took a large wooden box, tossed some dirt and rocks in the bottom, and broke a dozen or so Coca-Cola bottles and sprinkled the broken glass on top. If you were so inclined you could imagine that there were lots of used, smashed flashlights in the box. We filled out the necessary form to the effect that we were turning in what was left of 325 used, battered, and broken flashlights. Adderholt loaded the box into my jeep, took it to his buddy on the other side of the field, and returned with a paper authorizing the removal of 325 flashlights from the books.

It was important to remember what day of the week it was, as on the first surplus run of any week, we gave the guys in the surplus program one bottle of good bourbon, which I was able to procure for five bucks. If we didn't have anything that vaguely resembled what we were supposed to be turning in, we just filled the box with dirt and rocks and nailed a cover on top. We usually saved the closed-box drops for the day of the week when a bottle of bourbon was due, and we never had any of the goods returned. We went through those property cards one at a time and brought the final balance to zero. Roscoe thought I was golden.

But the main use for my jeep was transporting one or more pilots the ten kilometers up the road to the town of Bad Wildungen, where three hundred Red Cross people, almost all girls, were quartered in an exotic old German resort hotel that was disguised as European Red Cross Headquarters. The girls next door were a mixed batch, from lily-white hometown honeys to hardcore professional prostitutes from downtown. There was always music, booze, food, and girls to spare.

Lots of things changed at Fritzlar. We were told that the world's greatest fighter pilot, Col. Clarence T. Edwinson, was enroute to take command of the group. The word was out to all the troops that Edwinson was one tough cookie, who flew anything, and whose word was law in any outfit he commanded. He had been an All-American halfback, and he had shot up a storm with the P-38 outfit he had commanded in Italy. The word was out that he hated the name Clarence; that those who ranked him, and some of his old buddies, called him Curly; and that those who knew him from elsewhere referred to him as Big Ed, but never to his face. That was pretty academic to us second smokers, since to us he was obviously, "Yes, sir, colonel."

When Big Ed arrived on a Friday morning at 8:00, he wasted no time in establishing his authority. He called for all the officers on base to assemble in the group briefing room at 9:00 a.m. At exactly that time, the adjutant shouted attention, and I saw that Big Ed really was big but trim, and it was impressive to see how nimbly this obviously strong man moved as he strode to the front of the room. Holding the group at attention, he scowled from side to side, then said, "Just so you knockers get it straight right from the start, I want you to know that I can outfly and outfight anyone in this room." He paused for effect, then added, "At ease." He got everyone's attention right away.

As a very restrained group, we took our seats, barely looking anywhere other than straight ahead at the first thing we had seen resembling a for-real commander in some time. Before Big Ed could start again, the closed briefing room door squeaked, open and a somewhat shabby Captain McCracken tried to sneak in late. Big Ed took a few strides toward him, and I got my first full-face look at him. His eyes were piercingly sharp and squinted in concentration, and his rather large nose was hawklike: impressive. He was zeroed in on McCracken, who immediately froze in his tracks. Nobody had any trouble hearing Big Ed when he snarled, "What's your name, captain?"

McCracken came to rigid attention, something he had not done in a long time, and replied, "Captain McCracken, sir!"

Big Ed turned and walked back to the front so all could see him, wheeled toward McCracken again, and spoke calmly and icily: "Captain, when I say 0900, I mean just exactly that, 0900. You're fired! Go pack your B4 bag and report to the base adjutant's office. And either you're off my airbase by noon, or I'll personally kick your ass through the front gate." Big Ed and the adjutant traded curt nods of understanding that the formalities would be accomplished. McCracken saluted meekly, Big Ed returned the salute, and as McCracken turned and closed the door behind him, you could have heard the proverbial pin drop.

Nobody knew what to expect next, but we sensed the message would be clear. Our new boss spoke: "I've seen some things since I came on this air patch that tell me that maybe some of you knockers have forgotten that flying airplanes and being ready to kick Russia's ass, or anybody else's ass, is what this is all about. So, tomorrow you get a chance to show me what you've got here. I want a max effort from all three squadrons, with pilots and crew chiefs standing by their aircraft for inspection at 0700. After inspection, we'll scramble for takeoff on my command, and I'll lead the group with the 389th Squadron. You squadron commanders, report to my office for details."

Again, Big Ed and the adjutant exchanged curt nods, the adjutant bellowed, "Attention," and as Big Ed strode out the door, everyone silently agreed that things were going to be different.

The personnel situation had been improving over the past few months, and the squadrons were at or close to full strength, with quality enlisted and officer personnel. Each squadron was assigned twenty-eight Jugs, but they had been forced to pickle many of them when they had no crew chiefs to take care of them. Now they were systematically unpickling them and putting them back in flying shape. They still had a ways to go, so while warning them that it was far from his idea of a max effort, Big Ed accepted a twelve-aircraft show from each squadron, "just this time; we gotta do better." The components were there for a class outfit, and it sure looked like Big Ed was going to be the catalyst to make it happen.

At 6:45 a.m. on Saturday, the Jugs stretched in a single long line along the edge of the parking ramp, their tails to the runway and their noses to the hangars. My crew chief, Staff Sergeant Talkington, and I busied ourselves about our baby, FB-4, but we didn't have anything to worry about. Talkington had been up all night, touching up the paint and wiping her down with aviation gas, which resulted in a spotless machine, devoid of leaks, and a crew chief with gasoline-burned and blistered hands. She looked great with the 389th Squadron's red trim, black lettering, and a four-foot-square painting of *Miss* adorning the left engine cowl. It was just plain *Miss*, nothing else, since both Talkington and I were completely unattached. Our pinup girl was blond with a gorgeous figure inside a sleek black sleeveless silk formal, elbow-length gloves, and a single red rose. I had admired the artwork from the first time I saw it and scrounged it when the former owner went home.

Everybody up and down the line had inspected each other for personal appearance, and we were all sharp as tacks, from boots to goggles. At 6:55, without a word, we all moved into inspection position, and a pilot, suited up and ready to go, stood at parade rest in front of the left wing of each aircraft, while his crew chief stood in front of the right wing.

There was only one aircraft to the left of *Miss*, and that was FB-18, crewed that morning by our squadron line chief, and it would be flown by our new group commander, Colonel Edwinson. Each of the three squadrons had its own radio call sign, while flights within a squadron were designated by color. If this had been a single squadron event, without the group commander being involved, I would have been designated as Sailplane Red Two. But Big Ed's call sign was

Rupert; thus, for this mission our squadron was known as Rupert, and I was lined up as Rupert Red Two.

Our squadron commander, Roscoe Woodruff, was smart enough not to schedule himself in that lead flight. I had been flying pretty good formation, and I guess Roscoe thought a second-smoker wingman for the boss might be good politics, so he put me on the left wing as two, the ops officer on the right wing as three and deputy squadron leader should Big Ed's aircraft abort, and the assistant ops guy as four. I was excited.

A liberated German army sedan approached from the left with the new boss, alone and driving. As the second hand swung to 7:00, Big Ed, ready to fly, parked beside FB-18, took his chute and helmet from the car, and handed them to his crew chief. He was greeted by a stiff and formal Captain Roscoe Woodruff, dressed in Class A uniform, complete with his stiff, grommeted Brooks Brothers fur felt hat. Roscoe didn't get much attention from Big Ed, who had studied the lineup, knew that Roscoe had not put himself anywhere on the schedule, and would not be airborne with his troops. Big Ed already had a replacement for Roscoe on the way. Rupert Red Leader turned and started down the line, anxious to have a look at his new troops and their machines. I was the first one he met. To my surprise, he said, "I hear they call you Motto." He followed my "Yes, sir" with "Looking forward to flying with you this morning."

The flight was an ass buster, as Ed worked us hard for an hour, turning, changing positions, changing formations within squadrons, and most importantly, flying over the home drome so that our crew chiefs could see their charges in flight. After landing, our formerly fresh flight suits were black with sweat. I knew I had flown the best formation of my life and was all smiles as I parked and hustled out of the cockpit. Big Ed and our line chief were talking like old buddies as they put his gear back in the sedan. Then, Rupert Red Leader walked over to me and said, "Hey Motto, you fly good formation. Want to fly my wing for this tour?"

All I could utter was an awed "Yes, sir!" as Big Ed headed back to his car.

As he ducked back behind the wheel of the sedan, he waved back an acknowledgment of my ramrod salute and smiling, said, "OK, I'll tell Woodass, or whatever his name is, to schedule it that way. See ya at debriefing."

The debriefing was very critical, surgical, and personal, but constructive. Again, Big Ed generated silent, unspoken agreement. The 366th Group had a long way to go to get that magical excellence that our new commander demanded, but for the first time since I had come on board, almost everyone wanted it. There was also an unspoken realization that anyone who didn't want that excellence or couldn't hack it probably wouldn't be around for long.

After he had covered the mission, Big Ed looked at the adjutant and asked, "Is the 389th sponsoring the party at the club tonight?" When he got an affirmative nod, he turned back to the pilots and asked, "You guys got another max effort in you for tonight?" The ensuing verbal agreement was spontaneous, and the adjutant didn't even have time to call attention as the troops popped-to the instant the old man headed for the door.

As Rupert Red Two, I had it as good as it gets for a second balloon. When we went someplace in Europe, I got to fly Big Ed's wing. The learning curve was enormous, and all I had to do was watch and listen to get the best airborne leadership course in the world. One of my best lessons came when he took the group from Fritzlar down to Frankfurt for a general officers' retirement flyby. The weather was lousy, but we got the flyby accomplished. When we were refueled and ready to return, the local authorities told Big Ed that the weather was too bad and that he was not authorized to take off. Lesson: he simply called the new local general and told him that he was taking responsibility for his troops, and we were leaving for Fritzlar.

At that time, weather reporting was the pits, and communications were Stone Age. Instrument-approach procedures in Europe were inadequate to nonexistent. At Fritzlar we had a twenty-five-watt radio beacon, which you could dial in on your coffee-grinder radio, and when you got close enough it would point toward the field if you were lucky. Big Ed prided himself on being a super instrument pilot and a master of time and distance navigation, and I wanted to learn from him—which I think he knew. He briefed us that he had called the tower at Fritzlar on a land-line telephone, and they said they had about a thousand-foot ceiling and a couple of miles visibility: a walk in the park. Ed gave me his time and distance figures and said, "Motto, check me on each of these as we go. When I get over Fritzlar, I'm taking us straight down, because I believe we've got plenty of room underneath. If I screw it up, which I won't, I will leave one smoking hole in the ground, and I'll expect to see three other holes in perfect formation. Any questions?"

We ploughed through the murk to what should have been Fritzlar, and it was the toughest weather I had ever been in. You probably never saw a tighter flight of four. The radio compass needle flopped around and swung 180 degrees, Big Ed pulled us up and over in a neat wingover, and we headed straight down from 20,000 feet. We broke out about 1,200 feet, pulling streamers like mad in the wet, rainy air, and buzzed the flight line.

One of the social forces of the times in Europe was displaced persons (DPs), driven from their homes by war and still wandering in very poor conditions. Most of our local DPs were Polish, and they wanted nothing to do with the Russians, whose occupation-zone border was only a few miles away from us. The able-bodied male DPs were organized into paramilitary units and utilized to augment our MPs in guarding our property and equipment.

The commander of the paramilitary unit was a dashing young Polish captain of noble birth who was a graduate of the Polish military academy and who had fought gallantly trying to save his country. His goal in life was to drive the Russians out of Poland. Our officers' club was open to him, and every now and then he would burst in, yellow locks flying, in his brilliant Polish infantry full-dress uniform. Steve the Polsky loved to party, and he considered Sprag and me, as fellow academy graduates, to be among the few worthy of consideration as his special comrades.

In truth, Steve had nothing but the clothes on his back and his treasured dress uniform. He lived in the same shambles and ate the same slop as the rest of the DPs, but you would never know it. He delighted in dropping in on Sprag and me in the barracks so we could practice dueling. He assumed that we had learned to duel at the academy. We did in fact have a few mandatory hours of fencing someplace along the line, but very few of us ever got into it. With Steve, nothing would do but that we duel in the hallway with broomsticks, as was fitting for gentlemen of our ilk. The rest of the guys thought we were nuts. We usually had a stash of goodies for Steve, like booze, coffee, smokes, candy, and snacks from the base exchange. He always accepted it only for his people, but we realized it was a part of what kept him going.

Steve's other passion was telling us, in great detail, how rotten the Russians were. I was surprised by the degree of contact the Russians seemed to maintain with the DPs on our property, and Steve apparently had opportunities to confront them personally. One night he was especially wound up on how he was going to tell them to go to hell and to leave his DPs alone at some mysterious upcoming confrontation he was to attend. I told him he better be a bit cool and not get himself killed for nothing, but he scoffed at that advice. We never saw him again, so I guess he sounded off once too often and the Russians did him in.

Since the Fourth of July was on a Friday, it was going to be a long weekend, starting out with a Friday morning flyby. All the troops were getting used to the strict standards of Big Ed's inspections and flybys, and most of us looked forward to the challenge. He kept increasing the pressure by making the formations more difficult, but the pilots responded—most times. We would spell out names and numbers, and everyone on the airbase got into the spirit of perfection, with enlisted men becoming experts at rating the quality of the show.

We had already had one practice for the Fourth of July show. We had practiced out over the Edersee, because the routine Big Ed wanted was a tough one, and he wanted it to be right when we went public for the troops on the Fourth. Each squadron provided sixteen fighters, plus spares for the buzz flight. On the first pass we spelled out the Group's number, 366, which we had done before. It started to get sweaty after the first pass, as we broke up the 366 and moved into the salute for the Fourth which was forty-eight Jugs spelling out *BANG*.

The group ops officer was the flight monitor for the week, and he flew above the gaggle, calling this or that flight or individual up, back, in, or out. He also took pictures and landed ahead of the group, so the photo lab had prints ready for Big Ed before debriefing. He didn't have too much to say on the practice 366, but the first try at *BANG* was something else. It was sort of like a huge airborne accordion wheezing and wobbling out of step, and no amount of airborne coaching from above smoothed it out.

As we worked our butts off, hanging in there in tight formation, muscles aching, sweat soaked, we really didn't know what he was trying to teach us. We knew that as a group of young pilots, we were improving rapidly in gunnery, bombing, formation—everything we did. We appreciated the fact that the world of the moment was U.S.A. versus Russia, and that our forces were being cut back too rapidly. We didn't know how important our group was in the overall shrinking U.S. military posture in Europe. Nor did we appreciate how important each one of us was to the group, or how one bad performer could ruin the entire effort, be it an air show or a shooting war. We were about to get another lesson.

The problem of the Weehawken weave we were struggling through started with one pilot, Maj. Theodore Gray, who was Iceberg Blue Two, the second man back in the left leg of the A. Ted Gray had been trained as a fighter pilot, but he wanted to be an accountant and was more interested in his job in base finance than he was in flying fighters. Like all of us, he had heard Big Ed say that if you wore the wings, and if you were qualified to fly the bird, then you damn well better fly and be proficient, because we just might need you in a shooting war tomorrow. He was assigned to the 390th for flying, and their ops officer made plenty of flights available to him, but there was always something else that he needed to do, until this Friday morning, when the 390th needed a pilot for that slot and he couldn't get out of it.

Ted Gray was all over the sky. He would fall back, then overshoot, trying to get back into position, then slide sideways to avoid a collision, then slide the other way to try to get back into his spot. We were all tucked in pretty tight, so besides being dangerous, every out-of-sync move Ted made was magnified as he forced those around him out of position. Soon the back of the A was waving like a hula skirt, which quickly transmitted to the B and the N and the G, and the whole thing was a mess. We all kept trying, but it just never came up to acceptable.

The briefing room was buzzing, with all the pilots flying with their hands, trying to be assured that they hadn't personally messed up the drill, when the old man stormed in, eight-by-ten photos in hand, and his head down like a charging rhinoceros. We popped to and stood rigid and silent, and he let us stay that way, never giving us a command of at ease.

He never yelled at us, but he could turn on an icy tone mingled with a growl that cut right through you. He used it with, "Major Gray, are you in the room?"

A weak "Yes, sir," answered.

Big Ed continued, "Were you flying Iceberg Blue Two?"

The "Yes, sir," was even weaker.

"You're out of my outfit, Major Gray. Pack your bags and be off my airfield by three this afternoon."

The "Yes, sir," was almost inaudible.

"And the rest of you knockers . . ." Big Ed paused painfully. "You just lost the war." He dropped the photos on the table beside him and left just the way he had entered.

There was no inspection before we cranked engines on the morning of the Fourth at exactly 9:00. Each of the three squadron operations sergeants had huddled the night before and decided that they would add a different touch to the engine start, and they got Sergeant Adderholt to tap his bottomless resources for some flare guns, known as Very pistols, and some colored signal flares. In the morning the ops sergeants climbed to the roof of their respective ops buildings, and when they saw Big Ed's prop turn, to everyone's surprise, they started firing straight up, and red flares burst in front of the 389th, white star flares burst in front of the 390th, and blue bursts saluted the 391st. A few of the incandescent fragments bounced a bit close to machinery on the ramp, but that didn't seem like a big thing at the moment.

The flyby went great. There was hardly a wiggle as we flew by on the first pass with the squadrons in trail, with four flights in fingertip within each of the squadrons. A few minutes later we were back spelling out 366, and then everybody in the know was waiting for the *BANG*. It took one big, flat three-sixty, and we were in there, and Big Ed rolled out on course for the ramp. Just as we crossed the midpoint of the ramp at five hundred feet in a perfect *BANG*, the buzz flight of four screamed under us at fifty feet, and just for fun the three sergeants added another shower of red, white, and blue flares. The crew chiefs cheered, and we were already smiling to ourselves. Big Ed must have figured he just about had us ready to go to war in case the Russkies decided they wanted some of that.

Next on the schedule was a party at the Edersee. The place was packed, the booze and food were plentiful, and all went as planned until late afternoon, when everyone in the bar area suddenly froze. Moving from their car, to stand in the doorway, in full uniform, were a Russian lieutenant colonel and a Russian major, both wearing Russian wings. Root Pine, who had played around studying a little Russian, became the Edersee spokesman, and more through curiosity than anything else, we invited the Russians in. They both practically inhaled a bourbon and water offered to them, and immediately started speaking better English, claiming they were lost. But it was apparent that they knew where they were, and what units the pilots were from, though all the Red Cross girls were obviously a surprise to them. They were simply using a new twist in the game of looking for information, and since they were in uniform, the worst that they could be accused of was being across the border of the Russian occupation zone without authorization—though how they actually got across, with their car, nobody ever knew.

It seemed like a different game to play, so we took turns toasting them in rapid succession with loaded drinks. After several belts, the Russians made a big mistake when they insisted on toasting the Red Cross gals one by one. Those gals could knock the booze back with the best of them. By the time it got dark, the Russians didn't know who they were, and many of the air force group weren't much better off. The Russians were a mess by the time they got their car started and lurched into the night in the direction of the Russky border. The next day the Office of Special Investigations, which was supposed to be sort of like a military FBI, announced that the army constabulary people had found a completely wrecked Russian staff car with some blood in the front seat, in a ditch, on the far side of the Edersee and way inside the border. Mission accomplished. The other big story of the weekend was the rampant rumor of an impending change in the group's status.

CHAPTER 5

NEUBIBERG

In early 1947, Washington was going full blower on reducing American military strength worldwide. The cuts in force structure were ruthless and across the board, despite continuing massive Russian buildups. The flow of personnel ebbed. There was no new equipment in the mill. Spare parts were limited to what was left on the shelves or what could be cannibalized, and there were precious few funds to operate what was still operable.

When Gen. Curtis LeMay arrived in Europe to take over United States Air Forces in Europe (USAFE), he found that about all that remained of the once awesome American air armada was a handful of fighter groups scattered about the continent. He quickly decided that he simply did not have the resources to keep them all at an acceptable degree of combat readiness. At the same time, pressure from Russia was mounting on all sides. Their air forces showed little indication of shrinking, MiG fighter jets were being produced in quantity, and border thrusts and provocations were common. LeMay determined that one highly trained, combat-ready fighter unit with adequate support resources would give him better air-fighting potential than several struggling units. That's when the 86th Composite Fighter Group was activated.

General LeMay directed Big Ed to form an elite composite fighter group of P-47s and P-51s, with the best fighter pilots he could find. LeMay felt that from a strategic point of view, he would be most comfortable with his fighters near Munich, at the old Luftwaffe base of Neubiberg, where a P-51 group was currently operating. Once the new group was operational, they would be provided with reconditioned Jugs, and the Mustangs would be phased out. The reasoning was that the Jug was a better weapons system for pounding the Russian ground forces, should the bell ring. The Jugs couldn't turn as tightly as the Mustangs when both of them were down on the deck, but the Jugs could chew up ground forces, take terrible punishment, and often limp home. When the Jug went above twenty thousand feet and the turbo kicked in, she was a tough opponent. Thus, LeMay wanted his only fighter group to be a Jug group, and he wanted Big Ed to run it.

When somebody first heard from somebody that somebody thought that some changes were in the mill, we also heard that General LeMay and Big Ed went back a long way together. I even heard that Big Ed's original wife was somehow related to LeMay, but I never knew of anyone who ever verified that. We did know that Big Ed was quite comfortable referring to him as "the general."

Big Ed was in Wiesbaden conferring with the big gears about the move when the group personnel weenies called a meeting to announce, in their typical jargon, that the base at Fritzlar was closing. Those interested could volunteer for consideration to be assigned to a composite unit to be stationed in Munich, and to be commanded by Colonel Edwinson. All others, and those volunteers not selected, would be returned to CONUS (continental United States) with minimal delay.

Elias Spragins, Wilbur Pugh, Walt Dabney, Root Pine, and I beat most everybody else to the sign-up sheet to move out with Big Ed. When we got there, we learned that each of us had no choice; Big Ed had already put each of us on orders to Neubiberg.

Since we were moving out of the boondocks to the big city of Munich, complete with autobahns, it seemed like a decent set of wheels would be a good idea. I junked the purple jeep, and through a classmate I was able to buy a brand-new 1946 Plymouth, one of the first American cars brought into Europe after the war. Sprag, Wilbur, Root, and I were off to München in style.

We found our way to the base at Neubiberg and checked in to the bachelor officers' quarters, which was a typical blah BOQ. It took only a few minutes to claim our spot, unpack, and wash our faces, and we were ready to find the officers' club. It didn't take too long for new guys to meet new guys, and before too long a bunch of gypsies were on their way to becoming a new team. That sort of thing happens easily in the fighter pilot fraternity.

But the new outfit did not go together without a good deal of sorting out who was who on the pilot-superiority pecking list. At first, nobody knew who the hot sticks were, but within a few weeks, pilots were freely exercising their bragging rights at the bar. The Jug guys coming to town had been well screened, and Chester Van Etten, better known by his World War II call sign of John Black, had gone through a similar process as he pared three Mustang squadrons down to one. Pending the arrival of all the reconditioned Jugs, they kept a full squadron of P-51s, including a six-ship flight of specially equipped RP-51 photo reconnaissance Mustangs. The competition was fierce and fun.

As the Jug people began to arrive on base and the newly reworked Jugs started flowing in from the depot, the first priority for the Jug guys was shaking down their new aircraft and checking out the local area. First priority for the Mustang drivers was orbiting over the end of the runway then pouncing on the Jugs' tails the second their wheels left the ground.

The group evolved into three Jug squadrons, and the only P-51s remaining in the group were the six photo-reconnaissance Mustangs. The P-51 pilots then went through their P-47 checkout routine and reversed the roles off the end of the runway. I got to check out in one of the reconnaissance, or recce, P-51s, and when you were in a Mustang, it was indeed a piece of cake to suck up a Jug carrying a full fuel load. Great sport.

One of the many things Big Ed taught me at Fritzlar is that I should always have my own last-ditch plan on how to get back to the home drome when everything went to pot. The archaic navigation aids of the times were no better at Neubiberg, so I wasted little time in preparing for the time the weather moved in, the radio aids went down, and the control tower became useless. The strongest radio signal in all of south Germany came from the Armed Forces Radio Network (AFN) station, which broadcast twenty-four hours a day in the middle of downtown Munich. Listening to AFN was a ritual, and anyone who was into the great jazz of the day made every effort to be tuned in at noon, when a guy who became our personal friend, Muffet Moffat, came on with, "It's luncheon in München." So AFN seemed like a good starting spot for the survival drill.

Even if the coffee grinder radio in your Jug was weak, you could usually get a solid signal from AFN as you got close in, and that would point your radio compass needle at downtown Munich. When the radio compass needle swung around indicating you were over AFN, you wanted to be heading 180 degrees and at two hundred miles an hour and one thousand feet. Three minutes straight ahead was a distinctive bend in a normally dry river bed. Whether you could see it or not, that was time for a standard-rate turn to the runway heading while reducing power and dropping the gear and flaps to establish a five hundred–foot-per-minute descent at 130 miles per hour. The end of the runway was another three minutes straight ahead. It was fun to practice, and you could usually get tower permission to finish it with a good buzz job of the base. And it worked.

One day I was ferrying a Jug back from the depot at Erlangen, when all the weathermen must have gone to lunch at the same time. As I was getting airborne, a dandy ice and snow storm bounced off the Alps and descended on the Munich area. Neubiberg recovered all the local flights, and nobody else was cleared inbound, but there was ol' Motto, all by himself, heading for home with no nav aids working and nobody talking to him on the radio. No sweat. When I got Muffet on the radio compass, he was playing some good noise, but I had to turn the volume down and concentrate on maintaining a thousand feet as the clouds lowered and the snow got heavier. I was on course for a good compass swing and then in the soup for the leg to the turn point. Turned and descending, I was so busy being smooth and accurate that I hardly noticed the slop. Two minutes later, in radio silence, came the runway lights and a nice full stop landing.

As I parked, the big staff car met me, and Big Ed said, "Motto, I bet you had that all figured out."

I tossed him a salute and said, "Yes, sir, just like you taught me."

He cackled his exclusive laugh and said, "Good on ya. See ya at the club later." That was not the only time Big Ed met me after I landed. From flying as Rupert Red Two, I had developed a tremendous respect for Big Ed's superb navigational ability. It seemed that he always knew exactly where we were, and how to get to where we were going. He didn't have to be at altitude looking at a map to pinpoint our position. He seemed to be equally capable whizzing along on the deck, where things you could recognize whipped past quite rapidly. The Russians were becoming increasingly more provocative on their high-speed, low-level probes against our border, and we played the same game.

You needed to know where you were at all times, since crossing the imaginary borders between zones was a huge no-no. Thus, practicing low-level navigation was a productive thing. It was also lots of fun, since you had a license to buzz most anyplace.

I was scheduled to lead a late-afternoon flight with my West Point classmate John Karr on my wing, and a low-level run against downtown Augsburg seemed like a good idea. John slid out into tactical formation on my left wing, just a little bit higher than I was, and we were right down on the deck, going about as fast as those Jugs could go. There were enough good landmarks so I could tell that I was where I wanted to be, but the late-afternoon sun was sinking, glaring right in my face, and making it tough to see straight ahead. But, we were almost there, where we would pop up and break away, when—aghh! There was the biggest pair of highline towers I had ever seen, with tops above me and with drooping electrical lines that looked like they were a foot in diameter right in my face. I yelled break left and pulled back as hard as I could, but it didn't work. A line caught my left wing, flipped me on my back, and sawed through the wing to the main spar before stretching, breaking, and snapping back, together with the most God-awful electrical flash you could imagine.

It took a few seconds to get back to right side up, to determine that I had not been electrocuted, and verify that my Jug was flying OK. John had been just high enough above me that he missed the wires. I waggled my wings to bring him back in close so he could check me over as we swung back towards Neubiberg. I had all sorts of black thoughts about accident investigation boards, reprimands, maybe even being grounded. We didn't say much on the way home. I learned later that things were not at all quiet in Augsburg. It was evening commute time, and I had cut the main power source for downtown. According to one of our State Department friends, horns were honking, traffic lights were out, and the main source of transportation, the electric streetcars, were stalled out. It stayed that way for most of the night.

I knew that there were plenty of captains, majors, and lieutenant colonels between the boss and me, and that several of them would enjoy taking a chunk out of this hot dog lieutenant. I couldn't do much about that, but I was heartsick that Big Ed would know that I had screwed up. I drew a small crowd upon parking, the highest ranking of whom was a senior major who ran the base maintenance shops and who would be responsible for fixing my sliced-up Jug. He, for some reason, didn't fly our fighters, and since my squadron commander was not on the scene, he took off on me like I was his pet whipping boy. I had no idea that he disliked me that much, but he was into telling me the aircraft would probably never fly again, and threatening to get me thrown out of the service about the time I heard a motorcycle close by. The motor pool guys had scrounged a big old Harley-Davidson cycle from the army and put it into top shape for Big Ed. It was the only one on the reservation, and thus it had to be the boss approaching. I don't think I ever felt lower.

He parked, returned my salute, ignored the major and said, "What happened, Motto?"

All I could say was, "I flat screwed up, sir."

He motioned for me to follow as he walked around my injured bird and said, "So tell me about it."

I limped through my low-level practice routine, finishing up with "and I was almost ready to pop up over town, and I ignored the sun in my eyes, and I screwed it up."

Big Ed turned and addressed the major, in a manner that made the major pop to, with, "Major, you got a spare left wing in supply?" When he got a yes, he continued, "You got a night crew on standby?" Another yes, and he nodded his head with, "OK, I want that wing off this bird, and I don't ever want to see that wing again, and I don't want it on my airfield." The major wasn't sure he believed what he was hearing, but he was smart enough to remain at attention and nod in the affirmative. Big Ed concluded with, "I want that new wing installed and rigged tonight, and you will call the 525th and make arrangements for Lieutenant Broughton to test-hop it tomorrow. Any questions?"

He turned away from the major, motioned me to follow him back to his Harley, and said in a tone I will never forget, "Motto, don't ever fuck up like that again. You only get so many chances, and you used one up there." I've been close to the deck, going fast, many times since, and I never did forget.

One of the guys John Black had retained in his select Mustang outfit was a captain named Art Owen. Art had been shot down in World War II over France, then spent many long months evading and fighting with the French underground. He had harrowing tales to tell, but the trouble was, he wouldn't utter a word about those adventures, nor will he today, almost sixty years later. Art signed up to bring his wife and their newborn daughter to Europe as his dependents. Art was one of four children, and when both of his parents died, he found himself with his sixteen-year-old sister, Alice Joy, as an additional dependent. AJ joined the rest of Art's family as some of the earliest American dependents into the area, and AJ, to her surprise, found herself to be the youngest charter member of the newly formed 86th Composite Fighter Group.

We spent our time either on the flight line, in our quarters, or at the club, so it was natural that Art introduced his very attractive little sister AJ to the group at the club. She immediately became the entire group's dependent and the best-chaperoned young lady in history. She enrolled in Munich High School, and later, when she and a few other dependents from the area graduated, she had the largest and loudest rooting section of fighter pilots that the hall could hold.

One afternoon at the club, as several of us were telling war stories, she mentioned to Art that she wanted to go to their off-base house and change for the upcoming evening party. Since Art was in the middle of a hot card game, I casually pulled out my keys and told her she was welcome to use my pride-and-joy new Plymouth. Not until she returned a few hours later did I learn that she had never driven a car before, but she made it. On another Saturday evening at the club, I invited AJ to go tea dancing with me at three o'clock on Sunday afternoon, which was sort of an uptown thing to do in those days. She accepted, though we both knew there were no tea dances in that place at that time. I figured we could drive into Munich and hit the State Department's fancy club at the Haus der Kunst or someplace like that, but she thought I was kidding. When I came by to pick her up at three, I found that she had another date, and that Art's wife was fixing dinner for all of them. Oh, well.

It was late on a cold winter afternoon when Bob Spragins and I walked out of the orderly room and crunched through the snow toward our quarters. Art's car was parked across from the orderly room, with his wife in the middle of the front seat and AJ sitting by the passenger window. We waved, and AJ smiled at me and without warning something inside me went uluump, and I knew, no doubt, that she was the girl for me. It wasn't the right time, or the right place, but several years later we were married, and four children and fifty-plus years later it is still the same.

One of Big Ed's prize imports was his deputy commander and number-one guy, Stick Thorson. Stick had a bunch of combat time and victories from North Africa and was a natural to back up Big Ed. Rumors were that he had been a real skinny type, but that was long past. He was round faced, jolly, a friend of all—but like Big Ed, a fast and firm enforcer of Big Ed's code. Stick loved to gamble and was always ready to join in on whatever wild thing was brewing at the club. His passion was cards, be it pitch, hearts, or you name it. When Big Ed moved in, he took over a huge, stone German house located adjacent to the border of the base, and Stick moved into one of the many rooms in the house.

Though I didn't really know it at the time, Stick was different. Stick had been an orphan forever, and had been raised by a group of nuns, whose teachings he held firmly beneath the surface. While most of us who were unattached managed to spend every cent we got our hands on, Stick had a healthy chunk of his lieutenant colonel's pay going to the nuns.

We all knew that we were part of the 86th because we were among the best available, which naturally led to some unfortunate ego cases. One of the giants of the days was the thirty second traffic pattern. The trick was to come at the runway low and pitch up while completing an inclined 360-degree turn that would include flinging out your landing gear and flaps and touching down and rolling your wheels smoothly onto the pierced plank in thirty seconds or less. It was a neat trick requiring exceptional "touch" while generating a maximum-performance turn at marginal minimum air speed without stalling out and auguring in. The Jug, being big and heavy, did indeed require lots of that "touch" to accomplish the feat. We got a new captain in the group who was reputed to be the hottest thing to come down the pike in many moons. Shortly after announcing to all that he was the thirty second–landing champ, he took a few days off to welcome his wife and children, then came back to work still talking. It was a Monday morning, and my classmate Frank Lish was on mobile control, monitoring our airfield traffic. This new captain came screaming into the traffic pattern and said, "Clock it for me, mobile," as he pitched to land.

Frank said to himself, "Owhee, that's awful tight," as the captain passed twenty-four seconds, still not on the runway heading but in a more than vertical bank. At that moment, she stalled at about two hundred feet, snapped, and went straight in. Severe words to all from Big Ed augmented the image of the smoldering heap off the end of the runway.

The air-to-ground gunnery range was another area where ego could bite you. It was common to bet something like a nickel a hole for the ground-strafing target and a quarter a bomb for practice-bomb displacement from the bull's-eye. After a pretty good verbal buildup, a flight of four took off with my flight leader, a senior captain named Pop Turner, leading, and three contenders on his wing. One of the sharpest tongues in the group was a captain named Arnold, so naturally his nickname mimicked our air force chief, Hap Arnold. Hap considered himself among the world's greatest gunners and bombers and was very pleased to tell that fact to anyone who would listen. Since Hap had taken on an administrative job as adjutant, he had developed slight eyestrain and was doing the unthinkable: wearing glasses. His nickname immediately changed to Cousin Weakeyes, and the barbs were merciless. Hap had the pressure on to prove he was still the greatest, and Pop had the pressure on to prove that most anybody could beat a guy who wore glasses, even part of the time.

The bombs we used were small replicas, with a true trajectory and a shotgun shell that fired and emitted a smoke spotting charge when the bomb hit. Pop rolled in on the first pass, going to show them how it was done, and pressed in on the bull's-eye. His speed built up, and his altitude disappeared, and nobody ever knew if he released a bomb or where it hit, because all they saw was the explosion and foul black smoke as Pop Turner flew straight into the ground and exploded: "unscoreable at twelve o'clock." That news went through the group in a flash. But thirty minutes after they verified that Pop had indeed augured in with the aircraft, after sending Stick to tell Pop's wife, Big Ed set up a new gunnery and bombing flight, leading the three survivors himself. He upped the ante to a quarter a hole and a buck a bomb, and he waxed all three of them. That afternoon it was back to business, almost as usual. There is a lot to learn in the fighter business, and unfortunately there are lots of bad examples to learn from.

The trick is to learn quickly while avoiding becoming a bad example. That way it's a lot of fun.

It didn't take too long before Sprag, Wilbur, Rooster, and I got fed up with the Spartan accommodations of our old German bachelor officers' quarters. The BOQ was basically U-shaped, and one of the wings, which had apparently been guest suites at some time, was shut off and boarded up. We busted in and found that the plumbing was intact and operational and that there were plenty of gas and electric outlets to convert it to a four-bedroom superpad fit for four young fighter pilots. It even had kitchen facilities and a large living room. We easily convinced Big Ed that it was a great idea, and he allowed us to have at it, with the stipulation that he be the guest of honor on opening night. By modern standards it is mind-boggling to describe the power we had at our disposal with a pack of cigarettes or part of a pound of coffee or sugar—and the locals were delighted with our seemingly miniuscule handouts. We scrounged or bartered for all we needed to do the job and it turned out to be an amazingly modern and functional complex. We named it the Penthouse, and everyone wanted to be invited. The guest lists included officers of various nationalities and their women, nurses, Red Cross girls, State Department dollies, and, after one of Rooster's night solo missions of strafing the *strasse* down by the *bahnhof,* a big-chested Russian DP, to help Rooster "better understand Russian culture."

We all played hard, but only as a secondary thing to our flying, and there was plenty of that. One cold, icy Monday morning, as I was carrying my chute back across the snowy ramp after a Jug flight, Big Ed came driving down the ramp, stopped, and said, "Hey Motto, you want to go to Paris for a few days?" Since I had been there before after a "Battle Of Britain" air show out of Fritzlar, I knew that it would be a fun trip and was all for it. He continued, "OK, Stick and I are taking the Gooney Bird to a fakey little meeting, so get with it and meet us at base ops in forty-five minutes. I'll get a couple of other guys and clear it with your squadron COs."

Within the hour, the Gooney Bird was airborne, with Big Ed and Stick up front at the controls and Dick Briggs, Hap Arnold, and me in the back. Even though the three of us in back had packed in a hurry, we had included ample booze supplies, which we snipped at while playing cards and telling lies to pass the time of day. When Big Ed got bored up front, he left Stick to fly and came back and led us as we alternated trotting from the front to the rear of the otherwise empty goon, changing the center of gravity as we moved. We would get all the way back in the tail and watch the nose head up. As soon as Stick would retrim for level flight, we would move full forward and reverse the game.

It was all fun and games until it got dark and the weather unexpectedly socked in all around Paris. The French air controllers and tower operators would not communicate with Americans on the radio unless they felt like it, which was not often. The radio frequencies were all messed up, and we wound up badly lost in the weather. We got so low on fuel that we couldn't make it back to Munich, and when Big Ed came back and told us to prepare to bail out, he was dead serious. Stick and Big Ed finally found a hole and got down under the weather, figured out where we were, and made a visual approach and landing despite the French controllers.

We spent most of the time in Paris partying, dancing on the tables at Maxim's and living it up, except for Stick. He wouldn't talk about it, but the suspicion was that he had found more gambling spots anxious to take his American cash than he bargained for. The night before we were to head back, Stick gave up and went to bed early, sober and obviously depressed. Big Ed rounded up six whores, got the spare key to Stick's room from the front desk, and all of us burst in to sic all six of them on Stick at once. We roared with laughter as Stick fought for his body. Stick didn't think it was at all funny and rolled up in a prenatal curl until everyone left. Stick continued to pout all the way home the next day.

The winters were long and demanding, but in Bavaria winter was fun for those of us who liked to ski. Imagine a weekend amid the Olympic atmosphere of Garmisch, skiing the Zugspitze, with classic rooms, including huge feather beds, for twenty-five cents a night, and hot buttered rums and lavish meals for a nickel each. It was heady stuff, and a natural follow on was to take some leave and attend the first postwar Olympics held in St. Moritz, Switzerland. The Penthouse gang headed out, and even in good weather, driving my new Plymouth through the mountains from Munich to St. Moritz was thrilling.

We thoroughly enjoyed the competition and the taste of international life in the fast lane that our U.S. warrior status allowed us. It went all day and all night. One morning at five o'clock, I walked a singing, completely bombed Norwegian ski jumper partway back to his team quarters. He had no concern about the fact that he was scheduled off the ninety-meter jump three hours hence.

On the night before I was scheduled to head back for Neubiberg, two things happened: a blizzard moved in, and in the fierce weather, Root Pine stole the Olympic flag. That genuinely enraged the Swiss authorities, and as the searching and questioning began, I discovered that I could pull the driver's front seat out of my 1946 Plymouth and hide the flag between the stuffed seat and the seat springs. I then went on red alert, waiting to scramble with the first snow plows that felt brave enough to attack the pass and the road back to Munich. When the first plow moved out, I tucked into close trail and barely escaped back across the border with the flag under the front seat of my Plymouth and the Swiss police in chase. The Olympic flag became a wall ornament in the Penthouse.

The other guys got back a couple of days later, and since the Swiss were still making noises about their Olympic flag, Big Ed figured it was a good idea for me to volunteer for a month of temporary duty (TDY). He needed someone to set up and run a stopover facility in Athens, Greece, for Jugs that our group was to ferry to Turkey to give to the Turkish Air Force. We loaded up a goon with some light maintenance supplies and a few crew chiefs, and off we went to Athens. Even though Greece was in the midst of a civil war, Athens in the spring was business as usual, and the State Department social complex came alive at five each evening. The flowers and food were exotic, companionship and music were excellent, and food poisoning was readily available. I have never been so sick and so alone. I clearly remember crawling on my hands and knees from my civilian hotel room to the community bathroom.

One of the Jugs that landed at my pit stop was out of commission for parts, so the pilot left it with me and my small maintenance crew, and went back to Germany on the Gooney Bird. The next goon from Germany brought in the required parts, and the Jug was soon ready for me to test-hop. The test-hop was fine and even included a duel with a Spitfire that I bounced while he was taking off from the RAF base on the other side of Athens. He waxed my ass.

I joined up with the next batch of Jugs that came through Athens, enroute to Turkey. As we turned onto base leg to land and deliver the P-47s to the Turkish unit at Balikesir, a Turkish airman cut the throat of a sacrificial lamb on the end of the runway. That was but the first of a series of Turkish culture shocks, but it got your attention as you were lining up to land.

When I got back to Athens I found that my maintenance sergeant had gone absolutely stone blind from drinking prohibited local moonshine, and I had to arrange for him to be air evacuated back to Germany. I decided to try one more of the exotic local meals, and I recovered from a second bout with food poisoning just in time to greet my relief and head back to Munich.

As the only U.S. fighter outfit on the continent, we were constantly getting called on to show the flag on behalf of our postwar allies.

General LeMay wanted the Jugs seen around Europe, which resulted in lots of great cross-country gaggles, but not all of the show-the-flag missions were fun and games. The Italian government was less than stable, and the State Department thought a little U.S. P-47 buzzing around an air show in Rome might help. We were in the process of exchanging Jugs with the repair depot and had lots of birds that kept having bothersome maintenance failures, but we answered the call with a gaggle of twelve Jugs. They ran into some bad weather and unexpected winds over Italy, so they kept going higher to save fuel, and the winds kept getting stronger. Walt Dabney was part of the third flight of four, and his flight leader suddenly looked for him and found his spot empty. They were in the weather, above the Alps, at an altitude where oxygen from the aircraft's system was a requirement for consciousness and survival. We assume that Walt's oxygen system may have had a loose hose clamp, or a leak, causing a lack of oxygen that he did not detect prior to losing consciousness. He dropped from the flight and probably continued to descend. Locals reported seeing a P-47 fall out of the storm clouds into a valley between the mountains. Did Walt recover momentarily at the lower altitude? Witnesses said the aircraft stabilized and the pilot climbed steeply trying to avoid the mountains that surrounded him. He didn't. Witnesses further stated that an individual ran to the wreckage momentarily, then ran off. When local authorities arrived at the scene they discovered Walt's remains, one part of which was his left hand, with the ring finger amputated and his West Point and wedding rings missing. I had the sad duty of escorting Walt's wife, Charlotte, and her two infant sons back to the States.

The Berlin Blockade found the United States woefully short of both air and ground forces in Europe. General Lucius Clay, the American governor in Berlin, and General LeMay, the military commander, were in constant, direct confrontation with their hostile Russian counterparts. General LeMay knew he was down to minimum air strength, but decided to gamble on an aggressive response to the first of a series of crises engineered by the Russians, when they administratively closed the air corridor to Berlin. He ordered Big Ed to an increased alert posture and directed him to increase border-feint missions.

The big show came after the United States and Russia agreed to a high-level meeting at Tempelhof Airfield in Berlin. The U.S. generals set up a review of the local security forces of the four occupying nations, knowing that protocol would require the Russians to attend the review. They put up grandstands and reserved a block of seats for the Russians at the top of the center section. Then, General LeMay called for Big Ed.

Big Ed briefed us that this just might be the first chapter in another shooting war, and the adrenaline was pumping throughout the group. Each of the three squadrons put up twenty-four Jugs, and there was not one single abort in the entire exercise. Big Ed led, and I flew as Rupert Red Two. The group headed for Berlin right up the forbidden corridor, loaded with live ammo, ready to fight if required, and secretly hoping that it would be required.

We saw a few Russian fighters shadowing us from a distance, but the Russian bogies never challenged our passage. When we landed, we set up an alert system and got ready to respond to whatever might happen. The air was charged, and nobody had to be told that this was not a party trip. We all went to bed early in the huge Tempelhof barracks area, within sprinting distance of our aircraft.

General LeMay was at the morning briefing and had a few words to pump the group up, as if it were needed. Big Ed's briefing was dramatic, concluding with, "I'm going to be looking eyeball to eyeball with those Russian red hat bands in the center of the grandstand, and I'm going to blow 'em over, and you guys are going to keep 'em down. Everyone stack up on me, cause if anyone gets below me, you and lots of other folks are dead." Nobody doubted him.

As planned, there had hardly been a word on the radio since take-off, and seventy-two aircraft were performing as one. As Big Ed rolled

out of a long, sweeping left turn at a thousand feet, he was still five
miles to the east of the airfield. I was stacked about a foot above him
and tucked in tight, as were three and four. The trailing sections of
flights were only slightly higher. Rupert White flight was on his left,
and Rupert Blue was on his right, and it looked almost like a single
flight of twelve. Fifteen more individual flights of four formed the five
similar snarling sections in trail behind Rupert Red Leader. We fed the
big R-2800 engines a little more throttle as we gradually descended.
The ten-foot-diameter paddle props carved huge, noisy chunks out of
the air as Big Ed passed through one hundred feet on the way down
and with the eastern field boundary in front of him.

As he crossed the perimeter road, the bottom of his prop arc was
five feet above the flat field in front of him and the red pip in the middle of his gunsight was centered on a group of about fifty Russian
VIPs in the top center section of the bleachers. The air was smooth,
and it was almost like a slow-motion, quiet approach to a stack of
wood and steel pipes and people that quickly turned into a very real,
high obstacle close to Big Ed's nose. Red hat bands were falling, diving, and trying without success to go elsewhere.

The additional back pressure on the stick that was required to hold
position as we skimmed the top row was barely perceptible. While I had
no freedom to look other than at Red Leader, I knew we had done the job.

Once Big Ed cleared the stands, he started a relatively tight climbing turn to the left that took him back up to two hundred feet and
heading toward the north perimeter of the airdrome. Seconds later,
when the second section cleared the stands, they made a similar exit
turn but to the right, with the third section boring straight in on the
Russians and three more sections still inbound behind them. If a
Russian dignitary looked up, he saw Jugs in every direction, all
uncomfortably low, noisy, and too close.

The plan was for the group to go straight back to Germany, right
down the forbidden corridor. Each individual section stayed on the

deck until they had cleared the city limits, then climbed on course and headed for Neubiberg at max cruise. Just in case people were going to start shooting at each other over the rights of free access to Berlin, Big Ed sure didn't want to be sitting on the tarmac at Tempelhof, surrounded by Russians.

Spirits were high when we landed back at Neubiberg, still without a single abort or dropout, but there was little time for fun and games. Big Ed held a short, serious combination debriefing of the mission and briefing for the alert plan we were implementing.

After our aircraft were serviced, one-third of the pilots, crews, and aircraft went on five-minute alert, with drop tanks and a full load of .50-caliber ammo. Another third went on one-hour alert, with a combination of external tanks, bombs, and .50-caliber ammo. The remaining third went on two-hour alert, with instructions to get some sleep, which was close to impossible.

I volunteered for five minute. As I sat in the cockpit, setting up the switches, I was smiling, thinking, "My, my! I may have missed the last one, but it sure looks like I got in on the first real one in this Cold War thing. I guess the Old Man was right, we really haven't seen the last of those Russians."

I, for one, had seen the last of that Russian threat in Europe, since the personnel managers in Washington had decided it was time for several of us to move to new assignments in the still-shrinking air force. West Point graduates were in demand for a series of unattractive stateside assignments and Big Ed could do nothing to retain us. I at least escaped assignment to the SAC nuke bomber program, the fate of many, but the assignment I drew sure didn't look or sound like a winner. One day you're flying as Rupert Red Two, the next day you're on duty in Newark, New Jersey, with the 2231st Air Force Reserve Training Center, which in essence is what happened. When I told Big Ed of the assignment, he couldn't believe it. Neither could I, of course. I know he shared my bewilderment—resentment, more accurately—

that the personnel weenies thought so little of me, hard-flying Rupert Red Two, that they slapped me with a completely nonoperational assignment.

It was a Monday when I found my way to the Newark commercial airport, then roamed around until I located some dingy one-story buildings that looked old and tired, GI style, and a small sign verifying that it was indeed the 2231st. I encountered a captain who had the misfortune to be named officer of the day on a nonduty day, since reserves didn't train on Monday or Tuesday. When I asked about a place to stay, he advised me that all the big hotels in Newark were priced out of sight, and suggested a hotel in downtown Newark that was easy to spot because it was right around the corner from the Newark Burlesque Theatre.

I found the small place with its dirty, rundown brick front, parked my car on the street, half expecting never to see it again, and checked in. It was worse than I expected. The only single room available was on the third floor: stairs right over there, no elevator. There were four rooms on the floor, with a cozy, common bathroom with a rusted-out tub, a toilet, a small sink, and one weak light bulb. The predominant sound was that of two loud and crass-mouthed females talking and laughing in one of the rooms. I assumed they were employed close by.

I checked in on Wednesday and met the commander, a West Point grad of many moons ago, who was on his twilight cruise and singularly uninterested in airpower or aircraft. The 2231st was equipped with the same type AT-6s I had flown during basic and advanced training, and also with a twin-engine trainer designated the AT-11, better known as a version of the "Bamboo Bomber."

The unit's mission was to maintain the proficiency of reserve officers who had signed on to the reserve program at the end of World War II. Many, as I quickly learned, were low-time pilots who not only lacked operational experience but also maintained a dangerously low level of proficiency. They could stay qualified in the program by attending a couple hours of briefing every three months and completing three landings in either the T-6 or the AT-11.

I quickly got myself assigned as the flight-test maintenance officer for the unit, which meant that I got to fly all the test hops on the repaired aircraft and was not involved in the reserve proficiency game. I was also designated as the motor pool officer. I got checked out on every piece of equipment we had, and I got to drive all around the area going huden-huden, pow-pow, bang-bang with the best of them.

I could almost always get a T-6 or an AT-11 on our days off, so I spent lots of time flying up and down the East Coast practicing my strange field-landing techniques. The only real tight one I had was the weekend my friend Abie O'Conner and I decided to take our trusty T-6 to Chicago to visit a neat girl I knew there who had also arranged an attractive date for Abie. It got dark fast, and the weather went to pot in Chicago, but we didn't know that, since we iced up, lost our radio, and couldn't talk to anyone. Due to the ice, we were using full power just to stay airborne. Flying between cloud layers, we were running out of fuel, lost, and didn't have enough fuel to go anyplace else. Then, when the light pattern that shone through the undercast said that it couldn't be anything other than Gary, Indiana, and Chicago, we had no choice but to start down. We found out later that we were in no danger from other traffic, since all the civilian and military airports were closed due to low ceilings and freezing rain. We were the only idiots up there, and we couldn't talk to anybody.

We guessed where the navy runway should be and started creeping down as the freezing rain glossed over the entire T-6, including the canopies and windscreen. We slid both canopies open, and I leaned out the left side, and Abie leaned out the right side as we directed each other toward the parallel runway lights we thought we had spotted ahead. We touched down, or more accurately we concluded our powered glide, and skated gracefully only as far as the first turnoff. The field was closed, and there was nobody in sight. Finally, we saw a pair of hand light signals waving at the far end of the field, which turned out to be the navy transient aircraft area. We skated that way, and when we finally skidded to a parked stop, a navy crewman crawled cautiously onto the icy wing as I shut her down. He took one look at me and said, "Lieutenant, what the hell are you doing out on a night like this?"

All I could think of to say was, "Well, we both got a date in town."

For an entire year I flew or drove to every headquarters within striking distance to beg a transfer from everybody I knew or could introduce myself to. I wrote formal and informal letters, to no avail. And then, finally, the wheel spun in my favor.

The personnel folks decided that, "over time," the Newark unit would be phased out. I had enough irons in the fire and knew enough people not to have to wait for the "over time." When my transfer orders came through, I was still designated as an AT-6 instructor, but I was headed for Randolph Air Force Base in San Antonio, Texas. I knew there would be opportunities to move on quickly from there.

I was at Randolph only a week before Big Ed, now back in the States, did good work with the personnel people in Training Command Headquarters. I was assigned to Williams Air Force Base in Phoenix, where cadets were training in AT-6s, P-80s, and two-place T-33s. That was still not the desired answer, but I was getting closer.

I spent two weeks at Williams, droning up and down the radio ranges in the back of T-6s, helping cadets develop their instrument skills. And then Marty Martin (from Fritzlar and Neubiberg) wrangled for me the desired set of orders from personnel. Training Command was reopening the abandoned gunnery ranges in Las Vegas, Nevada. Marty got me assigned to his Fighter Weapons Squadron at Las Vegas Air Force Base, and I was on my way to joining the new and elite jet set.

CHAPTER 6

NELLIS

I drove into Las Vegas on a Saturday and checked into the BOQ. It was a run-down wooden two-story structure with a couple of swamp coolers on the roof and plenty of cracks between the wooden planks. There were holes in the wooden siding for the desert heat and the endless, wind-driven dust to circulate freely. Who cared? Not me; I was back in the fighter business.

I called Lieutenant Colonel Martin to let him know that I had arrived and shortly thereafter found myself poolside and meeting the gears of the base. Everything on base was old, just the way the army air force had left it when they shut down the massive desert gunnery ranges that had been used for bomber gunnery training during World War II. One of the few relatively attractive facilities on base was a small cluster of slightly better-than-average GI quarters surrounding a swimming pool, and that is where the base commander and World War II ace Col. Joe Mason and his wife lived. Marty and the group operations guy also lived there in the other two sets of quarters, and there always seemed to be a splash party in progress during the weekends. I was welcomed on board warmly, and nobody seemed to care if I was a lieutenant or a colonel.

I knew absolutely nothing about old downtown Las Vegas or the newly emerging and now world-famous Las Vegas Strip. People bandied about Bugsy Siegel and names like that, and there were major gangland turf wars in progress, but all we cared about was that there were some swanky new fun palaces emerging along the long, dusty road on the western side of town. Marty and his wife, Marian, took me on a tour, and everything I saw amazed me. They seemed to know everyone along the strip. By the time they had introduced me to the managers of the only two hotels on the strip, the El Rancho and the Flamingo, it was well into Sunday. My head was spinning in wonder when they dropped me off at the BOQ.

Two of my classmates and good friends, Bob Spragins from Penthouse days at Neubiberg and Corky Slack, were living in the BOQ, so I got a good, lieutenant's-level briefing the next day. Sunday night Corky took me on a bachelor's tour of town. I met the gambling tables and was amazed that the management could afford to feed everyone unlimited free drinks while they were gambling. I figured that one out when I got back to the BOQ. I had been in town less than forty-eight hours and had already blown enough cash that I was short on the upcoming payment for my new convertible.

The base had two missions: One was a finishing school to train advanced air cadets and student officers in the P-51 Mustang. The other was the gunnery squadron, which itself had dual functions. Part of the squadron ran an intensive fighter-gunnery and bombing course for selected regular and air guard pilots who came to Las Vegas on TDY to learn to be gunnery specialists within their home units. The other part of the squadron provided academic ground school to those same TDY students, as well as analyzing fighter tactics, equipment, and requirements, and distributing the results of their research throughout the air force.

The gunnery squadron did all their training in jet aircraft, primarily the P-80, the first of the air force's operational jet fleet. The P-80A was a bare-bones machine with a fuel system that made it easy to cook the tailpipe on starting. The plane responded to undisciplined cobbing of the throttle by simply blowing the jet flame out the rear end and becoming a poor glider. With its increased speed and altitude capabilities plus its voracious appetite for the limited fuel supply it carried, it certainly could have used an ejection seat, but Lockheed could only cram so much into the short development cycle. We had a few P-80B models, which were limited-production hybrids, with more weight in the form of dubious improvements. However, it included an ejection seat that might function should a potential ejectee be fortunate enough to get rid of the bubble canopy. We were just starting to get some of the new C models, which were quantum improvements, almost like a different aircraft.

We were responsible for towing all our air-to-air banner targets, which we did with our two sleek, stripped-down B-26s or with P-51s. For support and administrative flights, we used our T-6 or B-25s, helicopters, or an OV-10 Beaver, all of which the base support people maintained. We also had F-86As and F-84Es, which the academic side monopolized. I got to fly all of them.

Throughout the air force, most flying units were reeling from the postwar cutbacks. Pilot proficiency was generally low, since money, hence fuel and parts, was hard to come by, and flying time was at a premium. Not so at our place. The requirement to get the new jet set combat ready in bombing and gunnery was well funded, partly because of political instability in Southeast Asia and Korea. An eager lieutenant in our outfit got all the flights he could handle during the week and could almost always pick his aircraft for weekend cross country flights. Talk about a flying club . . . we had it.

My new boss, Maj. Dewey Bower, was running about one hundred miles an hour all the time. I immediately liked him, because he got right to the point, he respected your capabilities, and he delegated responsibilities and the authority to go with it. He told me we had two weeks before our next class of trainees came in, and I was to take a flight of four air guard officers when they arrived. In the meantime, I was to check out in the various aircraft, familiarize myself with our course of instruction, and learn the rules of the aerial and ground gunnery ranges. He continued, "For the moment, I've got a mail pouch that needs to go to the range crew at Indian Springs right away. Our T-6 is parked out front, so take it and deliver the pouch to their ops shack and check with me when you get back." When I reminded him that I had not had a local check in the T-6 and I didn't know where Indian Springs was, he hardly paused as he was striding away. Almost over his shoulder he said, "Hell, you gotta know how to fly a T-6, check yourself out. And there's local area maps up at the counter. Just go northwest, up the valley, keep the mountains on your left, and you can't miss it." So by 9:00 a.m. I was airborne on my first flight out of Las Vegas.

When I returned, Lt. Fred Mosier was waiting to tell me that he had the assignment of checking me out in the P-80. We went out on the ramp to a parked 80, and I suddenly realized it was very hot, and I learned that simply touching a sun-soaked aircraft without having your leather flying gloves on could physically burn your skin. I climbed into the cockpit while he reviewed all the switches. He had me practice three engine starts, which were tricky in the A model. If you didn't move the throttle and the I-16 fuel pump switch smartly and in rhythm, you got a puddle of fuel in the tailpipe that could do all sorts of bad things when it ignited. On one of my starts, I moved with less than grace and got a hot start. The tailpipe temp gauge peaked, and the tailpipe groaned and sighed for what seemed like an eternity, while everyone on the flight line watched to see if the FNG was going to destroy a tailpipe. Mosier allowed that two out of three wasn't too bad for the first time. He gave me a dash-one tech order to study overnight, and said I was scheduled for an 8:00 a.m. checkout flight in the morning. Back in ops, I had a message that I was scheduled for a P-51 Mustang flight at 1:00 p.m. The ground rules were the same as the T-6 checkout, and it felt great to fly the Mustang again.

The differences in the three P-80 models were significant. The C model was far superior to the other two in all operational aspects. It was coming out in production quantities and would be the version that we would later use in Korea. The C was also available as the two-place T-33, which holds records as the airborne training and administrative workhorse of all time. The few B models were just sort of there, and left the inventory rather early. But the A was the fun machine. If the C was the Cadillac, then the A was the sporty car. She was small, the cockpit was tight, and when you manually cranked that canopy closed and locked yourself in, there was no doubt that you and that bird were one. She flew the same way, just like she was part of your mind and body.

My favorite was 059, the shiniest P-80 on the whole flight line. Corporal Wilson crewed her and was so proud of that bird he bubbled. The only time she was out of commission was for something like a hundred-hour inspection. Some days I'd make three trips to the range and back in 059, shooting with the best of them, and I never got tired of flying her. One of our mutually happiest days was when Wilson got his third stripe and became a buck sergeant. That was a big deal back then.

Before I got my first group of trainees, I learned the master lesson of Las Vegas and the Strip. Most everyone learned it at least once, and the lesson was impressive. You were expected to stop by the club for happy hour. Then, it often seemed like a good idea to clean up and head for town. You could always grab something to eat a little later. First stop was usually the Shamrock Motel on the border between North Las Vegas and Vegas. The bar was the largest and busiest part of the place.

They usually had music, tolerated most anything, and it was a neat meeting place. If you had a date, or joined up with a single or a group or just went solo, it was usually off to the Strip from there.

There was so much to see and do on the Strip. The drinks were cheap. The music was loud, and the bar shows were great. Food was always available with all-you-can-eat specials for less than a buck, but the temptation was always there to hit just one more place and eat later. Then suddenly it was panic time; there were only a few hours to alarm-clock time, and no time to eat now. Then on the long, dark road back to the base there was a friendly bar called the "Tale of the Pup," and maybe one more, and some cheese and crackers topped with pretzels, then a dash for the sack. The relentless desert sunrise came quickly, followed closely by first-flight briefing. It was truly painful, but somehow the memory seemed to fade away every once in awhile. Thank God we were so young and healthy.

Vegas was a small town in the middle of an inhospitable desert. The few stores downtown were dedicated to providing little more than the necessities of desert life. The downtown clubs and hotels were concentrated along a stretch of Fremont Street. The potential that was to lead to the Las Vegas of today was evident along the magic stretch of desolate highway to be known as the Strip.

Few of us had any conception of what the underworld was up to, or what the locals had planned, or what the future of that desolate piece of desert might become. Sprag and I had become friends with a local policeman, who was also a U.S. Air Force Reserve lieutenant who pulled his short active-duty stints with us at the base. He had some idea of what the future held for the strip and out of friendship offered Sprag and me a deal. He could get us in on a combine that was just going together where the participants could buy into a land deal for a piece of that desert strip between the current farthest outpost, the Flamingo, and the still small McCarren Airport. We turned it down because it would have cost us one hundred dollars an acre, and who would pay that for a chunk of desert?

The folks who were there at that time were happy to see the military returning, and the small-town attitude of friendship had not left yet. That attitude was personified in our relationship with Herb McDonald, the on-scene boss of the El Rancho. Every other Sunday afternoon the officers from the base, in uniform, and their ladies or dates were the hotel's exclusive guests in the main dining room for a tea dance. Unlimited food and drinks were on the house. The band played for dancing, and the entire dinner show performed for us, with the likes of Sammy Davis Jr. and his friends. If you didn't have a date, no sweat; the girls from the chorus line were there to join the party. Those are fond memories of a place that was more fun before it got to be the fun capital of the world.

One of our other favorite spots was the Westside Elks Club, which was very black and very much a closed club. Late one Saturday night, Sprag, hearing fantastic jazz pouring from the place, walked in, uninvited, and somehow became everyone's friend. They invited him and his fighter pilot friends back, and he and I were there the next Saturday night. Things didn't really get going until after midnight, when goodly numbers of the musicians and entertainers from the strip would pour in, escaping the strip's atmosphere, and ready to jam until dawn. Completely free-of-pretense sessions with the likes of Louis Armstrong, Ella Fitzgerald, Ziggy Elman, Johnnie Ray—whoever was in town—were ours for the asking. And the food and drinks were usually free. No wonder we knew we had a good assignment.

The tables in Vegas got to a few of our officers big time, but most of us were smart enough to keep our gambling at the fun level. Four of us had our crack at breaking the bank at the local roulette tables when we discovered a foolproof system that was a guaranteed big winner. We each put up fifty bucks, selected a roulette table, and split into teams of two for round-the-clock duty over the long Labor Day weekend. All our bets were on black, and the system told us how much to bet, depending on the previous roll. Over three full days we sometimes played with sizeable stacks of casino chips. After a big winning streak, with a fair-sized crowd of holiday casino rooters looking on, a strange sequence unfolded. The next roll came up red— no big deal, but we barely survived the thirty-five consecutive reds. We shoved out what was left of our stash as they rolled the thirty-sixth red in a row. As we dusted ourselves off and the crowd around the table faded away, the dealer, cold as ice, caught our eyes as the thirty-seventh roll came up black.

We were small-timers, but our old friend Stick Thorson was still a serious gambler. He had been assigned as the air force advisor to the Rhode Island Air National Guard, flying Jugs, and he contacted us to say he was flying out to Vegas. He said he didn't care about seeing us, but just wanted us to know he was coming to town to break all the local banks. He wasn't flying much and needed to get some flying time, especially some nighttime, just to complete his annual hourly flying requirements. But mostly he was hot to gamble.

We were looking forward to greeting Stick and watching him attack the crap tables with his characteristic gyrations and noise. He was supposed to be coming into Vegas out of Lowry Air Force Base in Denver, and since he was looking for some night time, we expected him shortly after sunset our time. It got to be dark, and our base operations didn't even have a flight plan on him indicating departure from Lowry, or estimated time of arrival in Las Vegas. A couple of hours later we called Lowry, and they said he had indeed departed, and for some reason the flight plan had not been transmitted. He was indeed due in Las Vegas at that moment.

It was time to be nervous. The route from Denver to Las Vegas is desolate. The radio ranges, the only navigational aids available at that time, were few, far between, and not all that reliable. Since it was winter, a westerly flying aviator could expect strong winds in his face. If the winds caused you to fall behind on your planned fuel consumption, it was natural to want to climb and throttle back to obtain better fuel consumption. But, as you went up, the winds in your face increased and slowed you further. Once you passed the point of no return, there were no alternative landing sites available, and it was an easy place to panic.

Two hours later there was no sign of Stick, and there had been no radio contact with him. His fuel was long gone, and our friend was down and missing. All of us just went home.

Nobody had much hope for success of search-and-rescue attempts over that desolate stretch. We were not surprised when those attempts were called off and Stick was officially declared missing. Winter droned on over the western mountains. Then one morning a New Mexico rancher caught a silver reflection in the snow. He found a P-47, smashed and upside down, with the parachute canopy caught on the vertical fin. The shroud lines behind the tail section were twisted and knotted from countless revolutions and at the end of the lines was a parachute harness containing Stick's badly decomposed body. He had not been wearing a flight suit, but instead wore a wool Eisenhower jacket and wool slacks, both of which were stuffed with multiple thick packets of high-denomination bills. Stick had not been ready to fly; he had been ready to gamble. He lost. None of us truly knew Stick; we just knew he was a good guy.

Our boss Marty Martin, Mr. Personality Plus, got to know most everybody in town, including a couple named Kat and Jim Losee. They owned the property that had been one of the two original ranches in the Las Vegas area. The two ranches were built around the only two known natural springs. Kat and Jim's ranch was located in what would now be the northwest portion of North Las Vegas, and was originally the property of the Stewarts. The other original ranch was the Walker property, located well to the east of the Stewart property.

Kat was absolutely effervescent and seemed to be running all the time. Jimmie was a crusty old Scotsman, methodical and practical in all he did. He did all the provisioning and was a superb cook. He was an expert marksman and his frequent dove dinners were among my favorites. The living area of the ranch centered around the natural spring, which Jimmy had converted into a picturesque swimming hole. To the east of the spring was a large, comfortable, two-story house. The original ranch buildings were wooden, cottage-type structures, and their exteriors retained their original historic appearance.

One of the small outbuildings had been the original Stewart home, and it was truly historical. The storytellers had it that Mr. Stewart had been a nice guy, always interested in the welfare of others. Mr. Walker, on the other hand, had a rather unwholesome reputation, and his status with the law was somewhat dubious. One summer, during a searing desert heat wave, Mr. Walker had departed for parts unknown. Mr. Stewart, riding along the eastern boundaries of his property, had ridden up to the Walker house. Remaining on his horse, he had doffed his hat and inquired of Mrs. Walker if all went well with her and her children. Receiving an affirmative answer, he headed back to his own ranch. When Mr. Walker returned, it did not suit him that Mr. Stewart had ridden onto his property and had spoken to his wife. He rode to the Stewarts' dwelling, approached the front door, and began firing his .44 through the door, immediately killing Mr. Stewart. That door, complete with the bullet holes and with nothing modified other than a coat of paint, was still there to validate the story.

So what would a couple like Kat and Jim do with a place like that? They turned it into a divorce ranch. Most states required divorce proceedings lasting at least one year long, but Nevada only required a six-week residency for "the cure." The town was already dotted with quickie walk-in wedding places, and Kat and Jim went after the high-priced divorce trade. To obtain a final decree, it was necessary to appear in court with a witness who would verify daily observance of the petitioner during that six-week period. Kat and Jim offered a package deal for a lot of dollars. They provided comfortable, historic accommodations, excellent cuisine, sparkling and understanding fellowship, and a valid local witness for the cure hearing. Unspoken, of course, was the lure of all the wild times you could handle, including nightly tours of the tables as long as Kat was along to observe. They immediately started booking well in advance with the wealthy from coast to coast, seizing on the easiest of remedies for their problems. It didn't hurt that Mickey Rooney and several of Hollywood's cuties were early customers.

Enter into this Bob Spragins, Mike Johnson, and myself, three of Kat and Jimmie's favorite lieutenants. Kat and Jim had one wooden outbuilding on the ranch that was basically three joined single apartments, and not too suitable for the divorce-ranch trade. They figured we were due a respite from living in the beat-up barracks and asked if we would like to move in. We snapped it up for a minimum rental and lived well on the ranch with our dear friends Kat and Jim. We were welcome guests for cocktails and dinner whenever our schedules permitted. Kat usually requested our help as escorts the first time she took one of the heartbroken honeys out on the town. About an hour into that first night out, we usually noted a significant personality change as the bright lights got into their eyes. But we avoided anything serious, and even if one of them decided she liked us, all we had to do was be busy night flying for awhile, and she was long gone.

As good as the town was in those days, the flying was better. One of the captains on the academic side of the squadron was a serious and inquisitive type named Fran Bailey. Historically, fighter aircraft had fired their guns using something called a fixed gunsight, which was basically a metal circle with a dot, called a pip, in the center. In the open-cockpit days, the sight was mounted in front of the cockpit so the pilot could peer through it as he aimed and fired his guns. By World War II, the ring and pip were projected electronically toward the windscreen in front of the pilot. The ground crews had the task of physically adjusting the guns so the rounds that the guns fired converged on the spot the pip pointed to at a range of one thousand feet.

All that was great for strafing a ground target. You just rolled in on the target, let the pip slide onto the target by virtue of your control movements, then blasted away when your experience told you that you were at the right range. The only time it worked that easily in an air-to-air engagement was the unlikely situation of an enemy choosing to fly straight and level and allowing you to close in to firing range from directly behind him. But assuming that both target and attacker were maneuvering as dramatically as possible, it became a matter of using the ring and pip to measure angular deflection and the amount of lead required to put your rounds into the target.

The problem that Fran Bailey was working on was determining what could be done to improve the gunsight in the P-51. There were plenty of industry specialists working on new and superior weapons-delivery systems for the Century Series models that were emerging. But things were looking rather strange in Southeast Asia, where the Vietnamese were taking it to the French, and we had no idea what we might become involved in. We had lots of Mustangs that were still flyable and available to fight. So, Fran and Otis May, our non-pilot math whiz who ran the academic side of the squadron, decided to see if they could give the P-51 gunsight a ranging capability. If you could tell exactly the range of an adversary at all times, it would improve your chances of properly leading your target. Fran and Otis got a Mustang to work with and arranged a kaleidoscopic set of mirrors, lenses, and light sources that projected a light circle within the gunsight ring. Rotating a modified engine throttle handle controlled the diameter of this new light circle. If you kept the light circle on the enemy's wingtips, you could instantly read his exact range.

Fran needed another pilot to work with him on the project, and I got that spot. Besides being an interesting concept, it meant that on a good day I got two firing missions with my students: a mission dragging a rag, and a workout with Fran later in the afternoon. Fran and I would take off in a pair of Mustangs, with one of us the shooter and the other one the target, and go after each other with gun-camera film. We were making good progress when everything changed in a hurry in June 1950, and the project was cancelled.

I had managed to get myself an F-80C model for a weekend cross-country to visit friends in Chicago. My previous flight out that way had been during the winter months, and the A model I had drawn for the winter trip reminded me that those birds were indeed getting old. I departed Chicago on a snowy morning, and I knew I was in trouble by the time I settled into a climb to visual conditions on top of the snow. The cockpit cooling system was stuck in full cold, and I mean icy, frozen cold. Worse, the system had picked up a lot of moisture from Lake Michigan. The entire air system was frozen in position, and there was no way I could budge the air controls. The full-force blast of freezing air from all the cockpit outlets was numbing. I was quickly approaching the state where I could not maneuver the controls. The main air standpipe was blowing a particularly strong blast over my right shoulder and onto my right hand, which was grasping the control stick. I could make my arm move as a unit, but I had already lost all movement and feel in my hand and fingers. I needed to get on the ground, and setting up an instrument approach to Chicago from scratch was not a viable alternative. Milwaukee, to the north, was only partly cloudy, and I knew that they had an F-80 Air National Guard squadron there. I declared an emergency, descended to the only slightly warmer winter weather on the deck, and made a less than smooth landing. It took a day to fix my bird's cooling system and get me airborne again, with my right hand still aching from the cold.

But this time, departure went well, and my C model was purring smoothly as I leveled at altitude and headed west for Nevada. I tuned my radio compass to a commercial radio station ahead of me to get a directional steering assist and to see what was on the airwaves. Surprise! North Korea had invaded South Korea, and we were already into it, with the reduced and depleted resources we had left in that part of the world. The rest of the trip back to Nellis, I was obviously nervous. By the time I arrived, the base was already buzzing with planning sessions, and change was in the wind.

The largest immediate change was in the P-51 program. The Mustangs were fit to fight, and there were plenty of them on active duty, in air guard units or in storage. Within days our already significant P-51 inventory increased dramatically. New squadrons were formed, instructor assignments were shuffled to man the new units, and training programs were drawn up to qualify the influx of recalled reserve pilots (retreads) that were on the way. In two weeks we were bulging at the seams with pilots, who, like it or not, were going to Korea as P-51 jocks.

Some of the retreads had been fighter pilots in War War II, had maintained some degree of proficiency in their reserve units and were hot for the program. Others had never been close to a fighter, were proficient in nothing, had never expected to be recalled, and wanted only to be civilians. Worst of all, some of them were already scared of the airplane.

When I arrived at squadron ops on Monday morning, I was told to report to Maj. John England, the number-one Mustang guy, since I was now to be part of setting up and instructing in one of the P-51 replacement training units. I pouted for a few minutes, wondering how the jet gunnery program would ever survive without me, but that was short-lived. John England had been at Neubiberg, and we were good friends. By 9:00 a.m. I had moved my stuff to the other end of the flight line and was helping to set up a new squadron. I had also already volunteered to go to Korea.

The operational part of the program cranked up in a hurry, but the accident rate was horrible and unacceptable. The Mustang is a great bird, but it demands respect and does not tolerate carelessness.

Predictably, the noneager among the retreads, especially those who feared the aircraft, fell at a dreadful rate. Of course, the retreads had the option of refusing to fly and turning in their wings, which some of them did. The stigma connected with doing that was inherently offensive to anyone who had won the honor of wearing the silver pilot's wings. They could still be retained on active duty in a nonflying job, but in some cases fear ruled. Our active-duty regulars, officer and enlisted, were not overly sympathetic to the retreads, and sometimes little more than a few careless words would push a borderline retread over the edge. One afternoon, after we had lost a Mustang and a retread in the morning, one of those borderline pilots slung his parachute over his shoulder and walked apprehensively out to his assigned Mustang for a training mission. The crew chief greeted him crudely with, "Well, lieutenant, are you going up to get yours today?" The lieutenant paused briefly, dropped his parachute on the ramp, walked back to Major England's office, and turned in his wings.

Everything ground to a halt one Monday morning when we lost four Mustangs and four pilots before noon. Colonel Mason shut down flying and ordered all flying personnel to a general meeting at 1:00 p.m. It was a combination safety lecture, pep talk, and reminder that our fellow aviators and our nation needed us, right now. It was a sobering session that got the message across, but it would be hard to say that overall morale was high at the conclusion of the meeting.

About 2:00 p.m. I was just signing out in squadron ops to grab my chute and test-hop a Mustang with a brand-new engine. Marty Martin was running the flight line at that time, and he called John England, saying, "You are now under a simulated red alert condition. You are to flush all permanent party pilots in all available Mustangs and rendezvous over Indian Springs to await further instructions." Those of us on single missions like mine were immediately running for our assigned aircraft, while the ops folks hastily cancelled student training flights and matched available bodies and P-51s. Fifteen minutes later, the same scene was repeated for all the jet aircraft and pilots, ordering them to rendezvous over Lake Mead.

After another fifteen minutes, both forces were advised that the simulated air battle for the control of the base was on. There were no further instructions or restrictions as both forces dived back toward the base and the ensuing fray. I was at full blower and was one of the first P-51s back in sight of the runway, where some of the jet stragglers were still taking off. I clearly remember roaring past the orange and white checkerboard water tower and glancing up at the top of it as I turned behind an accelerating P-80 as he sucked up his gear after takeoff. I pulled up, did a roll in his face, and broke hard left to look for more.

The sky was full of fighters for about twenty minutes until Marty declared that the battle was over and that fighters were clear to recover. I wasn't quite ready to quit. I had recognized the radio voice of one of our wing headquarters weenies, whom I did not particularly admire, transmitting from one of the P-80s. He always talked a lot about his flying accomplishments but flew only occasionally, and then only on easy missions. He had apparently taken off late, avoided the fray, and was still close to their rendezvous point over Lake Mead. I was fat on fuel and still running close to full throttle, so I grabbed all the altitude I could get as I headed in the direction of Lake Mead.

I spotted him turning back toward Nellis, calling for landing instructions, and starting a big looping turn in the direction of the base. His jet cruised faster than my Mustang, but, at full throttle, I was trading altitude for air speed, closing slightly and cutting him off in his turn. I wanted the bragging rights that were immediately available. He turned on a long initial approach at one thousand feet and I was almost in position, but still a bit out of range and a thousand feet above him. I kept pushing on the already wide-open throttle and traded another 1,500 feet for enough speed to pass under him about half a mile before he got to the end of the runway to start his 360-degree overhead approach. I horsed my trusty P-51 as close to straight up as she would go, while punching the mike button and saying, "Bang, bang; you're dead, man." I did two tight rolls in his face before pulling over onto my back and clearing the runway area. I got a good laugh out of the obscenities he cluttered the radio with while flopping about.

I pulled the throttle back to coast contentedly out to where I could turn onto initial approach for landing. However, once I came off full power, my brand-new Merlin engine realized how tired it was and began spitting white puffs out of the exhaust stacks. I had popped the coolant, and she was about to let go; confirming this was the oil starting to cover the windscreen. I didn't bother with an initial approach or a 360 overhead. I just popped the gear, and with the tower's OK, coasted down to a smooth landing.

As I taxied into the parking area my crew chief initially hung his head in mock grief at what he saw and heard. Then he quickly started flying his hands in a trace of my conquest of the P-80 and the two rolls, then gave me a big smiling thumbs up. There was no doubt that the entire exercise had been nonstandard, would never have been sanctioned by higher headquarters, and was very dicey; we were fortunate that there were no accidents. But, for days, war stories abounded all over the flight line, the club was packed for happy hours, the safety record improved, and the fear-of-flying syndrome diminished. I test-hopped that same Mustang again the next afternoon, and that time I put the required thirty minutes of slow time on the second new Merlin engine before I did anything else.

One of our fun things was our base football team. Military leagues were pretty competitive in those days, with an abundance of college, semi-pro, and some pro players still on active duty. I had played on one base team or another after graduating from the Point, and as recently as 1949, Colonel Mason had insisted that I play for the Nellis team. We did well that year and were the host team for the first Silver Bowl sponsored by the town and the Strip hotels. That event, with a quantum-degree jump in sophistication and facilities, is now a major collegiate affair.

I had really had enough of GI football after that year, and the Korea push kept me in enough demand on the flight line that I could weenie out of playing ball during the fall of 1950. Our team was playing a small college in St. George, Utah, on a Friday night, and since he was still pushing P-51 morale, Marty Martin decided that there should be a Mustang presence at the game. He sent a four-ship flight of us up to that dark, mountainous place to buzz the football field before the game, land on their short plateau runway, attend the game in our flying suits, then launch off that plateau and come home. Naturally, we were Pigskin Flight, and we drew matches to see who would fly what position within the flight. On the way up at dusk, Terry Moore led, with Sam Hoffman as two, Howie Hedrick as three, and me as tail-end Charlie. The formation buzz job came off nicely, even though the mountain air was super rough, and then we all manhandled the crosswind and put our birds neatly onto the marginal strip.

Any time a fighter pilot takes his head off of a swivel while the engine is running, he is asking for trouble, and Sam Hoffman was about to ask for trouble for us. It had changed from dusk to very dark in a big hurry, and Terry, with his landing lights still on, was threading in an S pattern along an unlighted narrow taxiway looking for an unlighted place to park. When you taxi a Mustang, which is sitting back on its tail wheel with its long, pointed nose raised in front of you, you can't see what is in front of you unless you unlock the tail wheel and use the rudders and brakes to S back and forth. As number two, Sam had cleared the strip, slid the canopy back, and reached down into his flight suit to grab a cigarette and light up. He was taxiing too fast, too straight, and just plain not paying attention. Lack of attention and having a huge, multibladed meat slicer whirling around on your front end can equate to bad news.

In a deal like that, the leader usually lands on the inside of the runway, with the others taking alternate sides. That way you can peer out the side and check your spacing on the guy in front of you. As my landing roll smoothed out, I checked Howie in front of me, and looking farther right I spotted Terry on the taxi strip with Sam closing behind him. Sam was about to climb Terry's back. I punched the mike button and said, "Pigskin Two, watch it! You're about to ram lead." It worked, but barely.

The football game only lasted a couple of hours, but Sam must have thanked me twenty times, reminding me that without my call he would have killed Terry, his best friend. I think Sam ate a pack of smokes before the game was over. The other three of us outwardly ignored it and had fun with the local crowd and the game. Besides, we knew we had a black departure from a poorly lighted strip on a shaved-off mountaintop to look forward to, and we didn't want Sam any more nervous than he already was.

As we had previously agreed, we switched flight order for the trip back, which put me in the lead. That gave me the unique privilege of determining, without benefit of advanced statistics or study, how a mighty Mustang would perform on takeoff from a short, high-altitude mountain strip on a dark, turbulent night. I've been in situations like that several times in several places, and it is always a real thrill. You're on the end of the strip, and you've checked everything on the bird, and she is ready to go. The directional gyro is set on the runway heading. In this case, you can't see much ahead of you, since the nose is in the way, and the runway edge lights are few and dim. Hold the brakes, full throttle, and the tail wants to rise, which is OK. Release the brakes, keep the directional gyro centered with rudders, and note with periph-eral vision the edge lights. The tail pops up, the dull lights on the end of the strip are out there, and you're accelerating on the mains. It's sure black out there, since you're taking off into a val-ley, but the wheels want to lift, and you're airborne. Suck up the gear, clunk; flaps up; zip; artificial horizon OK, and I can see the mountaintops on both sides. I'm in the clear, and it's bumpy as hell. Punch the mike button: "No sweat guys, it's bumpy, but no sweat, and the moon's just coming up."

When everyone got on board, I spread them out into loose forma-tion, since the turbulence was as bumpy as anything I can remember. The moon was now full and brilliant, and it was a fun trip back to Vegas. It was as light as day when we got back, and there was no other traffic, so naturally we pitched off the deck for landing, and flew as tight a pattern as we could. Back in the P-51 locker room Sam was still nervous, but that was not unusual. Besides, it was Friday night in Vegas, and we all needed to clean up and head for town. Rendezvous at the Shamrock in an hour.

By that time the P-51 pipeline was full and flowing well, but more P-80 outfits were being moved into Korea and they were short on qualified jet pilots. We formed additional jet training squadrons, with my friend Fran Bailey getting command of the 96th Training Squadron. Fran selected me as his ops officer, and I was back in the jet business with an unspoken agreement that I would be on the list to leave for Korea as soon as we got organized and got our first class qualified.

Sam Hoffman had followed me to the 96th, and one of my first duties was to check him out in the B-26 for tow-target duties. Sam almost ended my plans in a hurry. We accomplished checkouts in con-junction with air-to-air towing missions, and we would tow, drop the rag back at the base, and then go through transition exercises and shoot landings before terminating the sortie. This one was also a functional test flight after some scheduled maintenance on the bird. I was in the left seat, with our B-26 line chief in the copilot seat. The tow operator was back in the rear stinger with his targets, and trainee Sam was riding a jump-seat arrangement we had installed on top of a large, rectangular auxiliary fuel tank we had installed behind the pilots' seats.

Sam looked over my shoulder and followed me through the engine starts and preflight checklists, and we took off to the north. I pulled the gear up, retracted the flaps and started to pull the power back, and that is when we launched into divergent courses of action. The chief and I went into an urgent emergency procedure, and Sam settled back against the bulkhead, slid his earphones back a bit, and lit up a cigarette. The chief and I felt it and smelled it. Our shoes were instantly sitting in a couple of inches of one hundred-octane aviation fuel, and the fumes were boiling under the instrument panel and into our faces. We had no idea where the fuel was coming from, but we moved instinctively, fast, and without a word between us. The chief's hands flew through the switch panels, shutting down all fuel tanks other than the main tank, and eliminating all electrical traffic except the command radio. I rammed the props and throttles full forward and cranked her around, as hard as she could turn with a full fuel load, back to the reverse runway heading.

Sam's short legs were hanging over the edge of the tank but were not on the floor, and he had taken his first drag on his cigarette. I couldn't believe it, but I smelled a mixture of fuel and cigarette smoke! Pulling on the heavy control column, I leaned over my shoulder and in a microsecond saw a smiling Sam with a lighted smoke, and I yelled, "Put that cigarette out, you idiot; you're sitting on top of a massive fuel leak!" Then, over the radio, "Nellis Tower, Mayday, Mayday, Mayday, Sailplane Tow making a 180, landing against traffic on runway two zero, right now. Clear any opposing traffic out of my way."

I got the gear down and started the flaps down as the chief punched the intercom and warned our tow guy to hang tight as I pulled the power back. We touched down on the very end of the strip, and I stopped her as short as possible, which was very short. The chief opened the bottom hatch and released the ladder while alerting the tow operator to use his emergency escape rope. I had the engines stop-cocked and all switches off as I tapped the chief on the shoulder and pointed at the escape hatch. He went immediately per my order while I was tapping Sam and pointing. Sam thought about giving me an "after you" bit, thought better of it, and I followed him out. The tow operator was on the runway and joined us as we all trotted to the edge of the runway while the fire trucks came screaming out.

The rest of the incident was routine and they tugged her off the runway without much of a traffic delay. Seems a fuel fitting had failed, and gravity feed did the rest. I never did know what Sam did with that lighted smoke, and I was so miffed at him for lighting up without checking with me that I never asked him.

Marty Martin cranked morale up another notch when he came up with another fun thing called shooting down the flag. Nellis, like all military bases, had a daily formal ceremony, with the bugler sounding retreat to accompany the lowering of the garrison flag at 5:00 p.m. Marty set up a rotating schedule, with each flying squadron on base charged with having one of their aircraft roar down from the Sunrise Mountain area and be over the flagpole, at minimum altitude, at exactly 5:00. We all practiced our time, distance, altitude, dive angle, air speed, initial run-in point, and whatever went into achieving an exact arrival over the flag pole. Observers were appointed, time hacks were issued, and a two-second deviation was ranked as bush league. The competition was intense, and it did add some spice to the ceremony. One of the troops pushed it a bit too hard and went "unscore-able at 12 o'clock." He cleared the main gate, but impacted in what was then open area on the other side of the highway.

We got our first class through the 96th as the end of the year approached and, as promised, I was on orders to go to Korea. Nellis had been a wild and wonderful experience for me, and I think I realized that Nellis and the training program would never be the same again. But I didn't care. I was off to win the war in Korea.

CHAPTER 7

THE PUSAN PERIMETER

We were back on our heels getting our butts kicked in Korea. The Chinese were spilling over the northern border of North Korea like water over a dam. We had been beaten back to the point that our surviving forces were pinned within the Pusan perimeter and fighting to avoid being driven out of the peninsula. We had been kicked out of our forward fighter bases, and those squadrons were now staging out of bases in Japan. I was assigned to the 49th Fighter Group at the airfield designated as K-2, near the town of Taegu, sixty miles north of Pusan, and thus at the far north end of the perimeter. Portions of our 49th had been forced to temporarily move about 220 miles south to the 51st Group's temporary base at Tsuiki, Japan, and were still doing some flying and support work out of Tsuiki.

When I had arrived in Tokyo, Fifth Air Force Headquarters sent me to Tsuiki, where I was supposed to get some local training. The ops guy at Tsuiki looked at my records and realized I was well qualified in what was now the F-80C, no longer the P-80C, and said there was no need for me to waste time there. They had two F-80s there that had been pulled back for maintenance work and were ready to return to K-2, and I could take one of them and fly a maintenance major's wing to K-2 in the morning.

I checked in at the maintenance tent in the morning and sort of met the major, who appeared to be mad at the world. He mumbled his name and gave me some headings and frequencies and an aircraft tail number. His preflight briefing consisted of, "We'll crank up in thirty minutes. Take whichever wing you want."

I stowed my B4 bag in the left gun bay, checked the bird over, and had my engine running and my radio on tower frequency when the major came on the radio and asked the tower for takeoff instructions. I followed him along the bumpy pierced-plank taxiway to the single steel runway that pointed out toward the water. He never acknowledged my presence or even turned his head to look at me. When he took the runway and started to run up his engine, still without noting his supposed wingman, I shoved my throttle to 100 percent and was ready to go when he silently released brakes for takeoff. Sitting on his right wing in close formation was no problem, and the gear and flaps were up as we passed the breakwater and headed out over the ocean. At about two hundred feet altitude he made his first and only transmission as he switched from tower radio frequency to tactical frequency. He pushed his mike button and said, "Go, G for George." I moved my right hand over to the eight-button radio-channel control box on the right console, felt for the second row of four round buttons, dropped down to the third button, and pushed it in for channel G. It was a good thing I didn't have to take my eyes off of him to find that button, for in that instant the huge, 260-gallon fuel tank on his right wingtip, with about two thousand pounds of fuel in it, separated from his aircraft. The tank instantly rotated to vertical and slammed into the leading edge of my left wing.

That ton of fuel and metal whipped into a 180-degree rearward spin and the pointed nose of the tank ripped through my left internal wing fuel tank, releasing a shower of ruptured metal and cascading fuel as it bounced off the main wing spar. I instinctively ducked as the mass continued to rotate backward and upward toward my canopy and the engine in my aft fuselage. I punched the mike button and said, "Mayday, Mayday, Mayday," but the major never acknowledged as he faded into the distance. Screw him, he wouldn't have been of any help anyway.

I stayed on 100 percent oxygen, as the fuel fumes were almost overpowering. I wiggled the controls to see if everything still worked and switched my radio to guard channel, which allowed me to hear the radio traffic on all radio channels operating in the area, and made my transmissions readable on all those channels. It felt like the tank had missed my aft fuselage and tail, and though my left wing was a frothing fuel fountain in a mess of mangled metal, she seemed to be relatively stable. It took all my strength to move the twisted aileron surfaces to turn the bird. The tower held all other traffic clear and alerted the fire trucks and the meat wagon, which was about all they could do.

I was still over the water and in a shallow left turn, which was the way the bird wanted to go. First priority was to get rid of the four thousand pounds of excess weight I was hauling in my external tip tanks. After the show I had just seen, I didn't have a lot of confidence in the tank-release maintenance of this new outfit, but I had no choice. I struggled with the ailerons and got the wings level. Then, rather than mess with the tip-release switches, I hit the salvo button in the center of the instrument panel, which immediately cleaned off all external stores.

After much pushing and pulling, I got her back around and lined up on a long, straight-in approach to the runway. I must have looked like a skyrocket with the frothing foam trail behind me. Getting the speed brakes, landing gear, and flaps down and still holding her on course and maintaining the proper descent was sporting, but I got her down and taxied back to the maintenance tent.

Amid much oohing and aahing, I found out that the major's aircraft had been there for troubleshooting in response to write-ups about shedding tip tanks in flight. It had been cleared with, "Could not duplicate. Ground checked OK." There was nobody there who was interested in an accident investigation, or even an incident report. I was told that there was a C-47 Gooney Bird leaving from base operations for K-2 in an hour. I popped the left gun bay open, pulled my B4 bag out, and took off to find base ops and the goon to K-2.

The back end of that tired, old transport plane was loaded with B4 bags and lots of boxes. Over my protests, they insisted that my dinky B4 bag be weighed and put with the rest of the cargo. About two hours later, we touched down on a dreary winter afternoon in Korea and taxied to an area out in the middle of the field. The pilot continued to taxi slowly as the crew opened the side cargo door and unceremoniously pushed everything except me out the door onto the mud, slush, and snow. We bounced along for another five minutes before pausing at group ops so I could get out. When I climbed down and stepped away, the C-47 was on its way back to Japan.

The headquarters building was a rectangular, one-story wood and stucco structure that obviously had been put together with local labor and materials. It looked like it could easily blow away. There were no people in sight, so I cautiously entered and found a master sergeant pecking away at a manual typewriter. When I introduced myself as a replacement pilot, he escorted me toward the end of the hall and advised me to wait as he knocked and entered an office bearing an oversize sign announcing that it belonged to Col. John R. Murphy, commander, 49th Fighter Group. Using the best military protocol, he reemerged to announce that Colonel Murphy would see me now. As I passed him to enter the office he stood at rigid attention and announced me to Colonel Murphy. The sergeant remained at attention as I stopped in front of the colonel's desk, stood at attention, saluted, and announced, "Lieutenant Broughton, Jacksel M., reporting to Colonel Murphy for duty, sir."

Murphy looked me up and down before returning my salute, at which time the sergeant came off his brace and closed the door as he left. Murphy kept me at attention as he stared some more, rustled some papers, then motioned to a chair and said, "Please sit down, lieutenant."

As I sat, I was thinking to myself, "What kind of crap is this for the Pusan Perimeter?"

When Murphy first spoke, I found out. He opened with, "I see by your ring that you're a West Pointer. What class?" When I told him 1945, he smiled wisely and said, "Oh, I'm class of 1941."

I already knew that game. West Point grads are often referred to as ring knockers. That implies that if there is a discussion in progress, the senior Pointer need only knock his large ring on the table and all Pointers present are obliged to rally to his point of view. I never saw it work that way. I have noted that when you meet a good guy from the Point who is dedicated to his mission, and he knows you are also a grad, he will usually go out of his way to be friendly, and if possible helpful. But, we have turned out some who don't operate that way, and if they graduated before you did, they will go out of their way to be obnoxious.

Murphy made light chitchat for a few minutes about how he had molded the 49th into a great outfit, then asked to see my Form Five. That is basically a military logbook that records the details of every military flight you have made. When I told him that it was in my B4 bag that was sitting out in the mud, he tut-tutted. Though he knew a month ago who was inbound, where we came from, and what we had done, he directed me to go find my Form Five and arrange another appointment with him. That figured.

I asked Murphy's sergeant if there was a jeep available that I might borrow, but barely looking up from his hunting and pecking, he allowed that there was no transportation available. As I left Murphy's office and walked past the two jeeps parked outside, the temperature was hovering around freezing, with rain falling on the mud, slush, and snow. The mile walk to the cargo area was less than comfortable, as was the unassisted one-hour search for my B-4 bag and the sloppy trek back to Murphy's office. The second appearance was only slightly less formal. Murphy spent about fifteen seconds pretending to look at my Form Five, gave it back to me, and ordered me to report to Lt. Col. Ben King, the commander of the 8th Fighter Squadron.

I walked down the dirt road, Form Five under one arm and B-4 bag in the other hand, past the maintenance and supply tents on one side, with three smaller, locally manufactured squadron ops buildings on the right. The 8th was the middle one. When I stuck my head in the door, the first face I saw was Nat King, my classmate who was the squadron ops officer. He clapped me on the back, turned toward the back of the shack, and yelled, "Hey, Colonel Ben, c'mon out here. We got some fresh meat." Ben King and I were friends from the first handshake. I asked him if he needed to see my Form Five, and he said, "Hell no. Just toss it on Nat's desk. The ops clerk will find it there. Nat, see if one of the airmen can find John Daoust. Jack, you know Johnnie Daoust. I want you to take over John's flight, C Flight, and I want John to brief you and get you a couple of rides up north. You ready to fly in the morning?"

I said, "You bet," and I knew I was back among my kind of guys.

The squadron barracks for pilots was of the same type frame and stucco construction as everything else at K-2, and was devoid of anything except GI cots covered with mosquito netting along two opposing walls and a couple of potbellied stoves in the middle. The guys welcomed me warmly, and I moved into my cot apartment.

Our barracks amenities consisted of a very young Korean houseboy who swept and did our laundry by hand; an outside, gravity-operated latrine; and a cold-water shower. The latrine was plumbed by a gasoline-powered pump that directed water to a fifty-five–gallon drum on the roof. In addition to urinals, the latrine housed a wooden fifteen-holer with a water trough underneath. Just like today's modern designs, flushing was automatic. The drum on the roof had a spring-loaded door on the bottom, and when it was pumped close to full, the weight of the water would overcome the trapdoor spring tension. The contents of the barrel would cascade to ground level, flushing all in its path. As the water left the barrel, spring tension took over again and slammed the steel door shut with a clang that shook the entire structure. Bob Hope visited and commented that K-2 was the only place you could get shell-shocked from having a bowel movement.

I was still trying to figure out where I was and what was going on when I got to the 8th ops shack in the morning. John Daoust needed two missions to finish his combat tour, and he already had his homeward bound orders. We planned on him and me flying two two-ship missions and doing a bunch of briefing, then Utah Charlie flight was to be all mine. We almost didn't make it to that point.

The first mission went well, as I got exposed to close air support of our ground troops, and some road recce behind the front lines. After the mission debriefing, John and I went over all sorts of details until we had both had enough for the day. During our discussions on survival techniques, John gave me his small Czech-made, derringer-type pistol to stick in my flight suit pocket. We climbed a small hill behind the ops building so I could fire a few rounds and check it out. I picked a pile of dirt for a target, aimed, and pulled the trigger, but nothing happened. A quick look showed a complete round, projectile and casing, jammed into the barrel and pushed forward by the round I had just tried to fire. The firing pin had been struck, and why the whole thing didn't blow up in our faces and kill us both was a mystery. We scraped a hole in the dirt and buried the stupid thing.

The second mission was supposed to be all the way up north to the Yalu River, so I could check out that territory and hopefully do some damage to the Chinese heading south. Most of North Korea had cloud cover right down to the ground. We crossed the bomb line that separated friend from foe, but a solid wall of clouds blocked our way to the north. Turning west, we spotted some breaks in the clouds along the coast. I dropped into trail close behind John. We went down to about two hundred feet, then began to fly S patterns along what looked like a well-traveled dirt road. It didn't take too long to figure out that the weather on both sides of us was rapidly getting wetter and lower. It took less time to figure out that the weather ahead was even lower and that we were in a box canyon. John blurted out, "Pull up, I'm Popeye, pull up! NOW!" He was in the clouds and out of sight, and we obviously did not know where the rocks were in the clouds. I immediately hauled back on the stick and shoved the throttle forward. Then it got real quiet.

My F-80 lurched upwards, and I was instantly on instruments. The first instrument I instinctively looked at for guidance was the gyro-stabilized artificial horizon. Our particular model of that al-important attitude indicator was not reliable, and sure enough, mine had tumbled and was spinning madly. Like it or not, I was flying by the seat of my pants. I kept back pressure on the stick, which trans-lated to pressure on my butt and meant that I was at least going up. In the world of white, gray, and rain, the air speed dropped towards stall speed, and the butt pressure got light as I eased her over the top onto what felt like she was on her back. I rolled the wings to what should have been right side up and level. I glued my eyes on my emer-gency standby instruments and nursed her into a slight climbing atti-tude. Then the clouds got bright and I popped out into the clear blue sky. The first thing I did was look behind me, and there were indeed lots of hard pieces sticking up through the tops of the clouds. We found each other, and John had me lead back to K-2. It had indeed been an effective indoctrination mission. Over the next seventeen years of fighter flying, I never got myself or my flights trapped in a spot like that. That was it for John. He left that afternoon, and I was officially Utah Charlie Lead. Unfortunately, a short time later, while John was flying the ungainly F-89, he had a major engine fire, had to bail out over the San Francisco mud flats, and drowned in the mud.

All of our birds were C models, and though we operated off of five thousand feet of a rough, undulating, pierced-plank runway, nestled in the valley of the dry Naktong River, right behind Mount Bustyourass, we could still carry two huge external fuel tanks and lots of bombs, rockets, and napalm. We topped that off with six very accurate .50-caliber machine guns in the nose, which gave us superb strafing capability. Our maintenance troops were working out of tents, and since nothing was paved, our operating surfaces were dirt, mud, or snow. Operational aids were about nonexistent, with no radio-range or instrument-letdown procedure, and no runway lighting. We had a close to worthless twenty-five–watt radio compass homer mounted on the roof of base ops. Fortunately, we were replacing our deficient artificial-horizon instruments.

If our mission was close support, we worked within a few yards of our troops. Since we had no radio contact with them, and the forward air controller (FAC) concept had not yet been fully implemented, we had to depend on the grunts' colored cloth panels to define the bomb line. We watched our grunts cheer from their foxholes as we hit the Chinese and North Koreans as they swarmed across the hills in seemingly never-ending waves. We blew the enemy away with our bombs, or watched them do the fire dance while covered with our burning napalm, or ripped them with pinpoint .50-caliber slugs.

The lack of forward air control capability was due to the economy crunch following the end of World War II. The Department of Defense had stripped the forces of everything they considered unnecessary, despite the service chiefs' protests. For its part, much of the army still thought it should have its own air arm for things like close support, while the air force leaned towards hauling nuclear weapons way up in the wild blue yonder. Things like joint training with efficient equipment that would allow an air force pilot and a couple of airmen to integrate with the grunts and put airborne ordnance precisely on army-designated targets had been mostly ignored.

Suddenly, the requirement for a FAC program was upon us. The Fifth Air Force began to reach into the squadrons to pull protesting fighter pilots out for temporary stints with the army units. They were given a jeep-mounted radio and two airmen and told to get on the road and report to a specific commander in the midst of some very filthy land battles for survival. Slowly, we were making it work, the hard way.

Sometimes we worked with pilots flying our old basic trainer, the AT-6, as "Mosquito" aircraft. The Mosquitoes would search out targets, then call us in and direct us onto what they had found. Many of the Mosquito guys were frustrated fighter pilots, and they did a superb job with their single-engine, two-seater training aircraft, whose only armament was a smoke rocket capability for target identification. It took a lot of balls to fly low and slow while searching for people who were anxious to shoot you down. But as our coordination improved, the enemy learned that to fire on a Mosquito, and thus identify their position was to invite a flight of fighters to come root them out.

Our other missions were long-range interdiction missions, where we took out bridges and supply points, or armed recce missions, where we ferreted out whatever moved and stopped it. Anything that moved north of the bomb line was fair game, and the recce missions almost always turned up some targets of opportunity. Sometimes, if they were way up north, the Russian-built MiGs would drop in on us.

Whatever the type of mission you were on, the briefing cycle was pretty much the same, with one morning and one afternoon general briefing. The pilots from all three squadrons who were on the sched-ule would assemble in group ops to be brought up to speed on the overall war situation. We discussed the location of the bomb line and things like radio call signs and areas of operations for all other air units. Somebody from the group intelligence section would have something to offer on what they thought was going on or might go on in the future, but that was mostly guesswork.

The weather gent would present his WAG (wild ass guess), which was indeed important but unreliable. There were very few weather-reporting stations to help them, and they obviously had no weather info from our target areas. Wind forces over the target were vital as regarded our dive-bombing attacks, since there were still no such things as precision-guided bombs. We had to "eyeball" an aiming point for the dumb iron bombs we were carrying, but if the weather forecasters got within ninety degrees of the actual wind direction or ten miles per hour on wind speed, they were lucky. We depended pretty much on things like smoke drift or dust patterns, or just plain pressing in and holding our dive as long as we dared. The WAG would finish up with the guess on what we might expect when we got back. He would always close with, "If you can't get in here, go to Pusan." That remark could be interpreted to mean, "If it's socked in here, you might as well give Pusan a shot. It's on the seashore, and there are usu-ally a few feet of separation between the clouds and the ocean. So if you can determine that you're close to Pusan, you can always let down outbound over the water and maybe break out with enough room to turn back toward land. Then you might find a place to land." From there, each flight leader took his three wingmen back to the squadron, where they clustered around a wooden table and did the important planning for their particular mission.

Debriefing always awaited us after each mission. Each flight would trudge back to the intelligence section of group ops, where a nonflying captain named Nalborski held forth. He and a few nonrated second lieutenants or enlisted men would join each flight of four and proceed to ask the same multitude of mundane questions about who you were, where you had been, and what you had done. About the only fun thing at debriefing was watching Nalborski. He had a crewcut, a big moustache, was very loud, and was quite capable of reaching dumb conclusions and saying very dumb things.

Nalborski was also in charge of the mission whiskey. Our mission whiskey was Old Overholt Rye, with a label that said something like specially brewed for the U.S. Government. We labeled it Old Overshoes and were sure that strange label just meant that they didn't bother to age it, because all who ever tasted it agreed that it was tough stuff. Theoretically, the intelligence officer or the flight surgeon was to dispense it to treat those troubled by the trauma of combat. I never saw a returning pilot who would have benefited from a double shot of undiluted hot rotgut in a wax paper cup. Most of the year, despite the outside temperature, we were hot, soaking wet, and smelly from sweat. There was no such thing as air conditioning, and the odor of the honey buckets of human fertilizer covering the paddies and the incessant onslaught of flies and mosquitoes did not create a cocktail lounge atmosphere. If you decided to imbibe, you needed to down it in one gulp, because if you let it stand, the Old Overshoes would melt the wax paper and glue, and the bottom of the cup would fall out. Nalborski had a very free hand with the mission whiskey and would freely dispense it for a good mission or a bad one, and he always felt obliged to join in. If you drew him as your debriefing person, you just leaned way back in your chair and talked real fast.

Back when I took over Utah Charlie flight, I flew several different F-80s on missions and decided that I liked the way 844 flew. Thus, I picked her as my first very own combat aircraft. She was crewed by Sergeant Ugerholt, and we communicated well. After all, the chief is the last guy you talk to up close and personal before launching, and it is nice to know that he is doing his best to get you and his bird back. I noticed that 844 flew even better once my name was painted along the canopy rail.

I flew 844 on a morning mission and wrote her up as OK before debriefing and heading to the mess hall for a little sustenance. With no write-ups on her, 844 refueled and rearmed quickly, and since we were always hurting for aircraft, she was needed for the next mission. She was assigned to an FNG on his very first mission. He panicked on takeoff, tried a late abort—too late—he yanked the gear handle up and ground to a stop with the entire nose section torn off. Never lend your aircraft to an FNG.

As things stabilized a bit, the army brought in airborne troops and used K-2 as a jumping-off spot for the bitter battles the paratroopers fought across central Korea. On their first thrust they jumped in and ran head-on into the seemingly endless flood of gray-clad Chinese. The next day we were giving them close support, as they were pinned down, outnumbered, and fighting for their lives. They recognized our yellow noses, and you could see them standing up in their foxholes, waving and cheering as we whizzed over their heads and past the orange and green panels stretched out on the ground, dividing friend from foe. As we bombed, strafed, rocketed, and laid napalm on the enemy along the craggy, nasty brown hillside, ahead you could clearly see hundreds of gray figures rolling over the peak of the ridge and swarming towards our lines, firing their weapons skyward. It usually didn't take us long to get our job done, and when the only gray figures you could see moving were those running back up the hill with their backs on fire, you knew you had given our guys a brief respite. We pulled their chestnuts out of the fire a few times, and it was a great feeling to see them moving forward. When they finally rotated out of combat and came back through K-2, we couldn't buy a drink at the club if there was one of them in sight.

The enemy had no regard for human life, their own or others. We knew that the Chinese were flowing into the area by the thousands, and one gray morning, after we did a particularly good job of cleaning lots of Chinese off of a ridge overlooking our troops, I took Utah

Charlie to the north behind that ridge. I picked up the main dirt road behind the ridge and headed north with a cloud deck above us, but good visibility underneath. I followed the twists and turns, and as I flew over a sharp rock ledge, I spotted some ground activity around smoke rising from a fire alongside the dirt road. I stood my bird on its left wing and looked straight down on gray uniforms—Chinese—around a fire and metal objects hung over the fire on timber supports. They were boiling large containers of water. I snapped the left wing back up and looked up the road, where I saw a large column of Chinese heading south. They were marching down the road, two abreast, and there were at least two hundred of them heading for lunch before they moved up on the ridge to replace those we had just dispatched. Our six .50-caliber nose guns were hot, and I always recced with my trigger finger lightly hooked around the red trigger on the stick. All I had to say to my wingman was "Shoot," and we raked the entire length of the column. When I pulled up and cranked her around, I expected to see the survivors diving for the bushes. They were still marching south, stepping over the fallen ones, en route to their bowl of rice. By the time I pulled up from a pass back to the south, there wasn't any more activity along the road, and I hit the lunch bucket bunch just for good measure. That unit had probably planned on attacking our guys that night, but it was not to be.

The United States made constant announcements and dropped tons of leaflets to advise the North Koreans that anything on the roads or in the open during daylight hours was subject to attack, but it didn't make much difference. Both the North Koreans and Chinese used any humans or animals that could walk as transporters of war supplies, especially munitions. A gaggle of old men, women, children, horses, donkeys, oxen, camels—whatever was moving along the roads up north, especially if they were close to the bomb line—were probably on a forced march, carrying ammunition to be used against our ground troops. Quite often, North Korean soldiers chose to travel disguised as civilians. They were not an attractive target, but most times they exploded when strafed.

The air traffic load at K-2 had been heavy during Pusan Perimeter days, and our wavy, bumpy, pierced-plank runway badly needed to be repaired. To leave the runway free for work, we had to fly an early morning mission out of K-2, then fly all the way back to Japan to land, refuel, and rearm at Tsuiki for a second mission. After the second mission, we would recover at K-2 late in the day, or else we would go back to Tsuiki for a second day. It was on such a mission that I saw support folks at their best.

Ed Reese was a sharp, vibrant young man who joined my flight and constantly emitted happiness. Ed had been working for Lockheed and had just recently been married when fighting broke out in Korea. He volunteered to come back on active duty from the California Air National Guard, and was doing a great job of flying combat with us. Ed was scheduled to lead my second two-ship element on one of those afternoon missions out of Tsuiki, and he was full of the sheer joy of good flying with good people. He had decided to try to stay in after his volunteer tour and apply for a regular commission rather than return to his civilian job and air guard status. It was a hot afternoon and we were jealous of Ed's air guard nylon mesh flight suit, which allowed what breeze there was to penetrate. We wondered why the air force didn't have that kind of a flight suit.

Getting airborne with the heat, the lack of wind, the bumpy and ragged pierced plank, and our max combat load of fuel, bombs, and ammo would require all of our skill. My wingman and I staggered into the air, with Ed's element to follow. Ed snagged an upturned, razor-sharp edge of pierced plank just as he was about to rotate for takeoff, and his right tire exploded, slamming the overloaded bird back onto the rough runway. The right wheel immediately disintegrated as Ed jettisoned his external load and the landing gear strut dug in, slinging Ed off the runway in a ball of flame.

The fire truck standing by for takeoff emergencies was manned by two spindly Japanese under the control of a black giant of a U.S. Air Force buck sergeant, and it was chasing Ed from the first puff of tire smoke. They screeched to a stop beside the orange and black billowing inferno, and as one, dived straight for the cockpit. One Japanese swung his fire ax at the canopy glass. One pulled the canopy release handle. The black giant snapped the belts loose and, with one hand, lifted Ed's charred frame straight up out of the armed ejection seat as if he were a doll. Ed was encased in melted, molten nylon from a flight suit that had been improperly researched, developed, and tested.

I led the rest of the flight to Korea and went through the mechanics of the mission before returning to Tsuiki and rushing to the hospital where they had taken my element leader. Ed was a fearsome sight, but what there was of a face smiled and whispered, "Don't worry about me; do good work tomorrow." Ed died a few hours later.

Red Byers, Bartow Thomas, and I were stuck in Tsuiki on a rainy Saturday night while waiting for some of our sick aircraft to be fixed. Adequate raw booze, chased with cigarettes and warm coke in the tent we had been given resulted in a decision to catch the train to the nearest town of any size, which was Fukuoka. We walked about a mile to the rickety wooden waiting platform and were joined by a fourth officer none of us knew. The train was twenty-two minutes late. While waiting in the drizzle, the three of us decided we could do better than that, and the new guy tagged along.

Commandeering the train was no problem, except that Red and I worried about our comrade Tommy, who chose to ride on the cowcatcher. The fireman inhaled two giant slugs of our booze as he checked Red out on keeping the boiler cooking before he passed out on the edge of the pile of coal. We gave the engineer what was left in one of our two bottles. He nursed it and sang happily as he checked me out on brakes, throttle, and other details. We missed a couple of stops, but with me at the controls and Red shoveling the coal, we slid smoothly into the assigned spot in Fukuoka station, having made up sixteen of the twenty-two minutes we were behind. We did not linger, as the MPs were approaching on the double after having been alerted by some spoilsport along the way. Red, Tommy, and I escaped cleanly, slumped over in the crowd at about average Japanese height, but the wimp who insisted on joining us at the last moment just stood there and sang to the MPs.

We picked up our repaired F-80s and went back to flying combat and forgot all about it, but the MPs generated a complaint that wound up in General MacArthur's headquarters in Tokyo. When the demand for disciplinary action got back down to squadron level, Ben King sent it back with an endorsement that we were all too busy flying combat to mess with it. That was the end of that.

CHAPTER 8

PUSHING NORTH

Our reinforced ground forces were able to break out of the Pusan Perimeter and once again move north. But some of our northern fighter bases were still not back to fully operational status. Thus, other groups often used our strip at Taegu as a staging base. My old roommate Bob Spragin's group, still flying out of Japan, would sometimes fly a mission, land at K-2 to refuel and rearm, then fly a second mission and recover back in Japan. Sprag and I met on the flight line at Taegu after each of us had led our respective flights on an early morning mission. We had breakfast and shot the breeze while Sprag's flight was being refueled and rearmed. On that second mission Sprag, working with a forward air controller, approached the target for a minimum-altitude napalm drop. It looked like enemy ground fire hit him, causing a napalm tank to explode and a wing to shear off. As soon as I heard the description of how we lost Sprag, I thought about my tip-tank incident at Tsuiki and wondered if he got hit, or if the scenario went like this: The FAC says, "Whisper Baker, go button G for

George." As Sprag punches the G button, the right tank breaks free from its rear mounting bracket, hangs tail-low for a fraction of a second, then wrenches free from its front bracket, tearing the right outboard wing like a sheet of paper. The tank rolls crazily inboard before it broadsides the rear of the cockpit and the fuselage fuel tank. But the other guys in Sprag's flight had no idea of what hit what, or what blew first; it was just a massive orange ball of fuel, napalm, and Sprag.

Sharing each other's airstrips was not the desired solution, especially when Fifth Air Force brought in another entire group to fly out of K-2 with us in what was laughingly called coordinated action. You could bet on chaos. Each fighter group would provide about twenty-four fighters. The group, or individual squadrens, would stage at either end of the runway and take off in opposing directions. The missions were usually scheduled for the hottest time of the day, ensuring that the takeoff show would be dramatic. More often than not, the air and ground would be saturated with tumbling bombs and disintegrating aircraft—from both directions. The group penalized with the tailwind behind them would take off first, and the guys at the other end would brace for the ensuing terror show of aborting aircraft, burning brakes, jettisoned bombs, tanks, and jet-assisted takeoff (JATO) bottles (the short-duration, rocket-like munition that gave us an extra takeoff push) tumbling toward them. On at least two occasions, fatally flaming and crashing aircraft were part of the show. It was utterly scary.

Probably the worst one came on a Monday after one of Colonel Murphy's "Sunday evening weenie roasts," when he would gather our entire group in the dirt outside the mess hall and tell us what a bunch of dumb weenies we were. It started out tragically for the 7th Squadron. They had a well-regarded captain who had just arrived from the States a few hours earlier. He had piled up a lot of P-80 time at Selfridge Air Force Base, and he was supposed to get a few quick missions before he took over the 7th's ops officer slot. They figured that he was so good that he could just jump in and go. Besides, they were short of pilots, so they put him on the big gaggle. He was tired and everything was new, and it was a dumb decision.

The 7th was scheduled to be the first squadron airborne, so as I strolled out to the section of dirt where the 8th's aircraft were parked and started setting up in my aircraft, I was surprised to see the new captain still outside his aircraft. Three people were hovering around him, and he was still fussing with his Mae West, dropping maps, and looking very red-faced and flustered. I gave them a casual wave as I passed, but they were obviously wrapped around the axle and didn't even notice me.

Colonel Murphy had declared that he would lead our squadron that day, which resulted in his taking my flight and my dropping back to fly his element lead. I briefed my flight in detail before Murphy showed up, and then we all dutifully listened to Murphy half-heartedly skip through the printed briefing checklist, while we tried to appear eager to fly with him.

As our flight taxied to the south end of the runway, the last of the 7th Squadron's flights was struggling into the air from north to south, coming straight at us. One of the 7th's wingmen couldn't get his external JATO bottles to fire, and without adequate speed to get airborne, he had jettisoned his load and limped into the air over our heads as his bombs, JATO bottles, and tanks tumbled past us into the rice paddies off the south end of the runway. Their last aircraft, the new captain, had finally made it to the end of the runway on takeoff roll and was passing the point where he was supposed to rotate his nose. He had never launched an F-80 off a pierced plank runway, flown an 80 with all that garbage on it, nor made a JATO takeoff, especially going downwind. People were yelling on the radio, things were flying off of aircraft in front of him, and he was in trouble.

Those of us watching knew it. The nose gear was too high, and the main gear was only flirting with the air while dropping back to the pierced-plank runway. The JATO bottles never fired, and the wings were stalled out as he passed the taxiway with only 300 feet of pierced plank left. The F-80 made a desperation lunge into the air, fell back, and rolled left. Then the tail came up and the orange and black curtain of fire was drawn closed before the rookie got mission one. In retrospect, he was dead before he pushed the throttle for takeoff, killed by confusion, disorientation, and improper preparation.

Murphy displayed a rare bit of reflex leadership as he punched the mike button and said, "OK, Utah flights, let's go to work. That one's behind us." The remaining flights of F-80s closed their canopies and started to lumber into position for takeoff to the north.

At best, Murphy was not a very proficient leader. In fact, he was a marginal airplane driver, and our flight of four felt a bit anxious as we lined up and made our final pretakeoff checks. But, there was a slight breeze from the north, the JATO bottles fired as commanded, and the takeoff was the normally sluggish, apprehensive event.

My element was just lifting off and retracting our landing gear as Murphy pulled abeam of Mount Bustyourass and called, "Utah Lead, drop JATO now." Murphy intended to depress the pickle button on the stick, which he should have had set up to drop only the expended JATO bottles. Instead, he hit the jettison external stores button, which cleaned everything off the aircraft. Since my wingman and I were right behind and below him, two 1,000-pound bombs, two full tip tanks weighing about two thousand pounds each, two large, metal JATO bottles from Murphy's aircraft, and two more JATO bottles from number two came tumbling, end over end into our face. Per my prebriefing, I broke left, and number four broke right, as Murphy's garbage split the airspace we would normally have occupied.

Murphy did not realize what he had done, and his mount, free of tons of drag, surged forward, while his flight, still in combat configuration, strained to catch up. Murphy twisted to peer over each shoulder, but there were no aircraft in sight. He barked over the radio, "Come on, you weenies, close it up!"

I replied, trying not to laugh, "Utah Lead, looks like you've lost your load. Might give us a couple percent so we can catch up."

Murphy, confused, pulled the throttle way back, and after peering at his wingtips that were now without tip tanks, slowly realized what had happened. Meanwhile, the rest of us at full throttle were gradually closing on Murphy. Without saying a word, Murphy threw his speed brakes down, and the other three of us went hurtling past, throttles at idle, boards down, approaching stall speed for our heavy combat load. As we passed him Murphy pulled the boards up and went to full throttle to catch his flight. His clean aircraft leaped past us, which was all Murphy could handle. "Utah Three, Lead, think I've got a fuel flow problem. I'm aborting; you got it." As Murphy pulled up and turned back toward the strip, the remaining three of us moved into position, all smiling, knowing the flak and MiGs ahead would be less troublesome without Murphy.

Once our overall effort of moving to the north got rolling, it only took a few weeks to get all our flying outfits back to their forward bases. It's a good thing we got K-13 at Suwon operational, or I probably would have lost Joe Frey out of Utah Charlie flight. As we climbed back through twenty thousand feet and headed back to base after a road recce way up north, Joe, leading my element, started to fly strangely. Four called and said, "Charlie Three, are you OK?" When there was no answer, Four called again with, "Lead, Three's all over the sky, like maybe he's got an oxygen problem."

I immediately pulled the power back and started looking for Three. I spotted him losing altitude in a shallow dive. I told Two and Four to steer clear as I cautiously moved up onto Joe's right wing and saw his head bobbing and swaying from side to side as he gradually descended. It was OK that he was descending, since I needed to get him to a lower altitude for more oxygen, but I badly needed to wake him up. I barraged him with radio calls like, "Hey, Joe, this is Jack . . .

c'mon, Charlie Three, Lead here, wake your ass up man, shake your head, Joe, flip it onto a hundred percent oxygen. Suck in some air."

Nothing changed until we were passing through twelve thousand feet, when his head motion changed like he was trying to respond. Then came a weak "Can't see; all black."

I called Two and said, " Two, check your map, I think K-13 at Suwon is the closest strip. See if they're operational and tell them I'm going to try and herd a sick bird there. I'm trying to set up a super-long straight in. Give me a heading check. Four, give me a good guess on how we're doing on fuel down this low." Then it was back to Joe.

I was sitting pretty tight on his wing, chattering at him constantly and trying to get him to respond. By ten thousand feet, he said, "Yeah, sort of see you . . . not clear . . . head hurts."

By eight thousand I said, "OK, Joe, now I want you to pull back on the stick a little bit—oops, not too much; just want you sort of level." We didn't have any more altitude to spare from this far out.

Then came the nut cruncher: "Joe, I'm going to ease out a little bit in front of you, and I want you to tell me if you can focus on my tailpipe, OK?" I was half holding my breath as I added a few percent and moved forward. "You see me OK, Joe?" I was delighted when he mumbled that he could see my tailpipe and sort of see my tip tanks, but not much else.

Two called, "OK, Lead, all clear for K-13. They've got traffic cleared for your straight-in. Crash crew and medics are standing by, and I'd steer about ten degrees right for about twenty five miles." The visibility was great for Korea, and I rogered that I thought I had the base in sight.

Four came on with; "Lead, he's hanging in steady behind you."

I was getting tired of yakking, but knew I had to maintain Joe's attention. I told him I was going to lead him right down to touchdown and for him to just follow my lead and do what I told him. He responded with, "Roger, I'm trying."

I called him with every throttle movement I made as I lowered my nose and started an easy descent toward the sliver of pierced plank ahead. Things were nervous and erratic as we put the landing gear down and got the flaps set, but we were configured for landing by two thousand feet altitude and five miles out. The air speed was creeping toward touchdown speed. As we crossed the threshold, I said, "OK, Joe, over the runway at ten feet, ease her back and flair . . . keep it straight."

I was beaming as he said, "Roger, I got it. Thanks." I slid out to the side, cobbed the throttle, and staggered back to go-around speed. I had to admit that I was proud of that one.

I was also proud of the time I got in on a little bit of history that has always been fun to remember. If you are in the middle of fighting a war, you are probably among the least informed as to what is going on in the world. We were better informed than the grunts because we sometimes got to see an old copy of *Stars and Stripes*, the military newspaper. But we certainly knew that our big boss in that part of the world, Gen. Douglas MacArthur, was in a running battle with President Harry Truman. Everyone knew that the civilian side of our government was the controlling entity over our military forces. But to know that there was open friction between those factions was a shocker to us. Most of us had entered the military as kids and the leadership, a nebulous "they," had always told us we were supposed to give our all to win. I don't think any of us ever thought that "they" had any thoughts other than to win, and I know that most of us never even considered that "they" could be a fractured assemblage at odds with each other. The fact that "they" actually wanted us not to win, and that "they" wanted to sack our super leader, whose only goal was to win, was incongruous to us.

So, when we learned that General MacArthur had been relieved, we did as much wondering as you can fit into a combat schedule. We wondered if we were going to keep pushing north and drive the Chinese back across the Yalu River. We wondered if we were going to destroy the communist North Korean government that had started all this, and if we were really going to make the Korean Peninsula a free democracy, like they told us we were. Certainly we were not going to just quit in the middle of the fight, and still get lots of guys killed, while the bad guys in North Korea remained in power, were we? Unthinkable.

Then, one morning after I returned from an early mission, Ben King called me in and asked if I wanted to fly another one in the afternoon—a different kind of mission. That sounded interesting, so of course I said sure. Ben said I was to say nothing to anyone, other than the three Utah Charlies I took with me, but General MacArthur was going to fly into Seoul on a farewell visit to his commanders before returning to the United States. I was to intercept his aircraft south of Wonsan, relieve the navy fighters covering him on the water route, and escort him to Seoul. We felt honored at the opportunity.

His big old triple-tailed C-121 arrived exactly as scheduled, and we had an effortless changing of the guard with the navy flight. My wingman and I took up a position off the C-121's left wing, with my element on the right side. The C-121 was much slower than our minimum comfortable speed, and we had to do lots of wiggling and throttle banging, but we never wavered while guarding our charge. As the C-121 started letting down into Seoul, I was close in on the left wingtip, and I could look directly into the first porthole-type window in the passenger area. I knew that had to be the big boss leaning back in the modified airline seat in his personal compartment and having a little nap. The change in cabin pressure as they descended toward traffic pattern altitude seemed to wake him, as he stirred and stretched. I was hypnotized; it was just like the movies. He reached forward and came up with his trademark floppy cap, put it on, and pulled his corncob pipe out of his jacket. As he lit up, he looked out the window, searched the sky and ground, and then studied us for several seconds. We never flew better formation. About that time the landing gear started down and he leaned toward the window, threw us a highball, and held it until I returned his salute from the wingtip. That meant we were relieved. As the C-121 dropped away to touch down, we pegged our throttles, and Utah Charlie rejoined in fingertip formation and orbited the strip until the ground-security vehicles surrounded the C-121 as it taxied in. Fun ride.

On the other hand, predawn missions out of K-2 were not usually fun rides. They could be demanding, especially if it was very dark and wet, as it was as I briefed Utah Charlie flight on a predawn mission for an armed recce in the Wonsan area. The weather had been horrid for days, but it was better than it had been. We were tired of sitting, so I decided we'd give it a go. I stepped lightly through the dark as I approached my bird to preflight it by flashlight.

I was still thinking about the routine that I had gone through on our flight's predawn mission four days earlier. As I approached my bird that morning, my crew chief had just spotted a Korean civilian preparing to stuff a handful of hacksaw blades down my air inlet. He yelled and charged the intruder, and as the Korean tried to run away, the nearby air policeman blew the intruder's belly away with his .45 pistol. I had tippy-toed past what was lying there, with, believe me, maggots crawling inside it. The current morning's preflight was much less eventful.

By the time we bounced down the pierced-plank runway on take-off, there was enough predawn light to outline Mount Bustyourass. I stayed under the scud and started a 270-degree turn to the left. My guys zipped into position as I approached the 270 point, and we rolled out at about two hundred feet, headed for the homer on top of group ops. The needle on my radio compass was flopping around, even at that minimum range, but the routine was supposed to give you a firm position and time hack to establish your outbound course. Actually, it was a good excuse for a neat buzz job that was sure to wake up anyone still in the sack. I eased back on the stick, and we were on the gauges as I set up a time-and-distance course towards Wonsan.

An hour and fifteen minutes later, we were still on the gauges, but time and distance said we should be someplace close to Wonsan. What maps we had were acknowledged to be inaccurate, and the printed height of the mountaintops was a mere guess. I always added a thousand feet, but even that was not comfortable as you sneaked down in the murk over unknown terrain. As we descended to drop-dead altitude, there were no breaks. I was about to pack it in when a few wisps of cloud broke apart and fluttered past my nose. After descending another hundred feet, I was looking into a three-mile-diameter bowl, with decent visibility and scattered rain showers. Sure enough, the surrounding mountain peaks were poking up into the clouds at just about my thousand-foot adjusted drop-dead altitude. We could work there, and what did I see straight ahead but a fat, black, steam-puffing live locomotive.

What's better than bagging a live loco? Not much, as far as I'm concerned. I've dueled the MiGs, and that's a kick, but there you're dealing with one machine that can only do one thing. A live loco can haul lots of stuff and deliver the goods that allow thousands of North Korean and Chinese infantry troops to spill over the hills and slaughter our grunts. I've blown lots of live locos, and while you don't get the "attaboys" you get for fighting MiGs, you know that each time you bust one, you're probably preserving the behinds of a bunch of GIs. I've always thought that wiping out a live loco or a tank should generate as much pizazz as getting a MiG.

That morning, those running the Vladivostok to Wonsan Rail Line figured the lousy weather would protect them and were not expecting any crazy Americans to be milling about in the storm-covered mountains. They were late in parking their locos inside the secure mountain tunnels that were at opposite ends of the railroad track that crossed the floor of the bowl below us. I called for gun switches on, and all four Utah Charlies were whooping as we realized that chugging blithely beneath us were not one, but five live locos waiting to be had.

I was already lined up on the closest loco in the southwest corner of the bowl. I stitched his boiler, and he went boom. My element hit the one racing for the northeast tunnel, and we took turns blowing two of the three caught in between the two dead ones. That left one spooked train driver madly alternating between forward and reverse as his exits closed and the chase narrowed. Finally, going full chug towards the southwest, he realized he had goofed and was heading full throttle towards a stationary, steaming, ruptured buddy. You could see the fire covering his molten wheels as he locked the brakes and ground the metal wheels flat. I blew him just as he ran head-on into what was left of number four locomotive.

All of us were out of ammunition and had done good work closing down that section of the North Korean transportation system. They could only move one way at a time on their single track, and with no alternate routes, it would be a while before they cleared enough of that mess to get supplies flowing to the south again. Fuel was getting low, and our operational bowl was shrinking as the rain and clouds thickened. It was time to join up, climb back into the soup, and figure out how best to penetrate the weather and get back on the ground at K-2. We needed to see if there was any breakfast left in the mess hall.

The longer the war went on, the more noticeable it became that our daily tasks were becoming more and more standardized. As an example, once each morning, at the same time, and once each afternoon, at the same time, one flight of four was ordered to run a horseshoe-shaped armed recce of the North Korean railroad system that was anchored in Pyongyang and went to the Chinese border. We all knew that Pyongyang was the flak capital of North Korea, and it was dumb to test their gunners on a recurring basis. But nobody could say our directives ignored the element of surprise, since one day the runs started at Pyongyang and went to the border, while the next day they started at the border and ended at Pyongyang. The recce flights found only what the North wanted us to find, usually flak.

Tom Van Ripen, a World War II Royal Air Force combat pilot and friend from Neubiberg, was Utah Able Lead. My classmate Corky Slack, who was about to take Tom's flight when he went home after a few more missions, was flying on Tom's wing. They both knew that downtown Pyongyang was a no-no of a vicious killer flak trap, even if you hit it on a surprise single pass. But, Tom, scheduled for a standard afternoon recce from north to south, finished the run right on time and dragged his flight right over the hub of the defenses in the downtown Pyongyang rail yards. Apparently the smothering flak irked him to the point of losing his smarts, since he pulled up and rolled in to duel a huge flak battery. They blew him to pieces. Corky escaped on that pass, but also forgot what he had learned about dueling flak guns as he pulled up in their face and rolled in again, on the same target, trying to avenge Tom. Predictably, they also blew Corky to pieces. Two neat guys, wasted on a stupid headquarters mission, who died trying to win the war all by themselves.

With plenty of good targets available, I was frustrated that we had no night capability and that nobody seemed to care. I got Colonel Murphy to let me fly a two-ship night-combat test mission. Murphy had no interest in the project, except that I knew he would claim credit for it if it worked, and he was quick to tell me that only owls and crazy people flew at night. His statement to me was, "I think you're nuts, but if you want to kill yourself, it's OK with me."

I got Maj. John "Andy" Anderson, our squadron ops officer, to fly the second aircraft and four crew chiefs to agree to help, and we readied two F-80s and four jeeps for the project. We had no field lighting, so the jeeps were stationed at opposite ends of the pierced-plank strip to spot the corners of the strip. Andy and I taped one of those little Mae West survival lights to each wrist, took an extra flashlight, and off we went, flying as two singles. Our only navigation aid, the puny twenty-five–watt homer, faded behind us. We had a high overcast with no stars or moon.

Man, was it ever dark. The radio was so quiet I thought it was out of commission, but there was simply nobody working but us. When I got up north there were lights, fires, and trucks moving around in every direction. I picked out what looked like a convoy of trucks moving south, rolled into the black, and pulled the trigger. I had intended to specify ball ammunition only for my guns, which would have meant that I had no tracer or armor-piercing incendiary ammunition, both of which can light up the sky at night. Since I had failed to specify otherwise, I got a normal, mixed load of ammunition. As the rounds of ball ammo from the six .50s began to run into each other and into the tracers and the armor-piercing incendiary rounds that were in the mixed load, the black sky and black ground in my windscreen turned into vertigo-inducing red streaks and flashes. I have no idea what I hit or missed.

I got the nose back up to level, feeling righteous that at least I had attacked the North at night. Then came panic, as the instrument panel erupted with a large, flashing red light. There I was, not knowing where I was, over the bad guys, and it looked like I had a fire-warning light. There was nobody to tell except Andy, so I gave him a call but got no reply, since his radio had quit working.

I turned south, took a deep breath, and thought, "What next?" Next was checking the lights and switches and realizing that I had not turned on my wingtip fuel tanks after takeoff, had burned most of my internal fuel, and that it was my main-tank fuel-warning light, not a fire-warning light, that was telling me that I was down to about eighty gallons in the fuselage tank. With the flick of two switches, the tip tanks began to feed, the big red light went out, and it was time to try to find the strip at K-2.

Fortunately, I had covered that route almost a hundred times, so after a while I had a fair idea of where I was. The radio compass beacon at K-2 was worthless, as the needle on my cockpit indicator spun round and round on the dial, but from my gradual descent southward I spotted the outline of Mount Bustyourass running between the end of our strip and the dry Naktong River. Further to the south, I saw the dull glow of the lights of the city of Taegu, so that black space between them had to be K-2. Weaving over that space, I was able to spot what I took to be the four sets of jeep headlights, so I set up a big looping, descending left turn to put me on a long final approach for landing. Trouble was that my descending turn put me at an angle where the jeep lights were no longer visible, and it was difficult to remember where that spot in the black was located. Additionally, I was now actually down to about eighty gallons of fuel total, and that big, red fuel-warning light came on again. I was able to rotate the warning light lens ninety degrees, which temporarily blocked out some of the light, but the message remained: better get this thing on the ground.

I tossed the landing gear and flaps down and made a weaving approach until I picked up what looked like the approach-end jeep headlights. Rolling steady, I kept my nose low so I wouldn't lose the lights again. But landing nose-down is guaranteed not to work, so when I knew I was close enough that I had to raise the nose and flare out for landing, the jeep headlights went bye-bye. At that very instant, my fuselage tank registered minimum emergency fuel, and the solid red warning light burned brightly, reflecting randomly off of the domed glass canopy. There was no way to mechanically dim that panic light, even if you had a free hand and the time to reach for the light. I did not have the fuel remaining to go around and try again in that inky black, primitive situation, even if I wanted to, which I did not. Hold on! After a short float, I got the welcome tickle of the main gear tires crinkling along the steel pierced-plank strip. There was no holding the nose off on this landing roll, and I eased the stick forward to get the nose wheel onto the strip so I could peer ahead and steer for the other two sets of headlights ahead of me. When I got to the far end taxiway and tried to kick in a big load of right rudder to steer the nose wheel hard right onto the taxiway, I realized for the first time that my legs were shaking so badly that I could barely move the rudder pedals.

Andy's story was much like mine, except he had headed back when his radio went out and had landed ahead of me. He was so uptight that he just left, talking to nobody and not waiting for me. As I hung up my flying gear, I found a note waiting for me that said if I got back, Colonel Murphy wanted to see me at the officers' club. The club was booming along as usual. When I walked in, Colonel Murphy raised his glass and said to all, "Well, well, here comes our gallant night warrior."

Hardly anybody laughed except him, but that was tough to take. I kept it short and finished with, "There's lots of targets up there in the dark, and we need to find out how to go get 'em." Not much happened to improve our night air-to-ground attack capability for a long time.

The overall skill level of our pilots was amazingly high, and the only one I had trouble with was Ernie Dunning. Ernie was a brand new West Point second lieutenant, but in his own mind he was ready for promotion to general and theater commander. I had him as my number two man on my wing on a recce along the Yalu River in MiG country. We were in the MiGs' backyard when I suddenly realized that Ernie was not in position. I spotted him about a mile out to the side and slightly ahead of the flight. Without saying a word, I hand-signaled my element leader to be quiet and fly straight ahead, then I slid to the side and moved silently up close enough to look into Ernie's cockpit. Ernie had his maps spread out across his lap and was staring straight ahead at the countryside, deciding how he would direct the air campaign if he were king. I pushed the throttle up and pulled up directly in front of him and transmitted, "Bang, you're dead." My jet wash rolled Ernie's aircraft instantaneously and violently, his maps went flying, and for an instant he probably wondered if he was dead. When Ernie recovered, he sheepishly rejoined the flight, and the rest of the mission was routine.

I was merciless at the debriefing, as I once again explained the facts of mutual support, especially in MiG country. I put Ernie on full-time mobile control for a week, where he was cooped up in a little glass box at the end of the runway, assigned the duty of looking at the landing gear of approaching fighters to be sure they were down. When Ernie came off restriction, I scheduled him as number two again. By coincidence, we drew an armed recce a bit to the west of the last one, thus a bit deeper into MiG Country. Number four had aborted with a hydraulic problem, so we were stretching our necks extra hard to clear the area.

As we approached the Yalu River and started a turn, I saw Ernie sliding out of formation, as before, just as number three blurted out, "Utah Charlie, MiGs at four o'clock, closing!"

I was already trying to close on my errant wingman and cover his tail as I commanded, "Break right, Utah Charlie." Too late—a MiG picked Ernie off on the first pass. I thought my discipline at the earlier debriefing had wounded his fighter-pilot pride enough that he would approach the combat arena as briefed—and as a disciple of flight integrity and mutual support. But, by repeating his carelessness and his disregard for the rest of the flight, we had lost him. And he had put George Womack and me in a spot that could easily be a triple kill for the MiGs. We were left with sixteen MiGs all to ourselves.

A lot of the MiG pilots were locals, and often not too well experienced, but their Russian instructors were usually good. We never had the opportunity to take inventory of those we faced that day, but it looked like at least the leader of their first flight knew what he was doing and was very anxious to knock me down. The odds were sixteen to two, and they had a huge speed advantage and the ability to yo-yo on us at will. George and I had both flown the F-80 enough to know how to get max performance out of our birds, and you could sure turn that jet tightly, especially with cannon fire coming from your six o'clock position. If we could hang together as a flight of two, avoid giving them a good shot at us, and work them far enough south so that their fuel state required them to go home, we might have a chance.

Their lead guy and his wingman were on my tail almost instantly, and George and I were standing on a wingtip and watching them miss. They just kept coming, element after element, and some of them were not too tough to beat, but there was never a break in their attack. When they did get close enough to pull the trigger, it seemed like their ammo, especially those big, red cannon rounds, went all over the place. Their guns must have been poorly aligned, which was fine with us.

We wound up tangling with those sixteen MiGs for the unheard of duration of twenty-two minutes, which was a real test of muscle, endurance, and acrobatic skill for us. I was sweating like a pig, my sunglasses wet and smeared, sweat burning my eyes. I did manage to blurt out a radio call in the blind for any help, especially F-86 MiG-killer help, that might be in the area, but nobody responded. I had just gotten rid of a MiG element and was breaking back hard left, when for the first time in a while I could not see any MiGs. Bad news. I rolled to inverted, and there he was, the lead guy, under me and behind me, nose coming up on my tailpipe and closing fast.

When he pulled the trigger, the sky lit up with a shotgun blast of tracers with no concentration on me. I kept pulling and rolling as his speed flung him past my right side. I was upside down, looking right down into his cockpit, a few feet away, and he looked frustrated. He was all hunched over, still staring at his gunsight and churning the stick around, trying to hit something, but he had no shot on me. I continued my roll, then kicked hard right rudder. As I skidded into trail, I clamped down on the trigger and let go with a six-gun .50-caliber blast right up his tailpipe. Since I was close to stalled-out from max-performance turning and he had a bag of speed, he wasn't in range very long. I don't know if I hit him, but he rolled into a split S and headed back to Antung with fifteen sloppy MiG drivers behind him.

Though we didn't know it then, Ernie had ejected from his aircraft, got a good chute, and was captured upon hitting the ground. The North Koreans brutally mistreated him, and when prisoners were finally exchanged, he came back a physical mess. Spunky young man that he was, he eventually recovered, got back on flying status, and was assigned to an F-104 squadron. Who knows why he was assigned to the most complex, temperamental machine in the business? Before long he was killed in an F-104 accident.

Not that long after my last mission with Ernie, I finished my combat tour in the F-80s, and, coincidentally, the group was retiring them and converting to the newer F-84.

Since I had flown the F-84 at Nellis, I was able to start flying combat again when I was selected as the flight leader for Project Swatrock, tasked to combat test a new Swiss antitank rocket manufactured by the Oerlikon Company. The rockets were a superb piece of equipment. They were easy to work with, easy to fire accurately, and extremely effective against targets like tanks, trucks, and locomotives. After a concentrated training period with our specially modified F-84s, we were obliged to demonstrate the rockets for General Van Fleet, the army commander, and for General Everest, our Fifth Air Force commander. I escorted those gentlemen, sans any of their staff officers, as we put on an informal show-and-tell, shooting up captured Russian T-34 tanks off the end of the runway at K-2. The generals inspected the battle damage our rockets had inflicted on the tanks, and they were impressed. General Van Fleet pledged full cooperation in giving us free range over all of Korea as well as intelligence help in locating appropriate targets. General Everest pledged full Fifth Air Force ground and air support. It was a done deal, and General Van Fleet departed in the back seat of his two-seat L-5 observation plane, while General Everest flew out in his C-47. There were no brass bands in sight. Today that would probably require a cast of thousands.

We shot up a storm, and our tally of tanks and trains surpassed all expectations. We picked up a bunch of battle damage, which was not unexpected for that type of air-to-ground dueling. We also lost my co-leader of the project, Capt. LeRoy Stanley, which took the edge off of the good results. The final project reports were superlative, and we expected to see the rockets as an immediate addition to our fighter weapons inventory, but it was not to be. The United States did not buy the rockets, but the Oerlikon factory went into full production and supplied the Russians with the rockets for many years. I thought I deserved a medal from the Russians for running a successful combat evaluation for them, but they never came through. All they did was shoot at me in the next war.

It was time for me to get out of there and head for the United States. I packed up my B4 bag and got as far as Itazuke in one of our group T-33s. My fellow F-80 pilot Joe Connelly and I bummed a ride out of Itazuke to Tokyo in a C-46 cargo hauler. Despite the fact that we thought the headquarters pilots were going to kill us in the landing pattern, we made it back into noncombat country.

When we checked in with Fifth Air Force personnel, we found that we were at the bottom of the totem pole. Each morning we got to the terminal early, only to be bumped by low-ranking army and air force enlisted men, obviously from noncombat units, with Japanese wives and generally undisciplined children. We were told that, frankly, combat returnees were bottom priority at that time, as the State Department wanted to get the Japanese women and children back to the States by Thanksgiving—despite the fact that those women and children had no idea what Thanksgiving was.

One morning we managed to make the cut and found ourselves as the only two passengers who were either commissioned or combat returnees. We squeezed into the minuscule seats on a contract carrier. It was a hastily converted surplus air force four-engine DC-4 whose purple and pink paint scheme identified it as Sunshine Airlines. The study in people was interesting, for about the first five minutes. The male passengers had probably been in the Far East for at least two or three years, yet there were few stripes on any sleeves to indicate promotions. The men seemed withdrawn and almost confused at what they had wrought. Some of the women were docile and some tough, but they were all talking loudly and excitedly in Japanese, to the exclusion of English. It was common practice in Japan to delegate the care and discipline of young children to hired or family-related mama-sans, leaving parents free of such duties. The kids on Sunshine Airlines, free from mama-san—with parents who did not know how to control them—were completely out of control. Chaos reigned supreme.

The first Mayday call came when that tired old machine, with obviously suspect maintenance, lost an engine between Tokyo and Wake Island. Sunshine Airlines, complete with very, very senior hostesses, limped into Wake, and Joe and I hung around a miserable Quonset hut for a day waiting for the required engine change.

The next day Sunshine was reported to be ready to go, and we went through a repeat of the undisciplined loading exercise. The scheduled flight from Wake to Hawaii was planned for ten hours, but the second Mayday came four hours and forty five minutes out, fifteen minutes short of half way, when we lost the newly installed engine. The rules say that if you have that kind of emergency, especially over that very large pond, and are less than halfway there, you will turn back. That seemed like a very long turn as we headed back to Wake Island. Theoretically we should have been able to maintain altitude on three engines, but we were not maintaining altitude. It was scary as we got lower and slower with nothing but ocean in view. It got terrifying when we lost another engine on the same side, and one SA-16 Albatross air-sea rescue aircraft joined in formation on each wing. They don't send Dumbos after you if they think you can make it. We sunk to just above the waves, where you could clearly see the breakers, before we touched down amidst lots of flashing red lights.

During the double-engine-change delay, Joe and I felt the need to get away from it all and set out on our own to tour some of the World War II history along the island's coastline. There were plenty of untouched relics to view, including a cluster of old wrecked Japanese ships in shallow water in front of a string of Japanese gun positions. Everything was still in the gun pits, including human remains. After our nature walk and history lesson, we found the well-concealed spot where the transient aircrews hung out, with a bar, decent food, and a swimming hole, and had a few comfortable hours. But when Sunshine was again reported as ready to go, the boarding and departure debacle was even worse than before, since the children were tired and people were nervous. That time we made it.

Safely on the ground in Honolulu, Joe and I decided no more Sunshine Airlines for us and we jumped ship. We roamed the military flight line and found a friend from Nellis who had just completed a P-51 tour in Korea. Forewarned about the likes of Sunshine Airlines, he had contacted a buddy before he left Korea and arranged to fly copilot on a C-121 cargo flight from Tokyo to San Francisco. We bummed a ride with them, and even got some stick time on that big machine as we headed for the States.

We got into San Francisco on Thanksgiving evening and checked into the Mark Hopkins Hotel, donned fresh uniforms complete with crisp, new combat ribbons, and took the elevator to the Top Of The

Mark, the famous bar on the top floor since 1939. When we asked the bartender for the 49th Group bottle, per tradition, he produced a fifth of Chivas Regal scotch that had about three fingers worth left in the bottle, and set it between us at the bar. We opened it, drained it, congratulated each other, and paid the bartender to set up a new bottle for those to follow. Free drinks were everywhere, and we were off for a night on the town.

CHAPTER 9

LITTLE RED SCHOOLHOUSE

The first thing I did was get an airline ticket to Spokane, Washington, where AJ was staying with her sister and her family. I had not seen her in a long time, but I thought I wanted to marry her if she would have me. I checked into the tradition-laden Davenport Hotel and called and asked her to meet me in the hotel's Silver Dollar Lounge. My brain was a hodgepodge of travel lag, lingering combat awareness, fatigue, and exhilaration as I paced nervously in the lobby by the lounge, with people passing by smiling and nodding approval of my silver wings and colorful combat ribbons. When she rounded the corner of the lobby and headed my way, everything momentarily stood still, then immediately changed for all times. I knew that I wanted to marry her, and though it took some convincing, I got her to agree.

Christmas was approaching rapidly, and my orders had me reporting in to Luke Air Force Base, on the northwest side of Phoenix, Arizona, right after the first of the year. AJ's brother Art, who had done the father duty for years, was stationed at Williams Air Force

Base, and AJ wanted us to secure his blessing on our marriage. AJ drove her car to Phoenix while I flew to Las Vegas to see Kat and Jim Losee before continuing on to Phoenix. Art was delighted with our plans, and I boarded the first leg of what today would now be considered the long and lumbering prop-driven commercial airline route to Rochester, New York, where we would be married.

It was close to midnight by the time I got to Rochester and caught a cab to our house, which still seemed very much like home. I had changed a lot, but it had not. My dad had already gone to bed, and as my mom fixed me her patented bacon and eggs, I casually informed her that I was getting married in three days to a woman she had never heard of. As I described AJ to her, she said, "My God, I was that big when I was thirteen years old." Somehow, within the three days my family put together a first-class formal wedding ceremony at our old Episcopal Church, with all the frills.

Rochester was sporting its usual late December cold and snow when AJ flew in a day later. She was dressed in Arizona chic, complete with high heels, and was suffering from weather-culture shock by the time she deplaned and fought to keep her balance on the ice and snow between eight-foot-high snow banks. Back at the house a day later, as she came downstairs for breakfast the first time, she was wearing red plaid Bermuda shorts and a light yellow jacket. My father, always an East Coast wizard with words, remarked, "That's the damnedest outfit I ever saw." But my family became her family instantaneously.

We were married at noon on the 26th, had a reception at the house, changed clothes, and were on the road to Houston by five in the afternoon. We had to get going in a hurry, since AJ's brother and family were suddenly rushing to an assignment in Italy, would be staying overnight in Houston on the 28th, and could not possibly survive without a visit with the newlyweds. Since it was winter, and since two-lane roads winding through each and every village along the way were the norm as opposed to freeways of the future, it was a tough drive.

Our brand-new Dodge two-door had the latest in transmission technology, called tip-toe-matic, which was a combination of stick shift and a sort of fluid-drive overdrive. We quickly found out that if you wanted to speed up to pass a truck on a two-lane road, and were in tip-toe-matic drive, stepping on the gas would automatically whirl the fluid drive at a fantastic rate, and you would immediately slow down by twenty miles an hour. We spent our honeymoon driving straight through to Houston and splitting two-hour shifts driving or sleeping. Our candlelight dinners consisted of cold sandwiches at whatever filling station we found open. If we found one of the then-common Stuckey's quick roadside stops, we got the extra benefit of a box of their sugar-saturated peanut brittle to pump us up.

We made it to the designated motel in almost exactly forty-eight hours. Art and his family never showed up. They had a change in plans, bypassed Houston, but never got around to letting us know. After some much-needed sleep, we moved in with good friends in town for a short visit and New Year's Eve at the Ellington Air Force Base officers' club. Since the girls became enamored of Singapore Slings, that became a short evening and allowed us to blast off for Phoenix early the next morning.

When we got to Luke, I once again reported to Colonel Marty Martin and found an extremely busy base. It had a twofold mission of training U.S. pilots for duty with the F-80 and the F-84 squadrons in Korea and with providing F-84 proficiency and gunnery training to NATO students. We had lots of aircraft and a high priority for getting good people and equipment; thus, the runways and the gunnery ranges were quite busy. Any time you find a fighter base where everyone is getting all the flying time they can use, you find happy people. Luke was happy, and we worked hard and played hard.

It was hot: so hot that by midday, touching the aluminum skin of your fighter without wearing your leather flying gloves would physically burn the skin on your hands. The excessively hot weather affected us most in the area of takeoff performance, since the hotter the runway temperature, the longer the takeoff roll. We carried different armament and fuel loads for different missions, so we had to pay attention to the details of each planned takeoff. Quick-reference charts would tell us that for a particular takeoff weight, at a certain altitude above sea level, with a specific ambient temperature, you could expect to lift off at a certain number of feet down the runway. Perhaps a more definitive calculation from those charts was the go/no-go number. When you went to the charts with your specific inputs, you came up with a simple fact that for those conditions you needed to have a certain speed by the time you got to a certain runway marker, or you were not about to get safely airborne before you got to the end of the runway. Sometimes, when you had to input numbers like 120 degrees runway temperature, the results calculated as impossible. Most pilots hate to abort a mission after going through all the preparation to get to the end of the runway for takeoff, but accepting the go/no-go criteria was a must for longevity.

All models of the F-84 were heavy and slow to accelerate, carrying monikers such as Hog, Super Hog, and Lead Sled, and the famous dirt sniffers got a workout on almost every takeoff from Luke. The earlier the model of the F-84, the worse the performance was. Within our huge inventory of F-84s, we actually had one F-84B, one of the very first production aircraft. It had flown once, on its arrival flight into Luke from somewhere, but was out of commission after it landed. It just sat on the ramp for months as the supply troops searched for seemingly nonexistent repair parts. The maintenance folks finally pasted it together for what was supposed to be a flight to the Weapons Test Center for duty as a target, but by regulation it had to be test flown first. I used to scarf up extra hours flying test hops, and they asked me if I would fly the B model. Since it was the only B on base, and since none of us had ever seen a B or known anyone who had ever flown a B model, I said sure.

The weather was hot, as always, but the takeoff charts said it was OK to go. To cut down on takeoff weight, we made sure the gun cans were empty and just put fifty gallons in each tip tank, so I could check that the tanks would feed. I checked everything extra carefully, lined up for takeoff, held the brakes, and gave her about fifteen seconds at 100 percent run-up, and all the gauges were in the green. The first clue of what was to come was that it took very little pedal pressure to hold the brakes at full throttle. When I released the brakes to roll, nothing happened; I mean *nothing*. The wheels didn't go round, and the aircraft did not move. I was about to pull the throttle back and abort when she eased forward ever so slowly. I had about ten thousand feet of runway to play with, so I just let her go. I had my go/no-go speed and runway distance pegged, and she made it, just barely. When it was dirt-sniffer time, I eased back on the stick, and as she grudgingly lifted off, I sucked up the gear and held on, sitting motionless and barely breathing. I didn't dare retract the takeoff flaps, and I could count the cotton bolls on the plants in the field off the end of the runway. What a dog!

With the flaps up, I picked up a couple thousand feet and staggered around the airfield perimeter, keeping the runways in sight and never pulling the throttle back any lower than 98 percent. There wasn't enough oomph to do much of anything other than remain airborne, and none of the systems worked very well. In twenty minutes my curiosity was satisfied, and when I got back on the ground I wrote up enough discrepancies so that I figured none of us would get tasked to fly her out of Luke. When I left Luke, I think she was still sitting in the bone yard, waiting to be hauled out on a railroad car.

The only way to compensate for the desert heat was to fly our training sorties early in the day. Supervisors and instructors were usually up about 2:00 a.m., with student flights lifting off at first light. We were supposed to be through around noon, but it didn't work that way, and if we closed down by four we were lucky. There was no such thing as air conditioning, and while evaporative swamp coolers helped some, it was a long, exhausting day.

Everyone was pushing real hard, and the accident rate in the training squadrons was terrible, especially among the NATO students. Some of the French students seemed to think that trying out the ejection seat over the gunnery ranges was good sport, especially since they could then watch an American F-84E impact and explode on the desert. Some of the Italian students seemed indecisive. It was my unpleasant duty to be one of the first on the scene of a burning F-84E on the runway as the fire crew extinguished the flames. The Italian student had vacillated on takeoff from go, to no go, to go, to no go, then melted the brakes, which torched the aircraft. While the canopy was rolled back, his rigid, blackened remains were still strapped in, erect in the cockpit.

The accidents were not limited to the students. We used B-26s to tow the air-to-air banner targets, and Herm Peters found himself trying to make it back to Luke from the range in one of them while fighting multiple emergencies. The base dispensary was located on the southeast perimeter of the base, and that is as close to the runway as he could get before bailing out, inverted at low level. He parachuted into the front entrance of the dispensary as his B-26 was impacting and blowing up behind the dispensary. We did have an all-hands flying safety lecture after that one, but there was a war going on, and we just kept charging.

I had the best job on the base, which was running one-week refresher courses for instructors. Our instructors were among the high-jet-time people in the fighter business, were good gunners, and were eager. Most of us knew each other well and had completed a jet combat tour in Korea. We called my place the little red schoolhouse, and our program was actually a week-long bombing and gunnery meet, with daily rat races for bragging rights as to who out-hassled whom.

Back when AJ and I had first arrived at Luke, the housing office assigned us to half of a one-story duplex that must have been glued together at the start of World War II. We had a bedroom, bath, living room, and a narrow kitchen with no shelves or cupboards. Since we didn't own a stick of furniture, the few pieces of GI furniture that came with the place worked for awhile, but a kitchen needs something more than bare walls, a stove, and a sink. A good cabinetmaker I am not, but I managed to hang some slightly lopsided things on the walls that sort of looked like cabinets. We painted the walls and ceiling turquoise with advancing brown footprints: nothing but cool. We fixed the place up to keep it from crumbling, and by the time we bought some decent furniture from town, it looked as good as a dinky cubbyhole can look. The couple in the other half of the duplex were transferred out, and I made a pitch to the housing office, with help from my boss. They were impressed with the improvements we had made. I told them that if they would assign me the other half of the unit, and cut a hole and hang a door between the units, AJ and I would polish up the other half as we had the first half. They agreed, and with more effort and furniture we had a relatively neat pad by the time AJ was five months pregnant.

I had some leave time coming, and neither one of us had been on the ski slopes since Germany, so we decided that AJ was still mobile enough for us to check out the new ski scene in Alta, Utah. We scrubbed the duplex up and even got enough polish to stick on the tired linoleum floors to make them a bit shiny. One problem that came with those old places was plenty of Arizona field mice. Not wanting them to take over our place during our ten-day ski session, I bought a dozen mouse traps and set them in the predawn before we took off for the mountains of Utah.

The powder snow was plentiful, and not many people had discovered that developing complex, so things went well. I probably skied the best I ever had, and I know it was the best I'd ever seen AJ ski. I even took her to the tippy-top and took off and stayed a fair distance in front of her on the way down, but where I could still keep an eye on her. It was a challenging run, but she was so miffed off that I had deserted her that she made it all the way down without a single stumble or fall.

She was still unhappy when I skied up to her on the flat stretch in front of the lodge, intending to tell her how great she had done. There on the level, with not a mogul in sight, barely moving, she fell flat on her back. It took a few hot buttered rums before there was more than one of us laughing about that.

By the time we had descended back to the desert floor, it was surprise time. As we unlocked the door of our place, a foul odor greeted us. All twelve of my mousetraps must have gone off as soon as we headed north, and after ten days there wasn't much left of the mice except for the smell. There must have been some chemical reaction between dead field mice and very old polished linoleum floors, because in twelve places the linoleum and what was left of the mice had become one. While we were considering how to approach that problem, Maj. Dewey Bower, my operations boss who lived next door, dropped by to invite us over for a drink and to share some news. I was on orders to leave my little red schoolhouse and go to Del Rio, in west Texas, to help reopen an abandoned airbase and start a new combat-crew fighter-training program. I said, "Dewey, I don't want to go to Del Rio, Texas."

He replied, "I'm afraid that doesn't make much difference, but maybe a cool one will make you feel better."

Del Rio is about ninety miles west of San Antonio, across the Rio Grande from Ciudad Acuña, Mexico. In good times it had been the capital of Texas sheep ranching, but they had not seen a drop of rain in seven years, and things were so bad that the town was about to forget about incorporation and close down the police and fire departments and the school system. Businesses were almost nonexistent. That would not do as long as Lyndon Baines Johnson was a very big man in the U.S. Senate. The old army air force training field had been shuttered for years and was home for multitudes of very large rattlesnakes that enjoyed sunning themselves on the ramps and runways broiling under the cloudless skies. The scorpions and tarantulas swarmed everywhere. When we drove into town, the only place my pregnant wife and I found to stay was a decrepit motel along the highway from San Antonio. There was a small Mexican food café close by, but tacos, enchiladas, and beans three times a day were not on her recommended diet. Things didn't look too rosy.

There were only a few officers and airmen there, but the pressure was already on us to turn this debacle into a productive site for the Korean pipeline. As a captain, I ran group operations under our group commander, Lt. Col. Clayton M. "Ike" Isaacson, of World War II and Korea note. Ike and I became lifelong friends from the moment we met. We worked for an old-time colonel wing commander named Tom Mosley, who was definitely not interested in winning a popularity contest. The fact that neither he nor his staff were up to speed on jet fighter operations of the day tended to create a sense of friction rather than cooperation between the wing staff and the operational training group. So Ike and I just started charging like we owned everything involved with the mission of the base, which we almost did. We wound up with three operational training squadrons turning out good, combat-ready pilots, but Ike had to spend much of his time dodging Colonel Mosley and his often apathetic staff.

The initial base housing effort consisted of a small settlement on top of a sand pile separating the base from the vast expanse of desert. On one side of the road was a rather large ranch-style house for the Mosley family, and on the other side were two duplex single-story apartments. The good-guy warrant officer who was stuck as Colonel Mosley's administrative assistant and his wife shared one duplex with us, and our flight surgeon Charlie Wheeler and his family and Ike and Nona Isaacson and their family shared the other one. At least it was a happy neighborhood on our side of the street.

AJ and I were faced with the fact that even though Charlie Wheeler was a super flight surgeon and friend, he did not have the military medical facilities on base to assist in the arrival of our firstborn. The local facilities in town were not a good option at that time. Even if the local facilities had been attractive, the air force would not have paid for them. I guess everyone knows that we were not drawn to the air force by the lucrative wages, and we in fact were dependent on the available military medical care for our families and ourselves. In this case, available meant Brooke Army Medical Center, in San Antonio, ninety-plus miles away on a two-lane highway interrupted with Texas hamlets. The closer the time came, the more carefully we timed our dashes from Del Rio to Brooke for routine examinations.

We chickened out when the forecast for delivery got down to the anytime-now stage. Gerry Weaver, one of the dearest friends we have ever had, and the mother of my West Point roommate Bud Weaver, lived in San Antonio. I went on leave, we moved in with Gerry, and our son Markham (Mark) was born in style.

It seemed like whatever Ike and I did was guaranteed to cause a confrontation with Colonel Mosley. We had a brand-new second lieutenant student pilot get lost one afternoon when he was on a solo F-80 acrobatic training mission. As he was running out of fuel, he spotted an abandoned dirt strip about a thousand feet long and over a hundred miles out in the desert. He bellied in his aircraft and slid off the end of the strip, but he was OK. One of our instructors homed in on the student's radio transmissions, pinpointed his position, and relayed it to Ike and me in group ops. It was getting late in the afternoon, and since we didn't want to leave him out there overnight with big thunder bumpers on the western horizon, it was time for action. Standby helicopters were not standard features in those days, but we did have a B-25 assigned to base operations that Colonel Mosely rode in when he had to go some place. Ike and I both had B-25 time, and Ike asked if I wanted to fly as his copilot. I was already grabbing a map as we headed for the flight line. Those two big R-2800 engines on a B-25 had a very distinctive roar, and Colonel Mosley called base ops demanding to know who was flying his aircraft without his permission. When they told him what was going on, he flew into a blistering rage, but we were long gone and had switched our radio off of tower frequency by then.

We easily found the forlorn-looking, gear-up F-80, and we made one practice approach to the tiny strip before going around and making the world's greatest short-field landing. We got the lieutenant on board, and since he was in some degree of shock, he babbled incessant apologies until we finally had to give him a direct order to shut up and hang on. Then came the fun part, since we knew getting out of there was going to be iffy. As we taxied back to the other end of the little dirt strip, Ike and I joked that if we creamed Mosley's B-25 and lived through it, we would at least be on our way out of Del Rio for sure.

We got so close to the end of that strip that our main gear was on the dirt strip and our tail was hanging out over the desert. Both of us stood on the top of the rudder pedals to lock the brakes against the power of the two big engines. We pushed the control yoke full forward to pin the nose wheel down as Ike palmed the throttle quadrant that sat between us with his right hand. With my left hand backing up his hand, he moved all six levers to the forward stop, so we had full throttle, max rpm, and full-rich mixture on both engines. The nose wheel tried to bounce, the main gear wanted to skip, and the entire machine twitched, shook, and wanted to go, but we held her for what seemed like ages but was probably ten seconds. Ike yelled, "Go," and we were both off the brakes. His right hand moved to the control yoke as my right hand came off the yoke and joined my left hand in trying to push the throttle quadrant through the front windscreen. We leapt forward, and as the little dirt strip disappeared under us, we literally jumped off the end. We landed back at the base as the sun was setting, and, since we had been successful, that was the end of that.

Then I painted one of our T-33s scarlet red, and the wing staff went bonkers. Crew Training Air Force (CREWTAF) was having a gunnery meet, back at Luke, as a qualifying session for the Worldwide

Gunnery Meet. The guys at Nellis were a lead-pipe cinch to win, since they were the only ones with F-86s and thus had a lock on the air-to-air portion of the meet. We were the new kids in CREWTAF and had zero chance with our F-80s in a competition where one of the events had the towed aerial targets at twenty thousand feet. We were scheduled to get some F-84Es at Del Rio in the near future, and with a few phone calls we managed to get cleared to pick five of them up from the depot before the meet. They wouldn't be much better for air-to-air, and we only had a few days to practice, but it was fun to try. The red T-Bird was to make it easier to see when it towed targets for us during practice but, again, our local leaders didn't relate to that.

The shootout was lots of fun, but the outcome was almost as expected: a tune-up for Nellis, but I surprised them in one area. I got to pick the guys on our team, and we each selected one of the F-84s for the competition. I also selected a real sharp armament crew chief, and he and I worked longer and harder than the rest of the Del Rio team. You could only load two of the machine guns for the air-to-ground strafing event, and he and I spent hours on the firing-in butt (a revetment where we boresighted the guns) and in the air, test-firing those guns until we had two of the four guns harmonized so they could hit a gnat's eyebrow at a thousand feet. On the opening event of the first day of competition at Nellis, I put an unheard-of 98.9 percent of my rounds into the twenty-foot-square target. That caught the attention of all concerned and made the papers with a picture of General Born, the commander of CREWTAF, admiring my shredded target. That was to pay off for me the following Saturday.

All the "attaboys" for best scores had been passed out by noon Saturday, followed by a gathering at the officers' club. I had been back with those of my ilk for a week, and I savored the experience. The thought of further servitude in Del Rio was tough to accept, and when I spotted General Born at the festival bar, I decided it was the time to act. I introduced myself by thanking him for posing for the picture with my strafing target, which provided the desired introduction.

He casually asked, "How are things at Del Rio?" and without a second thought for protocol, I was off to the races. He knew Tom Mosley from way back, and by the time I got to the scarlet red T-Bird, he and I were laughing together. He said, "What do you want to do?"

I said, "I want out of Del Rio, and coming back to Luke would be fine with me." He excused me by saying that he would look into it. We flew our F-84s back to Del Rio on Sunday, and on Monday I was on orders back to Luke.

When I got back to Luke, the first of the long-delayed swept-wing F-84Fs were beginning to arrive. Unfortunately, those birds had been through a politically complex development battle, and the result was a flight-control system with a split-tail stabilizer that was definitely Stone Age and required more arm muscle than it should have. Turning tightly at any altitude or air speed was a problem. Technically, they were supersonic birds, but the F version—which, after all, carried the moniker of "Superhog"—took hard work to bust Mach 1.0. The best bet was to go to full throttle and climb to thirty thousand feet, then roll over into a very steep dive. Then you got your gut check as the Machmeter slowly inched forward and the rough country below came alarmingly closer. If your technique was proper, the cockpit instruments would momentarily hang up at about .98 Mach, then shudder as the Mach needle wiggled to Mach 1.01. That was it, and no way was it going to go any higher. It was time to retard the throttle and pull mightily on the previously described heavy elevator controls. The reward for all that was a small certificate acknowledging your entrance into the still exclusive supersonic society.

Major Bruce Clark was commanding the first F-84F squadron at Luke and was running the first class of students through a transition and gunnery program. I was given the second F squadron, with a nucleus of key personnel, and was charged with forming a firepower demonstration team and with further developing the weapons-instruction program while we waited for more new aircraft and more student pilots.

One morning Bruce and I were comparing notes when one of his instructor pilots interrupted with, "Major Clark, I think we've got a problem." One of their student pilots was overdue, and they couldn't contact him on the radio. More ominous was the fact that he had been on his Mach-1 mission, and a state trooper had called base operations to report black smoke to the south of Highway 60, which ran between Wickenburg and Blythe, just north of the supersonic area. He said the smoke looked like it was just south of the first set of hills. There were still no helicopters on base for such emergencies, and if the smoke was just over the first hills, we could get to it on foot. We grabbed a couple of small bottles of water and jumped into Bruce's car, with one of our factory tech reps joining us, and headed north at max speed. We turned west at Wickenburg and headed for the highway mileage marker described by the trooper. After parking the car and starting up the gradual incline leading to the first ridgeline, we realized how slowly we were progressing and were reminded of how deceptive distance is in the desert. It was still only about 8:30 in the morning, but it was hot, and our short-sleeved military shirts were of little protection against the relentless sun. Our oxford uniform shoes were not built to combat the rocks and ravines of the desert floor. But it was only over that first ridge, and we could make that.

By noon, we were exhausted and were still just approaching that first crest. By 1:00 p.m. our water was gone as the top of the ridge melted into a plateau that still kept us from seeing down past the far side of the ridge. When we got to where we could look down the backside of the ridge, we were looking at nothing more than thousands of miles of the same nothing desert. That was when our tech rep fell down the first time and confessed that he suffered from an inner-ear problem that hampered his balance. We immediately turned around to head back downhill to the road.

By 2:00 p.m., Bruce and I were taking turns supporting our tech rep, and his weight hurt our sunburned arms and necks. We kept the sun to our left, so we must have been heading roughly north, but we were still laboriously wandering around the plateau, looking for the crest, and we were lost. It all looked the same. That is when our tech rep broke down and begged us to leave him to die. We gave him five minutes to collapse next to a large, shadeless boulder before staggering on. By 4:00 p.m., Bruce and I were having trouble navigating and supporting our load, then the plateau finally dropped away in front of us and we could see the highway and the little spot that was our car.

Going downhill wasn't much easier, except for the psychological realization that we knew where we were. About 6:00 p.m., two AT-6 trainers from Luke appeared on the horizon, weaving in a search pattern as they looked for us. We waved them off and made it to the road and the car, but we were not very spry. We headed for a rundown tavern we had seen along the highway while driving in that morning, and reaching that front door was the high point of the day. We slumped onto bar stools and spilled out our tale of woe to a sympathetic desert rat bartender. I can still remember instantaneously inhaling two Tom Collins and eating every sliver of ice before my eyes refocused and my fingers flexed freely. We were pretty dopey, but we made it back to Luke. We left our tech rep at the base dispensary for emergency attention, and when I got home I stripped to my shorts and lay on the couch inhaling ice water and applying sunburn spray for several hours.

Nobody else found the missing pilot and aircraft for several months. When the wreckage was located by chance, the only conclusion that could be reached was that he had gone straight in and disintegrated. That did nothing to enhance the reputation of the split-tail F-84F.

One thing the split-tail F could do was go fast. The aircraft was also badly in need of some good press, since the Department Of Defense and Republic Aviation had been fighting over requirements, dollars, and the lack of a completed product for quite a while, and they still did not have the desired slab-tail fighter in operation. All of that made the F-84F the obvious choice for the annual coast-to-coast Bendix Trophy Race, which was part of a grand old festival called the National Air Races. Since Luke was the only Training Command base that had F models, and since I had a few Fs and no students, I got to be the boss of the Training Command Bendix team. We were to field three entrants, and my boss, Col. Levi Chase, selected Capt. Ed Kenny, who was running the Luke ground school at that time, and Capt. Harley Cunningham, one of our maintenance officers, as the primary pilots. I got to pick my dear friend Lt. Ed "Lucky" Palmgren as the spare pilot to fly the number three aircraft. Colonel Chase gave me a free hand on the project, and I rounded up a goodly crew of flying and maintenance supporters for a month-long fun project.

Lucky and I took a T-33 out to the flight-test center at Edwards Air Force Base to see if we could pick up any hot tips from the acceptance flight-test records on the F or from the guys who had done the test work. The day we got there was the day the Edwards pilots found out that they would have a team in the race, so obviously they had no hot tips for us. In fact, their attitude was one of, "Why are you peons from the field bothering us super-smart test people?" That was OK, because it made us realize that we needed to be imaginative and different if we were to win. We brainstormed with all our people and came up with our game plan, which was indeed different. The first thing we did was put Lucky to work on the nitpicking details of flight planning, researching winds and temperatures, fuel management, and the like. Next, we addressed the fact that all aircraft look smooth to the casual glance, but they actually have hundreds of spaces between panels, recesses around fasteners, and other skin irregularities that cause surface friction and speed-reducing drag. While some of our techs fine-tuned every system on our three birds, others went to work with Bondo and filled every surface crack on our three race birds, then gave them a double-dose Simonize job. Our F-84Fs sparkled in the sun and were absolutely slippery.

Since the F-84F would not go coast to coast on a single load of fuel, the necessary pit stop loomed as pivotal. A fuel factor we considered was that fuel expands with heat, so if your fuel is cold, you can pack more into a given fuel tank. And, dry ice is super cold, and since it quickly turns into nothing, it would not hurt jet fuel. A mechanical factor we took into account was that the fields and runway complexes we considered for our pit stops had to be such that we could land in one direction, take on our fuel from a single-point refueling truck, with the aircraft engine running, then take off in the opposite direction. We also felt that we should have a different plan for each of our primary contestants, with the spare being prepared to fill in for either one.

Ed Kenny flew flight plan one, which was my favorite plan, while Harley Cunningham preferred flight plan two. Ed pegged the throttle on takeoff from Edwards and left it there. When he was a hundred miles west of the deserted field at La Junta, Colorado, he dropped the nose and kept her on the Mach bubble until he was three miles from the end of the east-west runway. He then chopped the power to idle and pulled up into an arching teardrop pattern, dumped his speed-brake and then his landing gear as soon as he slowed enough, and touched down heading back to the west. Captain George Kevil and his crew had been standing by on the west end of the runway since the afternoon before. They had two trucks, one a single-point refueling truck we had borrowed from Lowry Air Force Base in Denver, and the other a refrigerator truck loaded with blocks of dry ice cut to the right size to drop into the topside ports on the refueler. Those chunks had been going into the fuel all night, making that fuel as dense as it could get, and even making the outside of the fuel shell cool to the touch.

As Ed reached the end of the runway and spun around to face east, they hit him with the single-point hose, and the ice-cold fuel flowed. The instant the automatic disconnect spit the hose out, he was back at full throttle, and we figured he could stay that way all the way to the finishing line at Wright-Patterson Air Force Base, in the Wright brothers' old stamping grounds of Dayton, Ohio.

Harley's flight plan was a bit more conservative but could be a winner dependent on winds aloft and turn around time. He flew at a bit less power, which allowed him to make McConnell Air Force Base at Wichita, Kansas on the first leg. There the crew slid GI mattresses under his wing pylons, and he blew his external tanks off, took on full internal fuel, and dashed for Dayton. Once all the primary entrants had refueled, Lucky and the other spares were allowed to make the run, though their times would not be considered in the order of finish. Lucky flew the same route as Ed Kenny.

Captain Phil Fryberger, who had helped me with the details of running the team, and I had flown a T-33 into Wright-Pat and were sitting on the grass of the hillside that marked the official finish line. A multispeaker public address system relayed the radio transmissions between the control tower and the inbound racers. By coincidence, the two test guys from Edwards who had given Lucky and me the brush-off were sitting just in front of us. Phil and I had a copy of Ed's flight plan, adjusted to his takeoff time, and were monitoring our watches. I turned to Phil and said, "Any time now."

The PA system spoke, "Race Control, Tiger One is thirty seconds out."

Phil and I smiled at each other affirmatively. The two wise owls in front of us leaned back, sort of glancing our way, and one said, "Hell, he must be lost; nobody's close yet." About that time, Ed, still in a shallow descent and still with the throttle wide open, zorched over the top of that hill by maybe a hundred feet, physically stunning the crowd. We won, and though it didn't count, Lucky's time was even a bit better. Since our Bendix team was scattered from coast to coast, and since both the air force and the Republic Aviation folks were herding Ed through the publicity wickets, there wasn't much celebrating to do. Phil and I headed for the flight line to catch Smokey Catledge's next-to-last show as leader of the Thunderbirds.

CHAPTER 10

THUNDERBIRD LEAD

We were all back at Luke for work call on Monday morning, with the Bendix victory a happy memory. I got an 11:00 a.m. call to report to Colonel Levi Chase's office. Levi said he wanted me to take over command of the Thunderbirds, and I asked if I could have forty-five minutes before making a commitment. He offered me an hour forty-five, so I raced home, and over a sandwich secured AJ's full support. When Smokey got back from the Memphis show on September 27, I was Thunderbird Lead.

Smokey was not into spending a lot of time briefing me on my new job. He figured that since all our pilots knew each other and, hell, everyone knew how to fly acrobatics—I should be ready to go. He did agree to a demo flight, so on the afternoon of September 27 he put me in the back seat of the Thunderbird T-33, and we headed for Auxiliary Field Two, a small, abandoned field generally reserved as a Thunderbird practice site. Smokey flew a full demo show, with me in back, sucking up Gs, with nothing to hang onto and my chin on my chest most of the time. When we landed, he asked, "Well, did you get all that OK?"

I replied, "Smoke, I didn't see one damn thing after you pulled up into that first cloverleaf."

He chuckled and said, "Don't worry, you won't have any problems. The team's all yours."

My tour as Thunderbird Lead from 1954 until 1957 has to hold the record for changes in aircraft, pilots, and locations. Every time we approached "routine" status, we took off on a new course, but that made the assignment even more challenging and gratifying.

After a few practice sessions, we went on the road on October 8. Fortunately, Bill Creech on one wing, Burt Spalding on the other, and Bob "Zippy" McCormick in the slot, locked me into position and kept me pointed the right way, and I started to get the hang of it. I decided that I wanted a full-time solo pilot, and brought Lucky Palmgren on board for that spot.

Since Lucky was the first official solo pilot, we started out slowly on his routine. We would take off as the diamond, then Lucky would take off as a single. I would move away from the field and loosen us up with a few maneuvers while taking another look at the area and reaffirming my approach patterns. That was our new solo's time to buzz the strip, doing loops and rolls as the weather permitted.

On that trip we got a chance to beat up the Blue Angels' home airfield at Pensacola and spend the night as their guests. They entertained us royally, and that visit started, for me, a relationship with navy friends that still exists today. A few weeks later, they showed up to fly their best maneuvers over Luke, and we checked them into the best base quarters we had, got them some GI sedans, and gave them directions to my house.

AJ, Mark, and I had moved into town, and all my guys and their gals were at my place waiting for the Blues. We had sizeable quantities of noxious chemicals waiting for them, the gals had lots of food, and in no time the party was in full swing.

We really did have a ball. We drank and ate everything in sight, told every war story known to the two U.S. acro teams, and played most of the loud records in my collection at least once. Our house was never the same. Much later that night, when everyone had left and AJ and I had finished shoveling the place out, I opened the medicine cabinet for my toothpaste and was greeted by a one-foot-diameter Blue Angels sticker that was forever a part of that cabinet. But when the Blues held muster the next afternoon for their short hop to their next show spot in Alameda, each of their birds sported a large, very-difficult-to-remove red, white, and blue Thunderbird decal on the navy blue side of the fuselage. Zeke Cormier was leading the Blues at that time, and he and I never got very far out of touch until I helped bury him some forty-eight years later.

A few weeks after I moved in as Thunderbird Lead, Zippy McCormick completed his tour with the team. I had inherited a pilot from Smokey Catledge whom I did not know a whole bunch about. Jack "Speedy" Hoyle had completed a Korean tour and was instructing at Luke when Smokey brought him on board to ferry their fifth or spare aircraft and to do an occasional solo maneuver if the situation called for it. The old team had done some work with him in practice, pronounced him qualified, and promised him the slot position when Zippy left. He had been on leave when I came on board, but as Zippy was leaving, Speedy showed up to claim his spot. We hustled him into some quick practice shows, and when Burt and Bill said he looked OK from their spots, Speedy Hoyle was the new slot man. We loaded up and headed for the Toledo, Ohio, show.

The Toledo show was on the last day of October, and the light morning snow got a bit heavier as we approached showtime. The show layout was average, and our briefing was routine. As we stopped by the men's room before heading for our birds, I got quite a surprise. Speedy came up to me, and it was easy to see that he had suddenly become very upset and shaky.

"I can't do it," he said.

I shot back, "Can't do what, Speedy?"

He said he was not physically or mentally able to fly the show. Start-engine time was ten minutes away. About that time Lucky came through the men's room and I said, "Lucky, crank up and take off on schedule. Tell Burt and Bill to stand by for start engines, and I'll be there ASAP. We may be a few minutes late, so you just keep doing stuff until you see us take the runway."

I was all set to lean on Hoyle, but quickly sensed that the situation was delicate and that something overpowering was chewing on Speedy. I have little idea what I said over the next ten minutes, but I bet I touched on everything from motherhood to the guys we had lost in Korea, to the red, white, and blue. Whatever I said, my men's room homily worked to the extent that he reluctantly agreed to at least give it a try. There was more snow in the air as Speedy and I walked toward our aircraft, and he almost stopped once, but I gave him a swat on the back and said, "C'mon, Speedy, we're all rooting for you. You can do it!" I sure hoped he could do it, one more time.

Lucky was about halfway through his routine, for the second time, when I got the diamond to the end of the runway, but the crowd was still glued to Lucky's every move. Our show went pretty well until we got ready to do the bomb-burst. We accomplished the bomb-burst by climbing vertically as a flight of four, then splitting into four ninety-degree-opposed outbound headings. After separating a reasonable distance, we would each roll into a steep dive and head for a predetermined crossover point. Speedy made it to that point, but then he came unglued. The crossover was a mess, and the rejoin from the bomb-burst was frightful. As usual, I wound up going away from the crossover point in a gradual turn, calling out my air speeds so the guys could coast back into the diamond without overshooting. As I glanced from side to side, Burt and Bill were closing smoothly, but I wasn't concerned about them. I didn't know where Speedy was until my aircraft shook and my windscreen filled with the topside of Speedy's machine, a few feet in front of me, climbing almost vertically and going like the hammers of hell. As I caught my breath, I saw that my wingmen were not quite back in position. I pumped my rudders to signal them to stay out in spread formation as I called, "Heads up, guys."

We should have been back over the crowd by then to salute them with a roll before breaking into the landing pattern, but that was not my number-one concern at the moment. I punched the mike button and said, "OK, Thunderbird four, lead is continuing a left turn at two thousand feet. You got me in sight?"

As I paused for a reply, Bill interrupted with, "Look out lead, here he comes again." Speedy zipped past me again, but this time he stayed low and out in front of me.

I called, "OK, four, we got you in sight. Set up a thirty-degree bank to the left and hold three hundred." He did, and I rocked my wings to pull Burt and Bill in as I pushed the throttle up to cut inside Speedy's turn. My next call was, "Four, look at nine o'clock level, going to ten. Call when you're in."

We sweated silently until we heard, "Four's in." Landing was routine but still nervous. That was it for Speedy. I don't ever remember seeing him again.

I moved Lucky into the slot position and brought Capt. George Kevil, my ice man from the Bendix race, on as our new solo pilot. George had no problem moving in and doing the basic maneuvers that Lucky had been doing.

Lucky moved into the diamond with ease. He and I had flown together in the early split-tail F-84F days and, just for fun, had tried some formation acrobatics in that bird. We agreed that it was tough enough to lead smoothly in that awkward craft, but tougher still to hold a good formation position.

Lucky was the smallest of our gang and was meek and mild to the casual observer, but he was truly a great stick. AJ and I met Lucky when he arrived at Luke following a combat tour in Korea. He was a young bachelor, quite unwise as to what many called the ways of the world, and AJ and I immediately sort of adopted him. To me he was, and remained, like a younger brother. Lucky and I flew together to perfection.

Toward the end of November, a U.S.-approved coup erupted in Guatemala and we, as the "Ambassadors in Blue," were scrambled for Guatemala City with an intermediate stop in Mexico City. We did do some loops and rolls upon arrival over Mexico City, but were not scheduled for a show, due to the urgency of getting to Guatemala, as well as the fact that the planners had failed to provide any jet fuel for us. We stayed overnight, long enough to discover Montezuma's revenge, while our jets were refueled with regular aviation gas. If you have never launched a straight-wing F-84 fueled with regular aviation gas from a 7,500-foot-elevation airfield, you have missed a thrill. Avgas doesn't produce the energy that jet fuel does, and the air at 7,500 feet is a bit thin. Combine those two elements, and the F-84 had the thrust of a kitchen fan. Our departure was a harrowing demonstration by diarrhea-stricken pilots executing thrilling takeoffs as we blew dust off the departure end of the runway en route to Guatemala. We showed the flag in Guatemala as the personal guests of the new el presidente, Carlos Castillo Armas, a forty-year-old army colonel who had overthrown the closest thing to a communist government ever to spring up on the American continent. Jet fighters were a novelty in that part of the world, and our arrival was spectacular. They had a very beat-up, bumpy runway, barely five thousand feet long, at five thousand feet elevation, with a sheer three hundred-foot vertical drop into a rocky gorge on the far end. The fifteen-foot-high fence across the hard surface at the approach end was crowned with about fifty people standing on the top of the fence trying to touch our wheels.

On show day we took the president for a ride in our T-33, and then came a one-of-a-kind air show. A pyramid-shaped target had been set up near the runway for a strafing demonstration by the entire Guatemalan air force, which consisted of four P-51s. Some of the same type people who had tried to touch our wheels broke from the crowd and climbed on top of the strafing target, and the Mustangs got ten of them. The show went on uninterrupted. We had gone through another one-hundred-octane refueling, but we gave them a good show, landed, and were taken to a small house that served as the operations building, where the huge crowd could see us. The president and his wife stood with their backs to the front wall, and we took up positions on either side of them. As we waved to the crowd, a heavily armed guard stood by my right shoulder with a machine gun slung on his left shoulder. When the crowd of thousands swarmed through the police lines, they crushed all of us against the wall, and I shall never forget the feeling of that machine gun muzzle crammed against my right ear. Thirty months later, as Castillo and his very attractive wife were walking through the palace to dinner, a member of the palace guard, later identified as a communist, presented arms to the president with a rifle salute. The guard then lowered his rifle and killed Castillo with four rifle shots before killing himself.

Back at Luke, with a few days with nothing on the schedule, we decided to get George Kevil going on an upgraded solo routine. One of the things I wanted to introduce for the solo was a three-turn spin. That had never been done on the show circuit, and performing it with a jet fighter was calculated to be a crowd pleaser. Each of us had practiced it and agreed the maneuver was safe, mechanically simple and suitable for the show. To accomplish it, you flew down the runway in front of the crowd at reduced air speed and climbed so the aircraft would stall, nose high, at 3,500 feet. When you pushed in full right rudder, the nose would fall through, and she would start spinning to the right. After watching the runway go by three times, you kicked full left rudder and pushed the stick full forward while adding throttle. The solid-handling F-84G would fly out of the spin before the runway came by again. You recovered with at least a thousand feet to spare and could play the power and altitude to gracefully bottom at a few hundred feet as you crossed show center. George also fancied up the combination of rolls and loops and felt he was ready to show.

We were scheduled to leave for a series of shows on a Saturday morning. There was no student traffic at Luke, so I asked George to take off early, go to an abandoned auxiliary field, and burn some fuel while loosening up. He was then to come back over the field and show us his new wares. As we waited, there was a garbled radio transmission and a plume of ugly black smoke from a fuel-fed fire rising straight up from the auxiliary field. George had augered in. There happened to be a chopper at base operations, and I got him to take me the few miles to the scene. I walked the site, trying to act brave, and there was no doubt that the aircraft had gone straight in and George had gone in with it.

The chopper brought me back so I could do what had to be done. Then we had to go. Showtime was approaching. We did our duty, but we weren't much fun on that trip. We hurried back, and Lucky and I spent an entire day flying back and forth to aux two and doing spins, trying to determine what could have gone wrong. I scared myself pretty good exploring one theory. Our F-84s had a red T handle on the left console to the rear of the throttle quadrant. The T handle was normally pushed down, which engaged the hydraulically operated aileron-boost system, which made the ailerons feel light and easy to move. Pulling the T handle up disengaged the boost system and made the ailerons heavy and difficult to move. As I entered one of my many investigative spins, I pulled the T handle up, and I was immediately on red alert. That bird torqued into a very tight corkscrew, the stick felt tight, and I seemed to be going straight down like a bullet. I reached over with my left hand and slapped the T handle down, quickly went through the kick, stick, and throttle routine, and recovered, uncomfortably lower than I had planned. That airplane should not have done that, but it did. Lucky and I moved up a couple of thousand feet and were able to duplicate that improbable ride. The factory tech reps couldn't explain it, and the company engineers back in Farmingdale said that shouldn't happen, but it did. During our tests I had been primed to plug the boost back in if necessary, and I still didn't have much room to spare the first time I tried it from show altitude. If that had happened to George, would he have thought about aileron boost? Nobody ever thought much about aileron boost; it was just sort of there. Is that what killed George? I don't know.

Later, Bill Creech walked the site and found what could have been foreign-object damage (FOD), and since FOD had not been a major problem in propeller days not many folks paid all that much attention to FOD in the early jet days. As jet traffic increased, it became clear that a jet engine could easily ingest a nut or bolt or stone on the ramp or runway, and the object could quickly destroy the spinning wheels and blades in that engine. A tool or a small part left in the wrong place, then sealed inside an aircraft, could find its way to the most vulnerable of places and destroy an engine or bind and lock controls. Suddenly, FOD prevention became a very big deal, and it was not uncommon to see squadrons on a morning FOD walk of their area, or entire wings on a runway FOD walk. It was amazing to view the junk such efforts produced. Bill found a screwdriver on the ground at aux two. Where did it come from, and how long had it been there? You couldn't match it with any scars on George's aircraft, because there was absolutely nothing left but tiny pieces. Had that screwdriver migrated or floated into a position to jam George's flight controls as he hung on a nose-high stall? Did that screwdriver kill George? I don't know. The official accident investigation board finally concluded that they didn't know either. Regardless of what had happened, I needed to select a new solo pilot, since the summertime show schedule was on the books, and it was a busy one.

Selection of team personnel, scheduling of shows, and determination of the maneuvers we flew and the show format were treated very differently during my tour as Thunderbird Lead than they are at present. Today's increased visibility of any one facet of the military, the revolution in communications, and the monumental increase in the price tag of even small operations all justify doing things differently. Way back then, it was a given that the team leader would make the pilot and crew chief selections, with the approval of our wing commander. The assumption was that we would select people within our wing who were skilled in flying or maintaining our Thunderbird aircraft. An occasional exception occurred, as when I needed a new noisemaker and public relations guy. I needed a combat veteran fighter pilot that I could vest with the authority to talk and act for the team. I explained to my wing commander that I needed my compadre Don "Punchy" Ferris, already a combat veteran of World War II and Korea, who could have easily led the team as well as me, to fill that spot. Colonel Chase called CREWTAF Headquarters, where Punchy was stationed, and he, his wife, Lorene, and their daughter, Susie, were on their way to Luke within two days.

The scheduling of our demonstrations was under the control of a very supportive Pentagon public affairs colonel. He delegated our specific scheduling responsibility to one of his majors, and I received a letter each January that told me where and when I was scheduled to show during the following year. Except for occasional targets of opportunity, that was it, and the rest was up to me. I had some freedom regarding additions, and if someone wanted to see us perform, and if I could fit it into the schedule, I would call our Pentagon major. Unless he objected, which he seldom did, the show was on.

The choice of show maneuvers was strictly up to us. If one of us had a new idea, we would talk about it, and if it sounded reasonable, we would try it in practice. For example, returning from a trip and letting down towards Luke, Burt Spalding called from the left wing and asked if we could try his idea for an arrowhead roll that we had discussed. I pulled up to enter a normal roll, but as I started to roll, I called, "Arrowhead, now." Lucky and I maintained our normal positions. Burt and Bill dropped back as we were going over the top of the roll, and as we came down the backside, they were flying wing on Lucky. We liked it and tried another one over the field before landing. Our ground crews, who were our most severe critics, said it looked good. Punchy reworked his narration, and it was in the show, where it stayed.

Our approach to our audiences at show time was also far more informal than present-day teams. We always had a very thorough but private and informal briefing for each show before we went out to the flight line. There was no marching or music. Each of our primary crew chiefs had things ready, met us at our aircraft, climbed the entrance ladder behind us and helped us strap in. After landing, we discussed our aircraft condition with our chiefs and filled out the Form One flight log for the flight before individually working our way toward our appointed assembly point. We usually had a rope barrier to keep the crowds at a safe distance while the engines were running, but when we shut down, the ropes came down. We usually hung around as long as the autograph and question flow was significant, and we signed everything proffered to us. I remember being offered a wet Popsicle stick for signing, with a slight delay while the kid sucked off the last of the Popsicle fragments. Some questions from the crowd could be quite technical, some basic.

Burt Spalding and I were exchanging remarks after a show when we became aware of a young man, silently staring intently at Burt's flying suit. Burt said, "Hi there young fellow. You have a question?"

The serious youngster replied, "Yeah, what's all them zippers for?"

Master Sgt. Earl Young was my line chief. He and his guys thought that being able to leave a smoke trail behind us would enhance the show, so they turned one of the gun ammo cans in the nose into a tank they could fill with engine oil. They ran one-eighth–inch tube back to the tailpipe and put a control switch in the cockpit. With the flick of a switch, we dumped oil into the jet exhaust and had instant white smoke. The first time we tried it in the diamond, we put out four fluffy, snow-white trails. Lucky, in the slot, had to abort the practice, since I had saturated his windscreen and canopy with oil and wiped out his forward visibility. From then on, I only used smoke when there was nobody in trail behind me, such as after the break on the bomb-burst. The smoke added to the show, but it also made it a lot easier to visually pick up the other guys as we split on the bomb-burst and thus allowed us to generate a better four-ship crossover.

It seemed like the next step should be pouring out red, white, and blue smoke, so Capt. Bob McCutcheon tried to figure out how to make colored smoke. While he was trying to stir plain old grocery store Rit red dye powder into some engine oil, he found that Rit and engine oil did not want to mix. While he was stirring enthusiastically, a goodly desert breeze rolled in, and things began to take on a reddish hue. Before Mac realized what was happening, even his skin, through his flying suit, was dyed a brilliant red. For weeks after, every time he perspired, he dyed his underwear and flying suit red. Speaking of flying suits, ours started out as GI garments, dyed, embroidered, and cared for by our wives or girlfriends.

When the team was first formed, Luke provided some space in base operations. We were still working out of that corner of base operations, and we still had no hangar, but since we didn't know any better, that was OK. But one scheduling aspect that was not OK was the lack of our own support aircraft to haul our crew chiefs and gear around the show circuit. We did a lot of begging to borrow Gooney Birds from our own base operations or from nearby bases. Finally, after much noise and conversation, we were assigned a C-119 and a crew to fly it. Some of our maintenance troops who had to constantly ride in it complained that it was a loud, uncomfortable, noisy clunker, so I felt like I had to check out in the left seat to calm them down. I went through the checkout routine and made sure that all my guys saw me flying it. That calmed things down, and that loud, uncomfortable, noisy clunker made things a lot easier for all of us.

We were fortunate to be in the time frame of super good relations between the people who built fighters and the people who flew them. With a constant stream of new birds entering the fighter inventory from competing companies, having the team flying and thus advertising your product was a big deal. Republic Aviation Corporation appreciated that fact, but above and beyond the commercial aspect, they treated us like real friends, and there was a lot of mutual respect. You could spot a Thunderbird pilot by his gold Rolex watch with the team logo on the face, or by his silver engraved cuff links and tie clasp. Whenever the schedule fit, we had the best seats at Madison Square Garden or on Broadway. But there was a more practical aspect to that relationship. Travel pay in those days seldom met the demands of the travel, and advanced pay was not available. Quite often the team leader and the factory tech rep made things livable for the troops toward the end of long trips. And you know what? Such great relationships never did one bit of damage to the U.S. military-industrial structure.

By the time Republic got the slab tail on the swept-wing F-84Fs, making them operationally acceptable and suited for formation acrobatics, our straight-wing F-84s were showing their age. In the spring of 1955 we converted to the Fs, and the swept-wing birds looked sharp in a slightly revised paint job. Also, the red, white, and blue drag chutes added a bit of class to the landing rollout. We were still able to keep the show in close to the airfield boundaries, and even today, close examination of anyone's film will fail to produce any smoother flying performances than we were able to present with the F-84F.

The F model was a crowd pleaser, and we found ourselves making giant strides on the publicity trail. We flew for a professionally produced and filmed twenty-minute color film that was one of the top five contenders for Hollywood's best short subject of the year. *Life* magazine featured us, with startling photography of the diamond over Los Angeles, against the sinking sun. Sunday evening television variety shows were a big part of America's entertainment menu, and almost everyone watched them. We cracked that market when we shared the *Colgate Comedy Hour* spotlight with Hollywood's Gordon and Sheila MacRae, and Rhonda Fleming. We did lots of good PR work, and it was fun.

We did not perform in a vacuum, and we did have plenty of thrills and chills along the way. Our timing was very poor when we chose Armed Forces Day in, of all places, Washington, D.C., at Bolling Air Force Base, in front of a monstrous crowd, as a place for one of us to goof, big time. Bolling and the neighboring naval base at Anacostia were both operational in 1955, and only a chain link fence separated them. Except for the fact that the navy runway heading was offset thirty degrees from the air force runway heading, they would have met squarely at that chain link fence. Our crossover point for the bomb-burst was the center of the Bolling runway. It had been raining, and there were mud puddles here and there, but show weather was fine. Things went smoothly as we pulled up vertically and split to the four winds in our trademark bomb-burst. When the time came to split S and head for the crossover point, Lucky and I pulled through on opposing courses for the runway center. Bill Creech pulled through on his right side of the Bolling runway, as briefed, but Jim Matthews, who had replaced Burt Spalding on left wing in the diamond, pulled through on his right side of the Anacostia, not the Bolling, runway. A potential disaster was in the making. The game plan was that the wingmen would go as low as comfortable, with each staying on his right side of the crossover point, while lead and slot would stay on their right of each other and above the crossing wingmen.

Everyone concentrated on being precise while depending on the others to do the same, and the wingmen never have much wiggle room as regards altitude. We were all keeping track of each other as we approached the crossover, playing the throttle and speed brake and striving to gauge the perfect cross. As the other three aircraft came sharply into Bill Creech's focus shortly before the cross, to Bill's horror Matthews was thirty degrees off course and about to collide with Bill, which would surely have creamed Lucky, me, and who knows who else on the ground. Bill skidded sideways and pushed over into the few feet between him and the ground as Matthews flashed by. The only thing between Bill and an angled taxiway was the Women's Air Force band, wearing WAF dress white uniforms and tiptoeing as they marched through a large puddle on the taxiway. The sheer force of Bill's aircraft screeching a few feet above their heads scattered and flattened them, and Bill's windscreen was filled with the image of a falling lady bass drummer. Most spectators don't really know what's going on during the cross, and I never got any comments from outside the diamond after that fiasco. As we were shutting down and climbing out of our aircraft, the WAF band was passing the reviewing stand and the bass drummer, her white uniform covered with mud and with a fierce look on her face, was sure swinging those drumsticks hard.

I could have fired Matthews, but we were in the middle of a concentrated series of important shows, and I hoped that after the scare of the event, a sincere ass-chewing would take care of it. I should have fired Matthews on the spot.

By early July we were flying a series of shows that would wind up with the formal dedication and groundbreaking ceremony for the U.S. Air Force Academy. As we headed for the academy, we had a refueling stop at Ellington Air Force Base near Houston. Our landing routine included flying our initial approach to the runway in the diamond, then pitching out and up to the left in one, two, three, four order for landing. Fighter pilots always preferred left-hand landing patterns, a hangover from the torque of piston-driven fighters, but since the NASA space program covered a large area to the left of the Ellington runway, only right-hand traffic was allowed. I switched the flight over to squadron common frequency so I could brief them on the landing pattern. I told them we would break right and that the order of break would be one, three, two, four. I had each of them reply by repeating my message and acknowledging that they understood. Back on tower frequency we approached the runway and I punched the mike button and said, "Thunderbird Lead breaking right, three will break next," and out and up I went. Bill counted thousand one, thousand two, and out he came to find Matthews had rushed the count, was out of sequence, and was turning blindly into him with collision again imminent. Again Bill put on a one-man spastic evasion show, and we all landed OK after some on the ground witnessed a weird traffic pattern. But as a flight we were ruptured.

Now there was no doubt, Matthews had to go. But we were en route to the single most important show in team history. The historic event had a guest list including air force Secretary Talbott, our air force chief of staff, General Twining, governors, Congressmen, the attachés of fifty-eight different nations, and more. They all knew we were scheduled to perform, and I knew we had to perform. Matthews knew he was on the bubble, and I'm sure I added to his concern as I reminded him of what I expected from him.

We staged out of Lowry Air Force Base in Denver, north of the academy site in Colorado Springs. The weather looked good, our birds were in good shape, and we had a day to go until showtime. When we had free time, I never spent it babysitting my grown charges, but I was nervous about this one, and I slept restlessly that night.

I got a rude telephone awakening from the Denver police at 3:00 a.m., and it was gut-check time. Ignoring our self imposed disciplines, Matthews had prowled the mean spots of downtown Denver and teamed up with a woman well known to the Denver police. It seems that among her routines was one claiming her purse had been stolen and demanding money from management to be quiet. The bartender recognized what was going on and called the Denver police. When Matthews rose to defend her honor and interfered with the police, they gave him a personal paddy wagon ride to jail. They backed the wagon up to the padded reception room, and when they opened the door, Matthews rushed forth to attack two tough, baton-wielding trained receptionists. They called asking me to identify him at the police hospital ward. He was indeed a mess, and they advised me he was being held without bail.

By 5:00 a.m., I had left the hospital and was back at the hotel awakening Bill Creech and Billy Ellis. Billy was new to the team, on his first trip as solo, and I had only had a chance to try him out on two flights on the right wing of a two-ship element. He was good, and I hired him, but we had not yet stopped traveling long enough to get him into a four-ship drill. That made no difference. We were there for the most significant Thunderbird show to date, and Billy was now going to fly right wing as Bill Creech moved to the left side.

We did a few four-ship rolls and loops on the way to the site. Then it was showtime, and Billy made his debut in the diamond at 9:00 a.m. We flew the entire show except for the bomb-burst, and Billy in his new position and Bill in an unfamiliar position did great. We had a full slate of shows ahead, and Billy got his crash course on the run. Matthews was history, and I had learned a bunch. I should have fired Matthews in Washington.

In the latter part of August, our schedule took us towards the East Coast and included a show in Syracuse, the closest place to my old hometown of

Rochester that I ever showed. My mother and father drove to Syracuse for the show, and they got a kick out of it. It was fun to introduce them to my troops. One of the things that bothered me that day was a performance put on by John Burt, who had recently left the air force and signed on as a demonstration pilot for Martin Aircraft. He was showing for them in one of their B-57s, which was the American version of the British Canberra twin-engine jet bomber. We were waiting our turn to fly when he made a low-level, slow-speed pass in front of the crowd. He was so slow that he was literally hanging on a stall to the degree that his airframe quivered as he finally added power to both engines and left show center. It bothered me to the extent that I sought him out after we landed to offer a constructive thought. I tried real hard to be friendly and not sound offensive as I reminded him of the fact that if your narrator says you are flying at the amazingly slow speed of 110, the crowd accepts the fact that you are sure going slow, but they don't know, or care, if you are going 110 or 115 miles per hour. I asked him to remember that a fireball prang job would be bad news for all of us in the air-show business, to say nothing of the spectators, and urged him to give himself a tad more speed in case something went wrong. As we parted, I felt like I had wasted my breath.

The F-84Fs had been impressive all along the 1955 show circuit, but as we left Syracuse we headed for the individual summer highlight for us which was the Republic Aviation Corporation show at the "foundry" in Farmingdale, New York. We got there a few days early, which gave us a chance to enjoy a day of deep-sea fishing on Republic president Mundy Peale's plush yacht. The time spent with the Republic people was a real kick and by show time I truly think we had met and chatted with almost everyone who worked there. I have never seen so many people so proud of their product, their country, and, in particular their red, white, and blue Thunderbirds and the guys who maintained and flew them.

We flew a doubleheader on Sunday, and both shows were jammed. During the afternoon show, the Long Island parkways were gridlocked for miles, as people simply stopped to watch, and the police gave up and joined them. Before and after the shows, we trooped the flight line as Mundy Peale chauffeured us in his Cadillac convertible. That was the builders and the operators together, at their best.

We got a request for a write-in show for the annual picnic at Marine Corps Air Station in Yuma, Arizona. We had weekend shows on the West Coast, and they wondered if we could do a show for them on Sunday evening. After our other shows, we sent Punchy and the T-Bird on ahead to Yuma, while we took on a full fuel load. We could burn fuel en route to Yuma, do a show for them, then recover back home at Luke. The show site was to be the picnic grounds on the base perimeter, where Punchy would work his narration on the PA system, but without radio contact with us. We had a preset arrival time, so Punchy would know when to expect us, and the base control tower was to clear us in to perform.

It was a clear desert evening with the sun lowering, but with plenty of sunlight left as we spotted the base from way out. The control tower gave us a routine clearance, with no special instructions or advisories, and I easily spotted the picnic area. I thought it was real smart of the fire trucks and other emergency vehicles to be out in the picnic area with their rotating red beacons and white strobe lights flashing, so I would be sure to see where I was to show. Little did I know that I was looking at pandemonium and that Punchy was right in the middle of it, trying to figure out what to do or say.

John Burt was scheduled to put on his B-57 demo before our arrival time. He was hanging on the stall, above the picnic crowd, when one of those things that could go wrong went wrong. He advanced both throttles, and the right engine spooled up to full power, while the left engine failed to move out of idle. His B-57 instantaneously rolled onto its back, dived inverted into a sewage disposal tank next to the picnic grounds, and exploded. Punchy was on the makeshift announcer's stand watching screeching emergency vehicles, screaming women with wailing children, and upset marines looking on helplessly. Nobody was thinking picnic, and nobody was thinking Thunderbirds, but Punchy looked west and saw that we were crossing the field boundary and about to roar overhead and pull up into a cloverleaf over the crowd. Punchy, still trying to figure out the right thing to say, made his mark in air-show history as he squeezed the PA mike button and announced over the din of panic, "Ladies and gentlemen, while we can hardly expect to duplicate the spectacle you have just seen, may I present the United States Air Force Thunderbirds."

We flew a super show and knew nothing of what had happened before our show until we landed back at Luke and got the details in a phone call from Punchy. John Burt had been killed upon impact, but there had been no other injuries. Punchy admitted to what he had said on the PA system, but he was always amazed at his choice of words in that situation. I doubt that anyone on the ground paid much attention to what he said at that moment. Once again we all thought on the truism that precision aerial demonstrations are a very positive motivator, as long as the performers use common sense and observe the basic rule that aviation of itself is not dangerous, but it is terribly unforgiving of those who violate its basic rules.

In December we headed for Turner Air Force Base in Albany, Georgia, for one of our last road shows of the year. I was especially anxious to show well for my many F-84 flying friends at Turner and their commander, Col. Hub Zemke, super ace and leader of the World War II Wolfpack. It was very close to sunset as we crossed Turner at minimum altitude to pull up into our arrival show. We completed a loop and stayed low as we turned back to do a roll before entering the traffic pattern. We were headed west as I pulled us up easily and entered a big, smooth roll, with the artistic layered purple clouds and orange sunset sky filling my windscreen. Suddenly, it looked like I was back over Pyongyang again, as the sky became thousands of black blobs. But it wasn't flak; it was a solid wall of starlings migrating south for the winter. There was no place to go, and we collided with untold numbers of birds just as we got to the top of the roll. Hitting a bird of any size at about four hundred miles per hour is destructive, and by the time we bottomed in the roll, we had one Mayday and three emergencies. Billy flamed out due to an engine full of birds. He calmly rolled onto final and deadsticked, while those of us with shattered windscreens and canopies and restricted flight controls lined up behind him. It was not the entry I had planned. Hub gave us the full support of all his base repair facilities, and we had four sound birds ready for test hop thirty-six hours later, well in advance of showtime.

Air shows are not too much in demand between Christmas and New Year's, but we had one more duty before Christmas. Our birds were very early Fs, and there were a number of modifications that we needed to accomplish on them. Republic offered to take our machines back into the factory between December 20 and our first January show. They wanted to go through them from end to end while bringing them up to the latest configuration, and all on the house. Their only requirement was that one of our demo pilots be on board at the factory while the birds were there, to act as our rep and to coordinate with Jimmy Roye, their vice president of manufacturing. Jimmy was a special friend of all of us. After we delivered our aircraft to Farmingdale, Lucky, our only bachelor, volunteered to take the first shift over Christmas. Meanwhile, I went upstate to Rochester, where AJ and Mark had flown, so we could spend Christmas with my folks. After Christmas, Mark took control of his grandparents, while AJ and I headed for the Big Apple to relieve Lucky. Jimmy wanted to educate me, and he spent hours showing me how aircraft factories work and how the machines progress from drawing boards to flight test. When AJ and I checked in for duty at Republic, our first assignment was to take a company car and report to the front desk of The Tuscany Hotel, a small, semiresidential, top-of-the-line spot on Park Avenue in the big city. We were escorted to our first cabin suite, and the next ten days were indeed memorable. The amenities were strictly blue blood, with service, food, and dry martinis beyond experience or expectation. I did have to check in by phone every morning with Johnny Weeks, the Republic customer-relations gent, who also became a longtime friend. I had to specify our choice of events for the evening, and the best seats in the house always seemed to be available for the New York Rangers, or the best on Broadway, or the Friday night fights at Madison Square Garden.

The techs at Republic completed their tasks on schedule, and I summoned the guys back to Farmingdale. My instructions from Republic were to sign for the bill at the Tuscany. I almost gasped when I looked at the total, a king's ransom in those days, of over seventeen hundred dollars. I was silently calculating how many months and weeks worth of captain's pay that was, but I signed as if it were routine, thanked some of the staff for their hospitality, tipped the bellman, and filed away some neat memories.

Like all aircraft companies, Republic had their super-secret hangar where they generated plans for the future and turned ideas into mock-ups and hardware. Access was very tightly controlled, as a company's future might well depend upon activities within those shuttered regions. Republic's chief designer was the legendary Alexander Kartveli, whose parents had spirited him out of Russia to Paris when he was a small boy. After immigrating to the United States, he quickly gained his reputation as a design genius and was the guiding force behind fighters such as the P-32, P-36, and the venerable P-47 "Jug" of World War II. After our August performances at the factory, Kartveli had commented, "Now that is flying with a soul, something we can not design into an airplane."

Jimmy had worked from the top to get permission for me to meet with Kartveli in the inner chambers, and I was awed at what I saw. Everywhere I looked there were sketches, models, and parts of air vehicles of both the near future and the distant future. The main item of interest at that moment was a full-scale mock-up of Kartveli's conceptual hypersonic F-103. It was huge so it could accommodate multiple jet and rocket-propulsion devices. The small wings seemed like an afterthought, and it looked like a huge bullet, angled up at thirty degrees and perched on top of two main landing gears and a towering nose gear.

I gazed and said questioningly, "It doesn't have a canopy?"

Kartveli half snorted and replied, "Canopies are ugly, like the bumps on a pickle. We will use a periscope. Come, I will show you."

We walked to the underside. As I was about to ask how you got into this monster, he pushed a handheld control device, and a section of the lower fuselage separated from the underside, and an elevator that appeared to be the rear section of a pilot's compartment descended to the hangar floor. The ride up was quick, and as the elevator stopped, there was a "klunk" that told me it was now locked in the bowels of the machine. Straight ahead was a single pilot's seat, power and control handles and gauges, and sure enough, where a windscreen should have been, a viewing screen showing the roof of the hangar. I had to think that it would take some time to get comfortable with a presentation like that at Mach 5.0. Back in the bright sunshine, I kept thinking about flying at that speed while looking at a periscope.

Then we went Hollywood when the air force teamed up with director/producer Mervyn LeRoy for the feature film *Toward the Unknown*. The story concerned personalities and activities at Edwards Air Force Base, where we shot all the action scenes. The cast included Bill Holden, Virginia Leigh, Lloyd Nolan, Mushy Callahan, and other interesting personalities, and we enjoyed the experience. Most of the characters in the cast were portraying senior officers, and it seemed like all we did the first morning was salute as they roamed the flight line.

Then Lloyd Nolan hailed me and said, "Hey, you guys are the most senior officers on this set, so how about telling your troops to forget saluting. Besides, it's embarrassing to old civilians like me."

We flew dry run after dry run while Mervyn and his camera people figured out what they wanted. I did have to straighten out one cameraman regarding the physics of the bomb-burst when he said, "Now, on that thing where you go straight up, I'd like you to hold that, you know, going up, for another ten or twelve seconds before you go all different ways." The film came out great and was a hit with the critics and the public.

The heavy show schedule was taking a toll on our F-84Fs, and it was getting tougher to keep them in commission and make our show schedules. We were anxious for something new and had the itch to become the first supersonic acrobatic team. We were in that glorious time frame where new and more capable equipment just kept entering the inventory at a rapid pace. As fate would have it, we limped into Randolph Air Force Base late one Sunday afternoon, trying to get back to Luke after a long string of shows. All of our birds were sick and tired. As I walked into Base Ops, our big bosses from CREWTAF, Gen. Frank Robinson and Gen. Charlie Born, were about to leave on a flight, and they congratulated me on my promotion to major. As we talked, they asked how we were doing, and I replied that we were just trying to paste things together and get home for some more maintenance. General Robinson didn't like that, and asked what I wanted to do.

I said, "General, I want to go supersonic, and the sooner the better." I was on the right track. He said he only had North American Aviation F-100As at Nellis at the moment, but he could get his hands on a few new F-100Cs. Did I want to give the A models a try in anticipation of the far superior Cs? I said we could be at Nellis, ready to fly, by Tuesday morning, and he said to give him a call after we flew the A models. It was a done deal, 1956 style.

The F-100 was a relatively new airplane, and the A models had some mean characteristics. The people at Nellis were skeptical that we could harness the monster into an air-show routine, and even if we could, they figured it would take months of practice. What better way to challenge four fighter jocks? In the morning, we each got a quick cockpit check, strapped on an F-100A, and launched. After about thirty minutes, I rendezvoused with Lucky Palmgren, and we had a ball pulling our guts out in formation. That afternoon I got us four aircraft for another ride and Lucky, Billy Ellis, Bob Anderson, and I joined up in a diamond as soon as we were out of sight of the field. We put in a half-hour's work on loops, rolls, and wifferdills: our turn-around maneuver that we executed to keep us in close to show-center after we pulled up after each pass. A good wifferdill required lots of muscle as you pulled the stick back into a climbing, rolling turn to the right, then rolled upside down and descended in a rolling turn to the left—and there you were, heading in the opposite direction, and lined up for the next maneuver. I brought the diamond back over the base, did a few loops, rolls, and wifferdills before pitching up for landing. The Nellis guys were real nice after that. I called General Robinson, and all was go.

We were to pick up our new aircraft at the Los Angeles factory. Our first F-100 show was scheduled in a month. We went back to Luke and resumed the F-84F show schedule, and we didn't miss a show, even though Punchy Ferris had to belly in one of the F-84Fs he was test-hopping when the engine quit on takeoff. Since our new birds were still being built, none of us had flown a F-100C yet, and about two weeks before the first show we really hit a big snag. Our C models made it through production and acceptance flight checks in record time, but they were hung up on getting painted with the Thunderbird colors. I was told I couldn't have my aircraft for another week, one week before the first show, which was on the East Coast at Portsmouth, New Hampshire.

Since I knew I had the backing of James H. "Dutch" Kindelberger, Mr. North American, I called his secretary, and she arranged an immediate meeting with the North American executive staff. I reminded Lee Atwood (the boss during Dutch's temporary abscence) and his staff that lots of Washington dignitaries would be attending our first show for the dedication of Pease Air Force Base, and the show was being advertised as the demonstration debut of the F-100C. I explained that it looked like I was going to have to call the Pentagon and cancel the show, since North American was unable to deliver. He quietly asked when I needed the aircraft, and when I said that 9:00 tomorrow morning would be fine, the meeting ended. I don't know what happened during the next few hours, but at 9:00 a.m. we strapped on six gleaming red, white, and blue F-100Cs and launched for Nellis. We moved everything, families included, to Nellis, figured out how to get the job done, and made our first show. It may not have been our greatest performance, but we were on our way in style. We even had a multiple-room wooden building at Nellis that was all our own, and we held title to part of a hangar.

The F-100Cs were excellent show machines, and the afterburner added a new dimension to our performances. I managed to make a connection with the air force clothing lab, and they tailored some nifty white custom flying suits for us. The first time we wore them, Billy Ellis was a standout crowd attraction. He wore boxer shorts with red hearts, and they showed very clearly through the new flight-suit material. Then, at Maxwell Air Force Base on July 25, we had our first major problem with the F-100C.

We showed regularly at Maxwell for Command and Staff College graduations, and that time we got there a day early. Since this was our first show there in the F-100, we scheduled a practice for the day before. We had only been airborne in the diamond for a few minutes when, as we were coming over the top of a loop, Lucky called, "Mayday, Thunderbird four's flamed out."

I kicked Billy and Andy out into spread formation, and then as soon as I spotted Lucky, I told three to join on two and stay clear of Lucky and myself. Lucky was over the city, full of fuel, and sinking like a rock. I called, "Lucky, you may have to punch out, 'cause you're not going to make it back to the field."

Lucky calmly replied that he would not eject due to the congestion on the ground. As I coasted up toward him, he spotted a short, narrow strip of green field a couple of miles south of Maxwell. It was less than a thousand feet long: way too short, but it was clear that he wasn't going to be airborne long enough to try anything else. He already had a glide set up and barely got to that pasture before slamming into the ground at about 150 miles per hour. Three hundred yards down the field was an embankment running perpendicular to his course, with a railroad track on the top. His aircraft was bumping and jumping and somehow lurched back into the air and over the track to strike the road on the other side. He slid for another two hundred yards, cutting off both wings as he collided with power and telephone poles. Narrowly missing a house, his plane ground to a stop.

I flew over him, and he was slumped forward in the cockpit with his head down. I kept making passes over him as Andy described the situation to the Maxwell tower and urged them to get their emergency vehicles to the scene. Lucky didn't move a muscle for five minutes, and then just before the first ambulance arrived he stirred, undid his shoulder harness and seat belt, and climbed out of what was left of his aircraft. No amount of description on our part ever convinced him that he was out for five minutes. His mind was locked on the view that he just slid to a stop and climbed out. Lucky flew the show in our spare bird the next day, and North American Aviation had a replacement aircraft ready for us by the time we got back to Nellis.

Our schedule stayed full, and we had three blockbuster events coming up where we really looked forward to showing with our new F-100s. The first was the Seattle Seafair show during the first week of August. While the unlimited racing hydroplanes were the stars of Seafair, both the Blue Angels and the Thunderbirds—the Blues and the Birds—were on hand, and an air force colonel named Russ Schleeh was about to shake up the exclusive, unlimited hydroplane organization. The entire week was a ball, with good things happening day and night. Those monster racing hydros are very temperamental, and at that time they all used the Rolls Royce Merlin engine, the same power plant we had in our P-51s. When you heard old Merlin roar, you just knew you wanted to give it a try. Most of their engine problems centered on a small gear, only about an inch in diameter, that basically connected the power-producing components to the driving components. The difference was that in our Mustangs we were driving a large propeller in air, whereas they were driving a much smaller propeller in the heavier medium of water. I don't think I ever heard of a quill-gear problem while flying Mustangs, but the hydros destroyed them at a high rate. Zeke Cormier had a navy connection to *Gale V* and got to drive her during a practice session. Russ Schleeh, a rookie in that league, was driving the relatively unknown *Shanty* and had been publicly described as a plumber by some of the more experienced drivers. I was set to get my try by driving *Shanty*, but Russ blew a quill gear in practice, and it was a scramble until starting time of the first heat to get her running and back in the water.

On race day, thousands of boats lined the Seattle floating bridge and every other vantage point available, while the shoreline was also jammed. Zeke and I alternated flying first on the Saturday and Sunday race days, and we had crowds of five hundred thousand each day. After landing, both teams were escorted to the course so we could avoid the crowds and traffic and catch the races. The title was decided on the last heat of the second day when Russ won the Seafair Cup in *Shanty*. As he cruised by the finish line and judges' stand on his way back to the pits, the rookie they had called a plumber reached into his cockpit and withdrew a plumber's friend, which he waved victoriously for the half million watching.

The second of our anticipated blockbusters was billed as the last ever National Air Show, at Will Rogers Field in Oklahoma City. That

American tradition moved from city to city each year, glamorizing our civilian and military technology and airmanship with racing, acrobatics, and all the hoopla of the world's greatest air show.

We were one up on everyone else at the show, as the local Pontiac dealers provided each of us with a Pontiac convertible decorated with the Thunderbird paint scheme. North American cranked up their Los Angeles–based plush Gooney Bird, picked up all of our wives and girl friends at Nellis, and flew them to the show. When we drove our hot dog convertibles out on the ramp to meet our gals, we figured that they would be dressed fit to kill, which they were. We did not know that North American had loaded the Goon with all the good delicacies and strong grog that you could imagine, or that the crew would include test pilots Bob Hoover, Chuck Graham, Art DeBolt, and Earl "Nasty" Blount. I have often wondered if there was a designated flyer on board. Anyway, when the side door of the Goon opened, they all came floating out, and it seemed like their feet barely touched the exit ladder. We had a ball. Everybody loved it. It was the last of a great tradition of military and national pride expressed through excellence and air-show fun.

General Bobbie Burns, a good guy, was the show coordinator. He was getting a bunch of heat on enforcing all the restraints on where, when, and how you could fly. Those rules were new at that time but are now commonplace. At our first briefing he explained that his instructions were to have a spectacular showing of airpower, but not to make any noise or fuss. We had the Blues and the Birds and the full spectrum of our national capability on call, and on the first two days of the three-day extravaganza, we flew nice shows.

Everybody knew that something was up when General Burns personally conducted the briefing for the third and final session of the air show of air shows. He announced that he had submitted his intent to retire, and that he had made the decision that there would be no performance restrictions on the final show. Since we were closing the show, he thought a last event supersonic pass by our solo man would be in order. That was a license to steal.

We were the last event on the schedule of the three-day show, and as we pitched up to land, the announcer said that the Thunderbird solo man, Lt. Bill Pogue, would now shoot down the flag with a real, live, supersonic pass. The fascinated crowd paused as Bill lit his burner and started a smooth, descending left turn toward the runway. Passing through Mach 1.1, he took out most of the shelves and containers in two local supermarkets. Next came all the glass windows of the airfield control tower. The boom and Bill rolled across the crowd, and they loved it, and headed for home.

After we climbed out of our aircraft, North American tech rep Bill Brooks came panting up to me. Guess what? One of the two bolts securing Bill Pogue's recently supersonic horizontal slab was broken in two, and since that could have been catastrophic, it was fleet-wide bad news. We refueled Bill's sick machine, and he launched for the Los Angeles factory at half speed.

North American expedited the fix on the slab tail on our birds, and we didn't miss any scheduled shows, but there was a bunch of change in the wind. Lucky was ready to leave, which was fine, since he was now a married family man, and Miss Jones, his bride, was deserving of knowing him as something other than a roving acrobat. She and their two daughters only had him until early 1968, when he was shot down while ramrodding the first F-111 deployment into combat in Vietnam.

Bill Pogue, our math and physics major, moved from slot to solo when Lucky left. Our practice area at Nellis was a remote crossroads in the Parumph Valley that was surrounded by mountains. We worked Bill out in the diamond one morning, and as we headed back to Nellis, he announced that he had flamed out and was unsuccessfully attempting to restart his engine. It was déjà vu with these slot guys. I coasted in on his wing as we both realized that the inhospitable mountains below were way too close, and he ejected. Once I saw that he was clear of the ejection seat, with a good chute, I checked his pilot-less aircraft and saw that the aerodynamic changes caused by the departure of the seat and canopy had caused the nose to come up. It was descending gradually rather than continuing its steep descent into the mountains, and that unmanned vehicle was headed for the end of the Vegas strip. My first thought was that I better shoot it down, but we had long since removed the guns from our demo birds. She was truly on course for big trouble, so I lit my burner and dove under her and pulled up as close in front of her as I dared. The turbu-lence did the trick, and she shuddered, nosed up, stalled, and went into the mountains. The accident investigation was a snap. They found a large section of a red football jersey from Palos Verdes High clogging the main fuel tank feed valve. It had been used as a rag at the factory, had escaped FOD inspection, and had been riding with us since the first day we accepted the birds. North American's production chief, John Casey, told me that the discovery caused them to conduct a spot check at North American, and they found lots of FOD, includ-ing an inspector's badge in the main fuel tank of another aircraft. After Bill Pogue finished up on the team, he went on to be a math pro-fessor at the U.S. Air Force Academy and a distinguished Space Lab astronaut, but he never forgot that red football jersey.

Punchy Ferris moved on, and Bill Scott took over as noisemaker. Billy Ellis checked out from the right wing and left en route to a two-star military career. Later, he enjoyed a distinguished civilian executive career, followed by his ordination as a Roman Catholic priest. Billy was replaced by Doug Brenner, who, nine years later, was to be one of my fellow Dirty American Air Pirates attacking downtown Hanoi in our F-105 Thuds. John "Bart" Bartley, our ex-marine enlisted grunt, was flying solo and waiting to replace Bob Anderson on left wing, and I hired Sam Johnson as Bart's solo replacement. Later a senior con-gressman from Texas, Sam eventually wrote *Captive Warriors*, describing some of his more than seven years of torture by the brutal North Vietnamese after he was shot down and taken as a prisoner of war. One must admit that I was privileged to deal with some neat guys and their special gals.

The third blockbuster came when I finished up my tour in February during Speed Week at Daytona Beach. We had developed a neat relationship with speedway president Bill France and his staff. My last show, and also Bob Anderson's last show, was also the last year they raced on the beach racecourse at Daytona. We got to hang out with all the competitors and drive a car once in a while. The organizers set up a match race between the top five NASCAR drivers, where each of them drove the same car over the flying mile on the beach course, with a significant cash prize for winning. They wanted to get the Thunderbird pilots involved, but there was cash involved, and neither air force nor NASCAR rules would allow that. So the five NASCAR drivers raced, and Lee Petty won that competition at 144.928 miles per hour. Then the five of us raced with the same car and same rules. I momentarily had the fastest time of all the pros and amateurs with 145.396, but thirty minutes later, somebody named Bob Anderson eclipsed my time by .003 miles per hour.

We showed over the beach racecourse on qualifying day and both main race days, and the crowds kept getting larger with each show. We had a normal seaside problem with seagulls on Friday, which, because of garbage accumulation, was worse on Saturday. We combated that by having the solo make frequent runs in afterburner to chase the birds away. But by noon on Sunday, all the accumulated garbage plus what was being strewn around by the huge Sunday crowd was attracting large swarms of seagulls. We solved that by putting one C-119 pilot a mile north on the show line and the other one a mile south on the show line. They were each armed with a case of hastily confiscated hamburger buns, which they fragmented and bravely tossed into the air as fighting seagulls swarmed them. The buns and the burners kept the gulls clear of our paths, and we finished up with a dandy show.

As I parked and cleaned up my last Thunderbird-show cockpit, I shrugged with the feeling we all get of "OK, so now?" To my surprise, a Western Union messenger came bounding up the ladder and handed me the yellow and black envelope that was familiar in those times as a telegram. It was from Dutch Kindelberger, on behalf of the directors of North American Aviation. It thanked me and everyone on all of our teams for what we had done to present the excellence of America's air power. That was exactly what my psyche needed at the moment, and I hit the ground running, since it was time to head back to Nellis and hand the reins to Jack Robinson. That ceremony was handshake easy, and we all hurried off to change clothes and head back to the Nellis flight line with our gals. The world's greatest plush Gooneybird was waiting, and we were all off to Squaw Valley, California, for a fantastic ski break.

CHAPTER 11

MOVING ON

If there ever was a job that required you to move on when you finished the assignment, it was the job of Thunderbird Lead. It's not
like you were a big deal in international affairs or a financial tycoon,
but you were about as big a fish as you can get to be in a little pond.
Your word was law in your corner of the flying business, and you came
pretty close to controlling most aspects of the pilots and support people who worked for you. Most senior officers had either left you alone
or tried to be helpful. Some of the top aircraft-industry leaders liked
you as an advertising asset, and others liked you as a friend. You had
definitely been a big man to the huge crowds watching air shows and
had generated more publicity coverage in ink, sound, and screen than
you ever thought possible.

But that's not the usual way the world turns for a thirty-two-year-
old air force major, and I was fortunate enough to know and accept
that truism. I was also fortunate to be part of an air force that was
bubbling with changes and challenges at a time when new equipment

and new technology seemed to be emerging almost daily. I was ready
to move on, and the only time I looked over Jack Robinson's shoulder
as he took over the Thunderbirds was when I was cleaning out my
flight locker after we got back from that ski trip, or when he asked me
a specific question.

I was already on orders to report to Air Command and Staff College
in Montgomery, Alabama, as a student in the next class, but the reporting date for that class was about three months away. Doc McGee, our
wing commander, gave me a goof-off job as special assistant to the supply group commander, who had no idea what to do with me. I found
plenty to do. I learned a few things about running an air base, and there
were always some aircraft that needed to be flown. Our good friend and
air-show great, Bob Hoover, was working for North American at that
time, and I volunteered to be the public address announcer for his daily
shows at the Worldwide Gunnery Meet. The Ford Motor Company had
supplied the Thunderbirds with engine-tech reps for the F-100s, and
since Henry Banks, the former Indianapolis 500 winner, was working
for Ford, I got to meet him. He took me on for the 1957 Indy 500, and I
got to work in the pits. Since we didn't qualify a car in the first thirty-
three, I switched to the crash crew on turn three on race day. Meeting
most of the big names in open-wheel championship racing as I tagged
along with Henry was quite memorable.

If, as advertised, the upcoming year in Montgomery was supposed
to be a mid-career review and a time for thoughts and decisions about
future career planning, it came too late for me. I was unwinding nicely
from the Thunderbird years, and about all I could find to fidget about
was when we should start packing and how much longer did we have
to wait before we could get on the road to Alabama. Then one day,
Jimmy Roye, our good friend from Republic Aircraft, called from the
factory on Long Island. He was flying out to Los Angeles and asked if
he could spend the upcoming weekend with us. We were anxious to
see him again and looked forward to a few fun days.

Jimmy was usually the happy Irishman, but he was serious on that trip. He was vice president for manufacturing at Republic, and he told me that he needed help in the form of an assistant. In addition to the F-84s rolling off the production line, they were involved in exploring the potential of further development of Kartveli's far-out F-103. The new F-105, which was supposed to be in production, was encountering serious contract problems with the air force, and the A-10, dubbed the Warthog due to its ugly appearance, was on the drawing board. All of that made for a full plate for Jimmy, but now they were becoming deeply involved with a French aircraft company regarding production of a series of jet-powered helicopters. The travel back and forth to France on top of everything else was wearing on Jimmy. He was running out of gas and was worried about his health. He did not have anyone on his staff that he felt could accept the degree of responsibility he felt he needed to delegate. Jimmy asked me if I would resign from the air force and come to work for him in Farmingdale as his deputy vice president for manufacturing.

He offered to personally teach me all he knew about aircraft manufacturing and said he had been authorized to tell me that I could expect to be considered as his replacement when he retired in a few years. Even the initial salary offer would put me in an income bracket with the air force chief of staff, and Jimmy had some fantastic houses in mind that they could assist me in buying. I could keep my hand in the flying game with their flight-test section. We had some fun in Vegas over that weekend, but most of the time my gut was rumbling with possibilities I had never thought about before. Jimmy needed an answer rather quickly, so that cranked the pressure up a bit more.

Like it or not, I had to do some serious mid-career thinking. I had been trained to evaluate situations and to make decisions promptly, but I had never been in a situation like this before. I was at a loss to make the right call. When I had gone through West Point, there was an unspoken understanding that we were in the military for a career of at least twenty or thirty years. When we entered the Point, we had signed up for an absolute minimum of four years on active duty after graduation, but not many of us had any thoughts of getting out after only four years of service. There were a few classmates, often from military families whose parents had forced them to accept appointments, who disliked the entire scenario and resigned their commissions as soon as they could. There were a few who yearned for the chance to trade their West Point credentials for good-paying civilian positions, which was not hard to do, but most of us had no thought of getting out. I have always found it interesting that most of those who served the minimum number of active-duty years are among the more prominent alumni association supporters.

I was completely enthralled with what I was doing in the air force. Despite the fact that it had been fifteen years since I joined the military, I had never given any thought to a career review. Who needed that? I was a gung-ho fighter jock flying the best equipment in the world. But suddenly a good friend had made me a most generous offer that would put me in a significant position in the American aerospace industry at age thirty-two. AJ was right there with full support for whatever my decision was to be, but all I had to do was look around to visualize the difference between our one-thousand-square-foot, one-bathroom GI Wherry housing and the comforts money could buy on Long Island. Obviously I had a serious decision to make.

I was delighted with my air force flying record to date, since I had managed to at least sample most every flying machine in the inventory. If I accepted Jimmy's offer I could expect to do some flying at Republic, and while production test flights aren't like leading the Thunderbirds, nothing else is either. I knew that flying at Command and Staff was limited to the one hundred hours a year you needed to stay on flight status, and I never felt that was enough flying time to keep a guy sharp. I had to be concerned about what my assignment might be after graduation from command and staff. Many graduates went to the Pentagon or remained at Maxwell as instructors, and in those cases you might as well forget about flying.

I had seen superb leadership in the air force, and I had seen leaders whose attempts at leadership were a joke. I couldn't have asked for better leaders than Big Ed in Europe, Ben King in Korea, Levi Chase at Luke, and Doc McGee at Nellis. Some of my past bosses who were on their twilight cruise and some who were star-happy rank climbers had shown me the other side of the leadership coin. From what I had seen at Republic over the years, I knew that the same contrasts in leadership style were probably present there. If I went to Republic, I would be working for Jimmy, and I always enjoyed a great relationship with Republic president Mundy Peale, who had authorized Jimmy's lucrative offer to me.

My thoughts kept running in circles. It concerned me that the air force seemed to be more and more inclined to separating itself into warriors and staffers. I had always been proud to consider myself as a warrior, and I wanted to remain a warrior, but that designation seemed not to be a favorite in some of the higher echelons of air force command.

The term *warrior* was not to be construed as a description of a less-than-sophisticated brute, capable of doing nothing more than swinging a club in battle. Neither is it a rank-sensitive term, since a warrior can be anyone from a corporal to a general. A warrior never loses sight of the fact that the primary reason for being in the military is to protect our nation against all enemies. In the case of the air force, that means always being physically, psychologically, and technically prepared to fly, to fight, and to lead when called upon to do so by the president, our commander in chief. Warriors know the people they command, and they understand the tasks they expect those people to perform. They delegate authority, demand success, and believe in two-way loyalty. Warriors know the technical details of their equipment, and they impose upon themselves the requirement of being able to operate their equipment to perfection. They lead their troops, and the tougher the mission, the more their personal leadership is mandatory. In a shooting war, a flight leader flies the lead aircraft in his flight, and a wing commander flies the lead aircraft in a wing strike against the enemy. Warriors do not send their people where they themselves have not been or would not go if practical. They are efficient administrators who delegate the appropriate administrative authority while personally monitoring directives issued and results obtained. A good warrior abhors the fallacy that other warriors are only capable of minimal rank while being required to do nothing other than fly an aircraft.

Warriors certainly do not dispute the fact that the air force needs multiple headquarters, staffed with motivated specialists and strong commanders, to coordinate the diverse operating units. However, there is also an obvious demand for strong and proficient leadership at the operating level. I was in the age and rank bracket for unit command. I felt I had demonstrated a talent for that type assignment, and I was dedicated to flying and leading in flight.

During the mid-1950s, two emerging personnel management philosophies were of concern to those at the operating levels. One concern was the growth in the size and number of headquarters, which led to larger numbers of professional staff officers who rotated within the staff culture and advanced each other in rank while acquiring only minimal, if any, operational experience. Those who followed that career path tended to generate ever-increasing numbers of regulations restricting operational freedom and demanding ever-increasing reports of myriad facts of questionable value. While the resulting administrative overload burdened operational commanders, various HQ staffs' assumption of control over the minute details of when, where, and how to fly a mission compromised unit efficiency.

The other troublesome tendency was the personnel management theory that to advance toward higher-level command responsibility,

officers needed to spend significant time in nonoperational assignments in order to learn and appreciate the importance of support
functions. This flew in the face of warriors' beliefs that an operational
commander was certainly smart enough to know that he could not be
combat ready if his supply officer ran out of spare parts or his refueling officer ran out of fuel.

This type of career conflict generated friction and threatened efficiency. It was not uncommon to see fast-track staff officers receiving
accelerated promotions and then, though not operationally qualified,
assuming an operational command for a short time, as a career stepping stone to higher rank. Combat flying units found themselves
commanded by aspiring individuals who seldom flew their aircraft,
were not proficient in their aircraft, and seldom, and perhaps never,
got airborne as their flying leader.

Did I have enough career-steering capability to remain a warrior,
or would Air Command and Staff College and subsequent assignments push me into becoming a staffer? Would I be wise to pull the
ejection handles now and accept a fat offer from industry, or should I
hang tough with the air force I cherished?

About ten days after Jimmy left, with decision day approaching, I
was still fumbling with my mid-career crisis. I wandered down to the
Thunderbird flight line and spotted my trusted line chief, Sgt. Boyd
O. Lambeth. Boyd was a husky, smart, tough, old-school sergeant,
whose dedication knew no bounds. He was perfect for the spot he was
in. We had a real frank discussion, and Boyd finally said, "Well, that
sure sounds like a fat deal, major, but do you think you could ever be
satisfied and happy if you didn't try to finish out an air force career?"
That was it: the crux I had been fumbling for. I knew I could never
answer yes to that question. I tossed and turned one more night, then
called Jimmy in the morning to gracefully decline his offer, with sincere thanks for his interest. Unfortunately, Jimmy's concerns material-
ized, and before very long we lost him.

Time was getting shorter for heading east as I walked into the supply chief's office one morning to make a perfunctory check-in and let him know I was still in town. He asked if it was true that the Thunderbird support C-119 had gone down. Without answering, I spun about and headed for the flight line. As I approached the ramp, I spotted a young airman who had been one of my assistant crew chiefs. His eyes red with tears, he was heading for the chapel. Yes, it was true; it happened someplace in Montana. The names came blubbering out, including that of Sergeant Lambeth. I wrapped my arms around that shaking youngster, who looked about ten years old at that moment. I didn't feel much older. I gave him a fatherly hug, patted him on the back, and silently shoved him on his way to the chapel. They had been returning from a show, fully loaded with equipment and the trip maintenance crew, when they apparently ran into high-flying Canada geese. That loud, uncomfortable, noisy clunker had gone straight into the mountains and exploded.

I had plenty of time to think about where I was going as we drove cross-country to Montgomery. I had taken the Thunderbirds there many times and been completely comfortable as we flew air shows for them. But I had very different sensations as we entered the city, got completely lost in a part of downtown Montgomery that frightened me, then, for the first time, drove through the front gate of Maxwell Air Force Base as a student. I knew that graduating from Air Command and Staff College was one of those things that I probably should be doing, but I wanted it to be over before it even started. I knew the change in tempo would be pronounced, but I was determined to make the best of it.

Attending Air Command and Staff College meant different things to different groups of people. The air force wanted the college to be an aerospace research and document center, bulging with academic excellence, that would provide students with a clearer view of the air force's view of the big picture. Some students saw it as a pause, approximately halfway through a military career, where they could simmer in a detached academic environment while evaluating where they had been in the military and envisioning what they could do for the air force and what the air force could do for them. Some considered it as a visa for release from flight-line activities and qualification for increased staff responsibility that would be the first real step on the stairway to the stars. Some of us wanted to find out how those of our ilk thought, how they acted, and how their experiences, combined with the college's academic overtone, could sharpen us for the future. Regardless, we all knew it was a big, mandatory X on the career advancement chart if we wanted to move ahead, and we all called the place Command and Golf.

From day one, the faculty was dedicated to the college's advertised goal of immersing us in the big picture. After several lectures to that effect, we were split up into sections or seminars of fifteen under the direction of a faculty advisor, who was usually a major or lieutenant colonel. Depending on the schedule, we met with our own group a few times a day to dissect the endless mass lectures, which we listened to at least twice a day. We accomplished our assigned projects, book reviews, reports, and so forth, at that level just long enough to get to know each other a little bit, then split into new seminars and repeated the process throughout the year. The course material was weighted toward strategic air, nuclear deterrence and long-range planning at major headquarters, which was as expected and simply reflected the overall air force priorities of that time period.

As students we listened a lot, were bound to absorb some of what we were exposed to, and mixed with each other as directed. Regardless of which section we might be assigned to, we usually shared our coffee breaks between lectures, lunch periods, and happy hours with those we had known before and who came from similar flying backgrounds. Our gang included three World War II aces, two fighter flight-test troops, a pilot from the very first jet acrobatic team, the Acrojets, a Thunderbird, and a fighter jock who was trapped on the college faculty. I doubt that there were many new, lasting friendships forged during that year.

Of the hundreds of lectures we attended that year, two were truly outstanding. Our gang did not accept the college's attitude that even if flying had to be tolerated as part of the flying force, it should not impinge upon academic accomplishment, but we knew we had to live with that attitude for a year. Then, along came that esteemed air pioneer, Gill Robb Wilson. What a guy! He soloed shortly after the Wright Brothers first flew, fought in World War I with the French Lafayette Escadrille and then with U.S. Army's aviation service. He covered the air war of World War II for the *New York Herald Tribune*, founded the Civil Air Patrol and the Aircraft Owners and Pilots Association, and was president of the Air Force Association and editor and publisher of *Flying* magazine. And he was more, including being a Baptist preacher and a real gentleman. He took the stage and talked to us for an hour, just like he talked in his three marvelous flying books. He talked about the glories of flying and the worldwide wonder of the skies. His recitation of the thrills only a pilot can know as he touches nature absolutely made you tingle and say to yourself, "Yeah, yeah, I know." When he tried to quit, we wouldn't let him. The auditorium discarded all the college's staid rules as we yelled, whistled, and roared in sincere appreciation. To hell with all the school's pomp; for this moment, every one of us with feathers on our chests were aviators again, and we loved it. When he took the mike again, he was clearly overwhelmed. He cried as he praised us and envied the technological aircraft wonders at our disposal. He gave us his blessing as he implored us to fly and fight to the utmost of our ability as we served and honored America in that proudest of professions, the military aviator. Academia went nuts as his wife helped him, exhausted, from the stage. None of us left. We just kept cheering, and I'm sure those cheers were still ringing in his ears as his party left the auditorium. I was thrilled to be part of that episode.

Our other day in the academic sun came when Gen. Russ Spicer talked to us. Those of us in the fighter business knew him from Europe, Korea, and most everyplace there were air force fighters. He would fly anything that could get airborne, and he was fearless in the air. If there were to be a single icon of the early jet fighter days, it would be Russ Spicer. He was lean and mean, with a handlebar moustache that fit perfectly. He could step out of a sweaty fighter cockpit and look perfectly groomed to meet any dignitary. He was very outspoken and never pulled his punches regardless of who he was talking to, but that never seemed to impede his progress toward the top. He told us personal war stories and reminded us that we were in uniform to fly and fight. To many of us that music was sweet.

For an hour, General Spicer fed us the gunpowder and raw meat I for one was starved for. The closer he came to the end of his presentation, the more he emphasized that academics and staff work were fine, but he begged us to remain dedicated to flying and fighting, which was not necessarily the party line of the college. Unlike Gill Robb Wilson, General Spicer was physically full of piss and vinegar. When he finished speaking, he popped to attention, saluted us, strode for the steps, and bounced down off the stage. Again, and only for the second time in a year, the auditorium rocked. Those of us who knew him knew he would not be lingering, and we rushed to the exit aisle and mobbed him on the way out. He greeted us with joy, remembering many of our names, smiling, slapping us on the back, and wishing us well. But Russ Spicer had finished that mission and done what he wanted to do, and he was on his way. It was a neat experience. For two days during the academic year, the warrior spirit had flourished in a foreign environment, and I thought that was just great.

Toward the end of the academic year, one of our seminars was completely devoted to forming two-man teams, selecting a research topic that passed muster with our faculty advisor, and preparing a detailed written and aural presentation. It was to be an elimination thing, with the class finalists to present their projects to the entire class and get a big "attaboy" on their year-end performance rating. I teamed up with an army major, and we explored a subject we both knew well. We decided to address the subject of air force close air support of ground forces. It was a valid subject that needed high-level attention, and it was a constant bone of contention in Washington as the service leaders jousted over roles and missions, and of course budgets. The stumbling blocks were obvious. The army wanted direct command and control over airborne support units that were to be assigned directly and exclusively to them. The air force contended that the army had no business commanding or controlling airborne equipment and personnel. However, the air force recognized a requirement to provide ground-force support, as an additional responsibility to its primary mission of long-range strategic nuclear deterrence.

My army friend and I knew firsthand that roles and missions meant little if you were trapped in the Pusan Perimeter. We had been a part of what had worked and what had been a waste. We had very specific suggestions as to what would work better, and our views were certainly firsthand and realistic. We gave both services bad grades, and in the luxury of academic freedom we did a fine job of telling both services how to straighten out their acts. When it came time to present our project the students who heard us thought it was great. However, since the air force impetus at the time was blue sky, Strategic Air Command (SAC), and nuclear weapons, the faculty was not too big on our conclusions. We did not advance very far in the "Attaboy, present to the class" sweepstakes. In fact, a faculty member drew me aside and advised me that I was not in tune with the air force big picture. Through recent personal contact, I can verify that forty-five years later the subject is still a bone of contention within the Department of Defense.

Introducing 2nd Lt. Jacksel "Jack" Broughton, sporting new pilot wings and second lieutenant bars, following graduation from West Point.

Flying a P-47, my first very own fighter, while assigned to the 366th Fighter Group in Fritzlar, Germany.

Colonel Clarence "Big Ed" Edwinson got people's attention. He was a great leader, a rough, tough commander, a superior pilot, and my personal mentor on how to fly and fight.

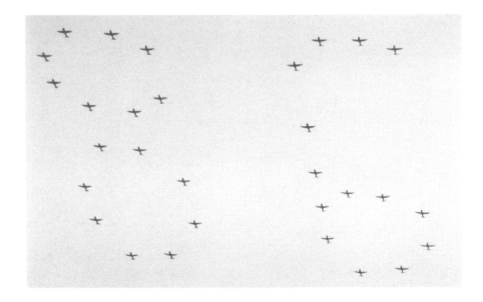

The top pilots in Europe were gathered together in 1947, under Big Ed's command, to form the 86th Fighter Group at Neubiberg, Germany. We were America's only European-based fighter force directly confronting the Russian Air Force as the Cold War became a reality.

In January 1951 I was leading Utah Charlie flight, as we flew our F-80Cs in support of our ground forces who were fighting to break out of the Pusan Perimeter.

Never lend your aircraft to a FNG. Here's what can happen if he runs it off the runway—while trying to takeoff!

My first Distinguished Flying Cross, pinned on me by my friend and commander, Pearl Harbor hero Col. Pete Tyer. He was promoted to general, but was killed in a T-33 crash shortly afterward.

After finishing my F-80 tour, I got to lead Project Swatrock during a highly successful combat test of the new Swiss Oerlikon air-to-ground rocket. The U.S. Air Force didn't buy the rocket, but the Russians did.

General Van Fleet, the overall commander in Korea, inspecting the old versus the new weapons.

Our Oerlikon rockets shredded the Russian T-34 tanks on the practice range at K-2 located near Taegu, South Korea. We did even better as we went after them for real up north.

Some cigarettes and candy replaced international diplomacy as Papa San and I agree on opening a new gunnery range in Korea.

AJ and I raise a toast following our 1951 wedding.

The Thunderbirds were flying the straight wing F-84G when I joined the team as Thunderbird Lead in 1954.

In 1955 we switched to the F-84 F, which was the Thunderbird's first swept wing aircraft.

Republic Aircraft's design chief, Alexander Kartveli (standing left), was noted for his futuristic concepts. He was a true Thunderbird fan.

During my three years as Thunderbird Lead, we flew a nonstop, demanding demonstration schedule, but we still had time for some fun.

We relocated from Luke AFB, Arizona, to Nellis AFB, Nevada, in 1956 when we were equipped with North American Aircraft's brand-new supersonic F-100C. We made the move and converted to the new aircraft without missing a single show.

Despite the vastly improved performance of our F-100s, we were able to bend them around and keep the show close to the crowd. Here we are halfway through a roll over the Nellis runway.

Initially our show flight suits were standard-issue flying suits which had been dyed and embroidered by our wives and/or girlfriends. We eventually got the air force clothing laboratory to provide us with some custom flight suits like the one shown here.

The 5th Fighter Interceptor Squadron insignia identified us as the Spitten Kittens. We managed to get a pair of lynx cubs for mascots, and naturally named them Spitten and Kitten.

The initial F-106 ejection seats were absolutely unsuccessful, and were justifiably known as the killer seat. We were stuck with them until the Spitten Kittens created enough fuss to cause the USAF to replace them.

We always had four fully armed F-106 Darts in the alert barn—manned, cocked, and ready to scramble in five minutes or less. Our primary duty was to prevent Russian trespass over the polar route.

This MB-1 Genie nuclear rocket, about to be loaded into a Dart, was part of our standard alert barn load.

When our schedule permitted, we enjoyed formation flying, which sharpened our skills and coordination. Here two flights of four fly over Minot to salute our crew chiefs and support personnel.

I was privileged to brief President Kennedy, as General Lee looked on approvingly. My prepared pitch was supposed to last thirty seconds, but turned into five minutes of memorable shop talk. I was impressed by the president's interest in and knowledge of aircraft and weapons.

General Thatcher, our ADC commander, stopped by for an informal surprise visit and got to meet Spitten and Kitten. Though he was a bit apprehensive at first, he and Kitten quickly became buddies.

When it was the 5th's turn to sponsor Saturday night at the officers' club, we chose a French theme and turned our can-can line loose, complete with fancy dancing slippers.

Here are the ramrods of my F-106 inspection program, Warrant Officer Dick Dalton (left) and Major Bob Smith (middle). That's me on the right.

On the step in a Grumman Goose, accelerating for takeoff.

Reaching for the water prior to landing.

Surfing out and avoiding casual boaters.

Climbing up onto the ramp for turn around and another flight.

All the Spitten Kitten aircraft of previous years fill the background behind my F-106. It would take a good-sized canvas to show the forty-six different aircraft I've been lucky enough to fly. *Painting by, and used with permission of, Staff Sgt. Jerry Roth, crew chief of F-106 number 002, 5th FIS*

The second half of the academic year at Maxwell was largely centered on the question of what was my next assignment. Several years in the Pentagon in lackey status was a real threat, as was retention at the school as an instructor, but those assignments were attractive to some, since they were indeed good for career development. I was suspicious when my initial draw in the assignment lottery turned out to be a staff job at the Air Force Academy. I got a sugary phone call from a colonel I had known for several years who was the one who had drafted me. He assured me of a supervisory position in a new academy project that would be meaningful to the academy and the air force. I was confused, and then troubled when he added that it would be "good for my career." As ex–Thunderbird Lead, I had good connections who called and alerted me that what the academy had in mind for me was about as mundane as a staff position can get. I had already become a pretty good personnel bandit and decided to use some of those connections to try for something better. With a little help from my friends, especially Colonel Ben King, my old squadron commander from Korea, and in spite of receiving an insulting telephone tirade from the Air Force Academy, I escaped with an assignment to the Air Defense Command Weapons Center at Vincent Air Force Base in Yuma, Arizona.

Our year at Air Command and Golf had allowed some of my classmates to improve their golf scores, but my outstanding memory of the local courses came on a Sunday afternoon late in the school year. I hooked an approach shot into tall grass off to the side of a slightly elevated green. Unbeknownst to me, it landed directly on top of an Alabama fire ant colony. I swished my wedge back and forth through the tall grass, alerting all the fire ant warriors, as I searched for my ball. Finding it, I took my stance, twisted my spikes firmly into the ground and waggled a few times. This must have further alerted the warrior fire ants, who, without my feeling a thing, had covered my legs up to crotch height. As I completed my back swing, the lead fire ant issued the command to charge. They all bit at once. My wedge went straight up into the air as I vaulted out of the tall grass. I somersaulted onto the green while ripping off my shoes and slacks. That caught a few people's attention. But as I jumped up and down, bouncing around the flagstick, flailing away from my belly button to my feet with both hands as I swept the fire ants away, play stopped on all the holes within view. Ladies turned their heads away. Fighter pilot friends laughed insanely. Classmates from SAC shook their heads and sighed. A distinguished-looking faculty advisor on the adjacent tee box exclaimed, "Well, we just try to do the best we can with what they send us." I didn't play over the rest of that round.

Finally school was out, and nobody was sentimental about that. Most of the SAC guys went back to SAC, where they wanted to go. Most of the headquarters guys went back to their old headquarters or some other headquarters, and my little gang all escaped the worst of assignments. Our mid-career exercise was over, and I for one was itching to head west and return to the real air force.

At Yuma, Colonel King welcomed me and explained our mission, which was evaluating air-defense command squadrons who were flying the F-86L or the F-89J. I was soon getting lots of flying time in F-86Ls, F-89s, and B-57s that we used to simulate enemy targets. Any model of the F-86 was a fun machine. I tolerated the limited time I had to put in flying the B-57, but the F-89 was not to my liking. In the first place, it had a guy in the back seat (GIB) running the radar. The F-89 was big and clumsy, with wheels that looked exactly like railroad car wheels. The summer heat in Yuma was breathtaking, and my checkout flight in the F-89 was in late afternoon. As we approached the end of the runway, we had to stop while two maintenance troops used hoses to spray water on the wheels, to cool them down so they didn't cause the tires to explode when I retracted the landing gear after takeoff. I can't remember any fighter pilot who claimed the F-89 as his favorite aircraft.

There were only a few houses on base at Yuma for the commanders, and housing in town was scarce and not so good. My arrival timing worked out well, as a local developer was just completing a cluster of tract houses. His guarantee included a clause that if you bought a house, then found within the first six weeks that you did not like it, he would buy it back, with no questions asked.

I signed up, and AJ, Mark, and I moved in while they were still applying the finishing touches, and we roughed it while waiting for our furniture to arrive from Montgomery. Those houses were set on scraped-out spots on the bone-dry, rock-hard Arizona desert, so my first chore was to try to get something green around the yard. Chopping the sun-soaked desert in 110-degree heat is a stupid way to exist. Getting some grass seed down and keeping it wet is grueling, and the stench of a load of manure imbedded in wind-driven dust is guaranteed to gag a serpent.

Administratively we were part of an air division, which also controlled another wing with a similar mission located at Tyndall Air Force Base in Panama City, Florida. The difference was that they were working with the new Century Series jets. They were flying F-102s and F-104s and were about to get some F-101Bs. I convinced Colonel King that we should know a bit more about their way of doing business, and he sent me there to check out in the F-102. The "Deuce" was a giant step ahead of what we had at Yuma, and I had a ball getting six quick flights. Colonel Dean Davenport was running the Tyndall wing, and General Milt Ashkins, the air division commander over both wings, was also stationed at Tyndall. The two of them were looking for a new commander for their weapons squadron, which was the outfit whose F-102s I had flown. They asked me if I wanted the job. I said I certainly did, but that I owed loyalty to Ben King for breaking me free from the Air Force Academy job and that I would want his concurrence before accepting. By the time I got back to Yuma, they had talked with Ben on the phone, and he had given his blessing on the deal. He met me when I landed, took me to the club, and roasted me over drinks with our mutual friends before sincerely wishing me well on what he knew to be a step forward. AJ didn't complain a bit when I announced our third cross-country move in fifteen months. I beat the six-week deadline, the real estate developer wrote me a check just as the green grass was popping up, and we turned around and headed back east.

CHAPTER 12

CENTURY SERIES

The Century Series jet fighters were clearly a different generation of flying machines. Starting with the F-100, which I had flown for a year with the Thunderbirds, they all had afterburners, which allowed them to transition to supersonic speed with ease, but at the expense of consuming huge amounts of fuel. Systems like flight instruments and radar now provided a new look in cockpit sophistication. Weapons-delivery systems were far more advanced than what we had used in the past. Long struggles on drawing boards and in wind tunnels were constantly producing dividends in design and performance advancements such as the F-102's Coke-bottle fuselage and the F-104's man-in-a-missile-concept. There were still several aircraft companies cranking out constantly improving fighters, and the air force was eagerly converting their operational units to Century Series capability. It was a fun and fast-moving time for fighter pilots, and the new birds were fun to fly.

My basic charge at Tyndall was to evaluate the weapons-delivery capability of each of the air-defense squadrons in Air Defense

Command. We had room to accommodate two visiting squadrons at all times, and they would rotate through on staggered three-week temporary-duty tours. I had separate groups of instructor pilot evaluators for each of the three types of aircraft assigned to the various squadrons. My guys would fly our aircraft while chasing their pilots in their own aircraft. We would put them through various tactical situations at all hours of the day and night. Our missions ranged from dry runs to live firings at drones on our offshore range in the Gulf of Mexico.

Harlan Ball, my ops officer, and I had the tough duty of flying all three of our aircraft. I will admit that we were both partial. The F-102 was a good, stable bird with a reasonable missile-firing capability. It was truly all-weather capable, and even though it was the oldest of our machines, it was the most reliable. One of the best ways to improve your own techniques is to chase and then critique another pilot, and I learned a bunch about the air-defense game in the F-102.

The F-104, the world's fastest tricycle, was the fun machine of the three. It was small, with tiny wings that had knifelike leading edges. The cockpit was tight and you felt like you were literally strapping on the entire aircraft when you closed the latch on your seat harness. The engine moaned and roared at every throttle movement, and she was even fun to taxi. But she was prone to doing weird things and could be a beast to handle when something went wrong.

One overcast day at Tyndall I was scheduled for a maintenance test hop in an F-104 following a routine inspection, and it seemed like a neat time for a max-performance climb. Traffic control cleared me to go as high and as fast as I wanted to go between the runway and the Gulf weapons range. I just left the burner plugged in and pulled the stick back as I went Popeye at about three thousand feet, looking for the tops that were reported at twenty eight thousand feet. In that little beauty, a max climb actually laid you on your back, but the physical pressure was solid, and the artificial horizon was steady, with the nose way up there.

I had passed through twenty thou when the cockpit lights, the radar, and all the electrical gauges hiccuped one time and went bye-bye. I knew the engine was still roaring nicely as I mentally discarded the now-defunct primary flight instruments. In my flight attitude, my primary target was the standby artificial horizon, since I needed to quickly convert to a less-demanding nose angle. The problem was that the standby artificial horizon was only the size of a half-dollar, and it was located top row, far left, on the instrument panel.

I came out of burner, and after some sloppy pushing and pulling and rudder-pedal pumping, I was sure that I was going down rather than up. As I fell through sixteen thousand feet, there was nothing out the window but white clouds, and I was still not in a stable, well-controlled descent. Then, as my left shoulder floated up and down, I saw a streak of blue off the left wing. It wasn't sky blue; it was water blue. I jammed the stick forward, kicked left rudder, and rolled in full left aileron. My F-104 zipped into a hole where I could level my bubble and set up a standby gauge's needle ball and air speed descent to visual flight rules on the bottom. Not your everyday descent.

Another time, I landed an F-104 with one hundred gallons of fuel showing on the indicator. As I coasted into the parking area, I pushed the throttle forward and flamed out on the ramp, with zero fuel in the tanks. Those kind of things happened with F-104s more often than they should have, but we loved to fly them anyway.

Then we got some of the first F-101B models. The F-101A was a single-seat tactical attack bird whose bad rap was that if you horsed the nose up just right, the wings and fuselage would blank out the tail, and she would pitch-up and depart control in all axes. The B model was a two-place interceptor wherein the engineers had addressed the pitch-up problem by ignoring history and placing a much larger two-place canopy topside, thus increasing the surface capable of blocking out the tail. I did not care for the overall feel of the aircraft, and no matter what attitude I was trying to maintain, I felt like I was trying to balance a golf ball on the point of a pencil. The nose wheel presented an additional challenge. When you got airborne and retracted the wheels, the nose wheel retracted forward into the oncoming wind stream, rather than rearward. It would not retract at all if your forward speed exceeded 260 knots. The tech manuals contained warnings to pilots covering both of these technological advancements. They advised us to pull the nose up smartly on takeoff in order that the nose wheel could retract, but not to pull up too smartly, or the enlarged overall forward surface might be likely to block out the tail and induce pitch-up.

The new, enlarged canopy introduced yet another problem resulting in the canopy going its own way without advance notice. In rearranging the internal electrical circuitry required by the two-place canopy, they had created a junction box that looked like a pineapple. It was covered with contact points that allowed the designers to bring a command signal into the pineapple at one point and transfer an electrical command out at another point, sort of like an order to buy or sell command. One of the problems was that the pineapple lacked any protective covering and was just sitting there, someplace between the engines and the bottom of the canopy. Thus, a floating washer, a stray scrap of safety wire, or a drop of rain could short-out or reroute a circuit, and something unexpected would happen. Most often it was that the canopy would fly off.

One dark, rainy night I was letting down to land at Tyndall with my most acceptable GIB, Nick, in the back seat and with my squadron administrator, Capt. JP Finch, on my wing. Happily, in my outfits, everybody with feathers on their chests flew our mission aircraft, and we liked it that way. I called to switch radios to tower frequency for landing and didn't get a check-in call from JP on the wing. I called, "JP, are you on tower freq?" It was sort of tough to see in the black night and light rain, but as I glanced left, there was JP, tucked in tight on my wing, minus canopy, with him and his GIB hunched over and hanging in there. His GIB had punched the radio channel selector when I had called the channel change, and the pineapple had dispatched their canopy to some undisclosed location in Florida. As I said, I flew them all, but I did like some better than others.

AJ, Mark, and I were enjoying the assignment when the personnel people called and said I was being reassigned to Turkey. I scoffed as I headed to Colonel Davenport's office, chatted with his secretary (who was a big item with one of our F-104 guys), and waited for my turn to talk to the boss. I told him that I wasn't interested in going to Turkey. Further, I had been promised a choice of assignment at the end of my Thunderbird tour, and still had not exercised my choice. He replied, "Then was then, and now is now; besides, Ankara, Turkey, is a choice assignment in some people's book." We loaded up for move number four in twenty-seven months.

After a grueling and very GI flight, on canvas bench seats in the back end of a decrepit old Military Air Transport four-engine C-54 prop-driven trash hauler, we arrived in England. Following a commercial hop to Istanbul, we had our first disgusting encounter with Turkish bureaucracy in the form of customs agents. I still smoked then, but I thought I had never smelled anything as foul as those guys blowing Turkish cigarette smoke in my face and demanding that I prove why we were there. I was wrong. It smelled much worse when they closed the door on the Turkish Airlines C-47 relic that took us to Ankara. We were met by a rotund lieutenant colonel, my "sponsor," who had drawn the duty of making us feel at home. After introductions, his first statement was, "You're going to hate this assignment." During the ride to town, he enlarged on why we were going to hate it, and advised us that the only things safe to eat were boiled eggs, borscht, cooked fish, jam, and bread. He helped check us in at the Bulvar Palas, on Ataturk Bulvari, took a twenty-dollar bill from me in exchange for a handful of Turkish lire, and pointed out the mile walk up the *bulvari* to the Military Assistance Group (MAG) building. Thus concluded his sponsorship.

Our cubicle was on the second floor of the four-story Bulvar Palas. It had a small bed, a cot, a sink, and a combination sort of toilet and shower. The toilet was actually a four-story tube; thus, all deposits from floors three and four passed our way en route to who knows where. AJ had decided that she was indeed pregnant again. Thus, all this was far tougher on her than it was for seven-year-old Mark and me.

Mark and I braved it in the morning and went to the dining room, where we each ordered a bottle of "good" water, a boiled egg, and a piece of bread with jelly. When I cracked my boiled egg open, out popped a three-strand piece of braided white string. I pulled it out for about eighteen inches worth and looked at the little bit of deformed egg left in the shell. Mark and I laughed like crazy, ate the slice of bread and jam, had a drink of water, and left. I checked into the MAG and immediately realized that there was nobody there of my ilk. I immediately started planning how I was going to get us the hell out of there.

I went through the process of meeting everyone connected with the job, Americans and Turks, and it was tough to decide who was the least impressive. Nobody trusted anybody else. It seemed that I was ticketed to be something like the number-two man in an operations liaison section assisting the Turkish Air Force, but my first duty was to get my wife and son out of that smelly hotel and into something like a house.

After several days of very frustrating house hunting, we found an almost completed apartment about three-quarters of the way up one side of the mountainous bowl surrounding Ankara. We rented the second floor two-bedroom apartment from the owner, a graduate of Michigan State University. The household goods we had shipped were somewhere on the high seas, but we moved in and roughed it. I got my brother Bob to pick us up a peppy little used Plymouth four-door sedan back in the States and ship it to me.

There were inconveniences: You could only count on the water running a few hours a day, and you couldn't drink it. All the fruits and vegetables were huge and looked enticing, but since that was the result of fertilization with human waste, you couldn't eat any of them. You could eat the lettuce, but only after you had soaked it in Clorox water then picked through the leaves to get rid of the dead gray bugs. There was a makeshift GI commissary in downtown Ankara, and one way or another, AJ took care of those details, and we existed well.

I could usually accomplish the busy work I had to do at the office in an hour or two a day, so it was tough to make the time move swiftly toward that date two years in the future when I might expect orders out of Turkey. We had majors on flight status and some enlisted men who were assigned to each of the fighter bases as advisors. They spent Monday through Friday at the Turkish bases and weekends in Ankara. That made it tough for me to justify going out to the operational bases, since the lieutenant colonel I worked for thought the downtown Ankara mission was far more important than the rest of us did. But I managed to break loose now and then on short-term visits to the fighter units. The other way to get out of the office was to fly the mail. I had to fly the C-47 Gooney Bird and the C-54 to get my flying pay, but flying them to deliver the mail at least got me out of the office for a day at a time.

After a particularly boring few weeks in the office, I reminded my boss that I, as an operational "advisor," had not yet been allowed to fly a single hour in a Turkish F-100. I hit a nerve, since he, as the number-one advisor, had not been airborne under his own control in anything operational in a long time. He arranged for me to go to Eskisehir for an F-100 flight. Having flown the A model and having led the Thunderbirds in the C model, I looked forward to a cockpit check in the D and a few days of fun flying. It was not to be. They scheduled me for one single backseat ride in a two-place D model trainer, flown by their most brash squadron commander. He was well aware that I had been Thunderbird Lead, and he made no attempt to hide the fact that he was determined to wring my ass out, big time. Putting the wringee in the back seat makes that a piece of cake for the wringor. The mission of the day was simulated low-altitude nuclear weapons delivery. That means you go in on the deck as fast as you can go, pull up hard, and at vertical you toss the nuke straight up and get out of there as best you can. I do not think I had ever been as frightened as I was as a prisoner of that asshole Turk. When we landed, I asked him if I could have a flight in one of his F-100s, alone, that would allow him and me to practice some one-on-one air combat maneuvers. He felt that such an arrangement would be impossible. Chicken, chicken, chicken.

One of the problems with our apartment came from the gypsies. The crudely paved road ended as it passed our place, and it became a dirt trail from there up to the top of the hills that formed the lip of the Ankara bowl. The gypsies lived in a crude camp on the top of the hills, and each morning about a hundred of them would come down the hill on their way to downtown Ankara to beg, steal, or scrounge whatever they could. In the evening they reversed course. There was nothing between our place and the top of the hills, so when the unkempt and unwashed gypsies started downhill in the morning, their first opportunity to mess things up came at our place. Our building was neat, smartly painted, with well-kept grass, bright flowers, and garbage cans. They would hit us like a swarm of fire ants, gibbering loudly in their unknown dialect, taking obvious glee in urinating and defecating all over the property, and without fail dumping the garbage cans and pawing through and scattering the garbage.

Turkey was a significant producer of sugar beets, and the city of Eskisehir had a large sugar beet processing plant. The plant had something quite uncommon in that part of the world: lots of pigs. Pigs were abhorrent symbols of evil not to be touched, and certainly not to be eaten. But the sugar plant had an economic as well as physical problem as regards getting rid of the massive slop and juice they squeezed out of tons of sugar beets. They had the happiest possible pig farm, as huge pigs wallowed in the waste and kept the place somewhat clean. The pigs also had little pigs, and the Turks capitalized on the fact that Americans and Europeans did not share their fear of pigs and would actually pay good money for them. Thus, by ordering a few days in advance, you could buy a gutted and cleaned suckling pig, head and all, for fifty cents. The next time I went to Eskisehir, I ordered two pigs and picked them up Friday before returning to Ankara. I got out my big butcher knife, separated the head and front legs from them, and then tried cooking the rest of them on the barbecue. I didn't think the culinary result was worth the effort, but that was not why I had bought the pigs in the first place. After dark I went out to our two large garbage cans, which were quite full, and packed one pig's head and feet into each can. I had their front legs draped over the rim of the cans, with their heads pressed down by the lids of the cans. The next morning the gypsies arrived on schedule, and as some proceeded to pollute the yard, others headed for the garbage cans. As they removed the pressure by lifting the lids, the piglet heads rose up, eyes wide open, and stared at them. The gypsies near the cans screamed, and kept screaming as they ran for the front gate. Others, who were in various stages of desecrating the property, clutched the skirts of their filthy robes and joined in the exodus. For the entire remainder of our stay in Turkey, those gypsies passed our house on the other side of the road, looking straight ahead, and never again set foot on the property.

Supposedly we were in Turkey to oversee the transfer of modern equipment to the Turkish Air Force and to assist them in mastering flying techniques and procedures that would make them compatible allies in any conflict arising out of the Cold War. We had approximately zero control of any U.S. equipment that was shipped to Turkey. Abuse of the system was rampant, and lots of Turks became very wealthy on a scandalous black market. On the flying scene, the Turks accepted what technical inputs they thought they needed, but basically, they flew our equipment the way they wanted to fly it. The most succinct illustration was in the missile field. We gave missiles to the Turks and to the Greeks. The Turks aimed their missiles at the Greeks, while the Greeks aimed theirs at the Turks.

I got a one-on-one look at the prevalent Turkish mindset following an F-100 accident at Eskisehir, when I was sent there to assist as U.S. advisor to their accident investigation board. A young Turkish lieutenant had attempted takeoff with a normal training fuel load. They had a NATO standard runway, which provided plenty of length for even a fully combat loaded F-100 on a hot day. The lieutenant came up to full power, lit his afterburner and rolled down the runway, but he never got airborne. His nose wheel never came up off the runway despite the fact that his speed when he ran off the far end of the runway was in excess of 250 miles an hour. Engineering calculations are that you can not force a normally configured F-100 to remain on the ground at that high speed. The Turks had a small Toonerville Trolley–type train that ran between the town and the base to transport civilian workers, and its route took it past the departure end of the main runway. It was fully loaded and passing the end of the runway when the lieutenant's F-100 left the runway, afterburner still blazing, and collided with the train and exploded. The lieutenant and some 260 train passengers were killed. It seemed to me that, in order to prevent similar catastrophies, it was urgent to investigate if the cause of the accident was some gross problem such as flight controls being rigged backwards or an extreme FOD situation.

When I arrived on base, I checked in with the Turkish general in charge, and we went through the approved routine of a salute, a handshake, and the sharing of a small cup of hot, sweet tea along with a cigarette. That done, I said, "General, I'm here to assist you in any way possible in the investigation of the recent F-100 accident."

He looked at me and, showing no apparent emotion, coldly replied, "Major, there will be no accident investigation."

I must have registered my surprise, because as soon as I said, "But, general," he raised his hands, signaling shut up.

"You see, major, you Americans do not seem to understand that the recent misfortune was clearly Allah's will, and it is not for us to question Allah's will. No, I repeat, there will be no accident investigation."

I could not resist one more, "But sir," and that was as far as I got.

He said, "Now, if you will excuse me."

When I got back to Ankara with my report, my bosses just shrugged and didn't seem too surprised or concerned. They were more interested in the fact that they had just solved a dispute between the Turkish and U.S. Air Forces. The United States was giving the Turks seventy-five F-84Fs to equip three fighter squadrons at Balikesir, where I had delivered a P-47 years ago. The aircraft had been shipped to Spain by boat, where U.S. maintenance personnel were preparing them for flight to Turkey. The United States had planned to provide ferry pilots to deliver the aircraft to Turkey, per terms of the country-to-country agreement. The Turks wanted to waive that portion of the agreement so Turkish pilots could deliver the aircraft. Our MAG had sided with the Turks, citing national pride, so the United States said OK. The lieutenant colonel in command of the first squadron scheduled to receive the new F-84s went to Spain with his pilots and accepted the aircraft that were ready to fly out. Despite warnings of severe thunderstorms, the first flight of four headed for Balikesir. The commander of the flight got lost in the thunderstorms, but they spit him out the other side, and he made it to Balikesir. But the other three pilots bailed out, so they wound up delivering only one of the first four aircraft. As soon as they had four aircraft delivered and flyable, the commander scheduled a four-ship air-to-ground gunnery mission to show off the F-84's strafing ability. That kind of mission is usually accomplished against four targets spaced along a straight line, with the targets being numbered one to four, from left to right. The flight takes spacing, in trail, behind the leader, and he rolls into a left turn to fire on target one, with each flight member firing on the next target down the line. In this case, the leader rolled in on target one, but the number two man also rolled in on target one. As the leader approached the proper range from the target to start firing, the number two man started firing and shot down his commander. Before they delivered the seventy-fifth F-84, the Turks had already destroyed twenty-five of them; thus, they started with only two squadrons rather than three. Yes, the Turks flew like the Turks wanted to fly, but Allah's will was sort of tough on their aircraft and people inventories.

Turkey was a hotbed of political unrest during our stay. The regime of Prime Minister Adnan Menderez was a cruel dictatorship, with only a thin façade of representative government. Corruption and atrocities were accepted facts of Turkish life. Dissenters usually shared the fate of the two hundred protesting university students whose bodies were found in a shallow, common grave a few miles outside Istanbul. The Turks in the know hinted that Menderes was done, but there was no outward evidence to that effect.

I had drawn the duty as sponsor for Maj. Art Hinkle and his wife and young daughter. They arrived about nine o'clock one evening after a very trying trip and just wanted someplace to bed their daughter down and relax. Thus, I took them straight to their room at the Bulvar Palas, where I had stashed some welcome goodies and a battery-powered radio, and said I would contact them in the morning. I went back to the apartment, and as I approached the door, Ahmet (my Michigan State University–educated Turkish landlord) walked by and casually said, "You might want to get up about four in the morning and go out on your back deck. It should be a spectacular sunrise." I understood his short statement, and AJ and I were in position with deck chairs, coffee, and binoculars to watch the Turkish Army swing into action and overthrow the Menderes government. The tanks, guns, and troops were in position, there was some well-placed gunfire, and the required butchery apparently was accomplished quickly. Menderes was already in Switzerland with untold fortunes and spoils, and most everyone other than his immediate cohorts seemed to be ready for the takeover.

The MAG sent out phone messages to U.S. personnel and dependents to stay home, and the city was locked down as the troops swiftly deployed to all key buildings and intersections. I was not proud to learn that the marine guards at our embassy had surrendered their weapons when the Turks arrived at the door, but who knows what instructions they had received from our American ambassador, who had bravely locked himself in the basement of the embassy. By four in the afternoon, all indications were that things had stabilized under martial law of the new regime.

I waited until five o'clock, then, dressed in my uniform and with a large paper sack of groceries under my arm, I fired up my powder-blue Plymouth and headed down the hill for the Bulvar Palas. The main intersection with Ataturk Bulvari was very red, and I was wondering if the obvious bloodstains had come from Menderes supporters or a whole bunch of ceremonial sacrificial lamb slaughters. At the corner, a tall Turkish Air Force two-striper, with a rifle and a sharp bayonet slung over his shoulder, flagged me down. I greeted him in Turkish, and he responded in English, asking for a ride down the hill to the Turkish Armed Forces radio station. I invited him into the right front seat and welcomed having an escort into town. I asked how things were going and, he replied that everything looked *tamum*. Tamum could mean many things in Turkish, but in this case it seemed to mean finished—OK. I was the only one moving on the *bulvari*, and the military tanks and truck crews along the way mostly ignored us as we drove by.

I dropped him off, and as I approached the Bulvar Palas there were several tanks parked along the curb at intervals in front of the hotel, with a group of soldiers grouped around the front entrance. I parallel parked between two of the tanks at the curb. The soldiers were watching me intently as I put the grocery bag under my left arm and walked between them toward the hotel entrance. A Turkish major with his hand resting on the U.S. .45 pistol on his hip was moving out of the entrance as if to challenge me, so I gave him a smile and a casual salute and said, "Merhaba major." He responded, and by pointy-talkie and a two-way mixture of Turkish and English, I indicated that I was going to our new major's room in the hotel to deliver the groceries, which was fine with him.

When I returned, the major and I again exchanged salutes, and his troops popped to with rifle salutes as I cranked up the Plymouth and made a U-turn up the hill. When I got to the turnoff, I glanced further up the *bulvari* towards Embassy Row and wondered if the ambassador was still locked up in his basement.

One of the grossest atrocities exposed by the revolution was the Ataturk Farm disclosure. The state farm sold flowers, livestock products, fruits and vegetables, chickens, and eggs. I did not trust the Turks enough to partake of their products, but we had a lieutenant colonel in the MAG who swore by the fresh eggs. He said they were the largest and best-tasting fresh eggs he had ever had. A couple of days after the takeover, the front page of the local paper broke the story, with pictures, of the raid on Ataturk's farm. The worst of the discoveries centered on the hen house, where the storage bays turned out to be refrigerator storage space filled with stacked, frozen remains of a large number of Menderes' enemies. It got worse. The area included a flat table and a large grinding machine that could have come from a commercial ground-meat processing plant. The Turk in charge of that facility had readily admitted that one of his duties was to grind up the frozen remains of the enemies of Menderes to feed to the chickens. He stated that he had felt a bit bad about it at first, but had become used to it. We labeled the lieutenant colonel a secondhand cannibal.

Fortunately, AJ's pregnancy was a healthy one, and the minimal U.S. medical attention she received was adequate, though not reassuring. An army doctor and two nurses, assisted by a staff of Turkish locals, worked out of an old Turkish medical facility that the army had taken over and brought up to our minimum standard. It was the best the medics had to offer, so obviously it had to be good enough.

AJ kept herself in great shape, and so her long walk down the hill to the doctor for a late-term checkup was in character. The Doc assured her that she still had a couple of weeks to go. She walked back up the hill, turned around, walked back down the hill, and asked to see the doctor again. He said, "What are you doing back here?"

She replied, "I'm back here to have this baby." That brought me into the picture for whatever a guy can do at times like that. We sat there, and it was hot, with no air conditioning, and the flies were bothersome. We knew delivery time was approaching, but the nurse asked me to hang in as long as I could, since the doctor had to do a surgical procedure on a woman, and the nurse needed to help him. She said when it was really time to just yell "Now!" and they would take it from there. I yelled "Now!" and I often wondered what happened to that woman in surgery because the nurse was right there. She wheeled AJ past the swinging doors, and literally in a matter of a few minutes I was looking at our not-yet-cleaned-up daughter Sheila, the first Broughton daughter in sixty-four years. An hour later I was looking at her in the newborn baby room as a Turkish lady gently swept a palm fan back and forth above the infants to keep the flies away. I ground my teeth and told myself again that I needed to get us out of there.

Then we got the break I had been working for. Our son, Mark, had undergone surgery for a lazy eye back in 1957, but despite a temporary improvement, the eye was once again in need of surgical attention. The local army doctor had been forceful in his recommendation that Mark needed to return to the States for medical attention. I assembled the required documentation and requested that my current tour be terminated and that I receive a compassionate assignment back to the United States. I had alerted my friend Ike Isaacson back in the States, and he had requested me for a specific assignment to his staff at Hamilton Air Force Base near San Francisco, where the appropriate eye surgeons and therapists were available to help Mark. Several weeks had rolled by before the MAG got a message through personnel channels that I was to be reassigned to Hamilton.

It took about six weeks more to get the administrative details accomplished. In the interim, I used a MAG conference I was scheduled to attend in London to visit the Jaguar automobile factory in Coventry and order my XK-150 drop-head coupe. Since I had called ahead, the vice president of marketing picked me up at the train station and treated me like I was a VIP. I was wined and dined in the executive dining room at lunch, and enjoyed my first-ever kidney pie. The MAG conference had dictated that I wear my air force blues with my medals and wings, and those adornments drew plenty of attention as the Jag VP took me on a tour through all the production departments in the factory. I shook hands and got backslaps and polite hugs every place we went. I even got to see the bare body of what was to be my Jag as it went through the first rough sanding station. I had given the VP my check for the down payment of a thousand dollars, but as I got into the limo for the ride back to the train station, you would have thought that I had just purchased half of the company.

We had our last rub with the Turkish bureaucracy after we rode the same smelly Turkish DC-3 from Ankara to Istanbul on the way out of Turkey. I was in uniform as we went through what seemed to be the same two customs police we had faced on entry to Turkey. After examining all our many U.S. and Turkish documents, they completely surprised us by snatching newborn Sheila in her tiny straw traveling basket and passing her over a counter to an unseen person. AJ went ballistic and, with young Mark in trail, charged around the right side of the counter. I lowered my shoulders and split the two guards, going around the left side. Behind the wall a fat Turk sat with our infant child on a desk in front of him, muttering that children born in Turkey, male or female, have dual citizenship and are subject to the Turkish draft. Though the dual-nation documents I had given them were well prepared and clear, he was not sure if he should release her or if he should detain her in Turkey. There was no hesitation on our part. I grabbed the ream of documents from the fat Turk, AJ picked up Sheila and her basket, Mark stepped between his mother and the fat Turk, and we just strode out of there, past their uniformed guards and into the commercial terminal area. The Turks just stood there. Before long we were back over the Atlantic, in what looked and felt like the same tired C-54 from the inbound trip, with our six-week-old daughter snoozing happily in the luxury of a cardboard box and a GI blanket.

Moving into Hamilton was a pleasure both professionally and personally. Ike Isaacson was running the current operations section of the 78th Air Division of Air Defense Command, and I hardly needed a briefing on my duties to slide into position working for him again. My primary job was to coordinate tactics and procedures with West Coast elements of the navy and Air National Guard who responded to the 78th in times of air defense emergency, or practice exercises for such an emergency. I did that, but my real primary job was to troubleshoot whatever problem Ike told me to attack. I was worse than a wing weenie: I was a division headquarters weenie. Therefore, whenever I flew out of Hamilton, I had to fly the T-33, which did the job OK for traveling. Once I got to a unit that supported us, protocol said that I should be current in whatever they flew, so I picked up flights here and there in the F-86, the F-100, the F-101, and maybe the most fun, the navy F4D. I even signed on as a crew member for a ten-hour-plus, all-night patrol over the Pacific Ocean in a radar-packed, four-engine RC-121C Constellation.

It took a little time, but my Jag made it to the port in Oakland as part of my household goods coming out of Turkey. It was a beauty in old English white, with a black silk weatherized convertible top and light gray and red leather trim; and my total tab was $3,245. It was so much fun to drive that even AJ enjoyed blasting off from a stoplight when challenged by local teenage dragsters.

Playing staff officer sure can get dull, and Ike and I confided in each other that we needed a break. His wife, Nona, was raising multiple youngsters, and AJ was doing great work with Mark and Sheila while expecting our third child: not family vacation situations. So Ike and I took some leave time and headed for North Dakota to do some crop spraying for a friend of his who owned Montgomery Spraying Service. Ike got to spray the wheat with a Stearman, while I drew the modified Super Cub. It was tough duty, with crazy work hours, and crummy living conditions, but it did two things for both of us. First, the strenuous demands made us forget all about the air force for awhile, and secondly, it convinced us we wanted nothing more to do with crop dusting.

We had great luck with Mark's eye treatments, as we got him involved with the best programs University of California hospitals and their associates had to offer. Skilled surgeons and therapists got the job done and avoided the bad things that another year in Turkey would have done to him. It seemed like no time until AJ was back in the hospital at Hamilton for the birth of Maureen. AJ had delivered Sheila in one of the worst hospital environments, and Sheila came through fine. She had Maureen in one of the supposed first-class air force hospitals, but Maureen and many others in the hospital at that time almost didn't make it due to staph infection. Fortunately, we had her home in good shape before too long.

Winter set in, though that was of little concern in California. But Ike and I needed to participate in a conference on the east coast of Canada on mutual air defense requirements. We cranked up a T-33 and headed east into a formidable-looking winter storm system. Ike was in the front seat as we flew over his native Dakota territories, and everything was white with a five-hundred-mile blanket of snow. We planned on refueling in Grand Forks, but before we got there we passed over a navigation fix labeled Minot.

As the direction-finder needle swung, Ike said, "Hey, that's Minot right down there."

I looked over the side and saw nothing but white snow, and said to myself, "Minot? Oh, OK." We let down through the winter stuff and refueled at Grand Forks. Somebody did something to our oxygen system while Ike and I were filing our flight plan, since as we climbed out on the next leg, we both got the bends. Man, that really hurt, but a week later we were back enjoying the West Coast.

Shortly after the first of the year, Ike decided that we should have someone checked out in the F-106 so we could better evaluate the performance of the one F-106 squadron that was assigned to our air division. I won the prize on that one and got a half-dozen good flights in the bird over a couple of days and nights. I was delighted with the way that F-106 performed. At the end of the second day, I was just beginning to learn some of its capabilities, and having a great time as I learned, but duty called back at Hamilton. Not too long after I had briefed Ike on my views of the aircraft and the squadron, he walked up to me, as I was daydreaming at my headquarters desk, and said, "This would probably be too tough duty for you, but ADC [Air Defense Command] is looking for a volunteer to take over the worst ADC squadron in the business. They're flying 106s, and it's located in Minot, North Dakota."

I jumped up and said, "I want that job." It was time to pack up and move again.

CHAPTER 13

SPITTEN KITTENS

AJ and I had to spend a bit of extra time going through the packing drill for our drive to Minot, North Dakota, where I was to assume command of the 5th Fighter Interceptor Squadron. The so-called back seat in a Jaguar XK-150 was close to nonexistent, and nine-year-old Mark and twenty-two-month-old Sheila had a dandy cross-country squirming match back there. AJ rode shotgun in the right front seat with five-month-old Maureen either on her lap or on the floor. The XK-150 did have a trunk, which was about as deep as the gas tank but a little wider, but it lost a bit of that space due to the graceful sweep of the rear end. Thus, there was not too much room for baggage. There was no direct route from San Francisco to Minot, and super highways had not scarred the reported natural beauty of the winding stretch of about two thousand miles of old-time roads through Nevada, Utah, Wyoming, South Dakota and the picturesque Black Hills, and finally due north to Minot, near the Canadian border. Late winter along that stretch was still very much winter. Obviously, the goal was to cross those miles with minimum delay, and the small, battery-powered radio that I bought, complete with ear plugs, helped ease the pain, for me.

Once we started down from the Black Hills and left the Badlands behind, everything got very flat. We made better time on the flat surface, and there was not much traffic except for us, but the wind started blowing a lot harder. Then came the snow—sideways. There were no signs as to destinations or distances, and the occasional mini-billboards that read, "Why Not Minot?" and "Minot, The Magic City!" were not really inspirational.

We found Minot in the snow and wind, but then it is hard to miss Minot when the only two roads and the only two railroad tracks on the map intersect in the center of town. The crossing of the rail lines, with attendant refueling and transshipment facilities in the potato-rich area, seems to be how the town got started. The Cold War Russians certainly had Minot on their target list, since it was on the direct attack route from Russia to the U.S. heartland, and was the home base for B-52 nuke-loaded bombers, Minuteman underground missile-launch silos, KC-135 aerial refueling tankers, and the nuke missile-equipped F-106 fighter interceptors of the 5th Fighter Squadron "Spitten Kittens."

The guys and gals of the 5th were primed and ready for our arrival. All our officers and most of our airmen lived on base, since we were the five-minute-alert guys who were expected to intercept the Russian threat. The quarters they had reserved for us were one-half of a wooden, two-story, frame duplex. The squadron already had survival stores in the apartment, baby sitters were in position, and we were the guests of honor at a welcoming party. I felt good about the way things were shaping up.

I was now officially the commander of the 5th Fighter, made up of fifty officers and five hundred enlisted men, and a goodly percentage of them had wives and children with them. The outfit was rich in history but currently rated as the least-proficient squadron in Air Defense Command. They were equipped with the latest and best weapons system in the inventory, and they had the mission of protecting America against attack by Russian bombers trying to cross over the North Pole and strike America. If you drew a line on a map from Minot to the North Pole you could see that there was not much civilization between the two, and looking north off the end of the runway confirmed that sensation.

The first thing I did the next morning was to call a meeting of all my officers in the operations briefing room. My first remarks were short and to the point, as I told them I was anxious to meet all of my people, learn about their duties and how they were being accomplished, and find out what we needed to do to improve our combat-readiness posture.

One of AJ's first duties was to find the commissary and stock up on food and housekeeping supplies. Since the base was twenty-five miles north of town, we were dependent on the commissary and the base exchange, especially during the long winters, when it was often impossible to travel between the base and town. AJ donned her leather coat, skintight matching leather gloves, fired up the Jag, and did the commissary chore. By the time she got home, her hands ached, and when she finally got the gloves off, it was clear that she had frostbitten hands. She got lesson number one in Minot weather, and forty years later her hands immediately ache at the slightest exposure to cold.

Minot was a huge base run by Strategic Air Command and commanded by a two-star major general. He was in direct control of the SAC bomber wing, tanker wing, and missile program. Air Defense Command's presence on the base included a semiautomatic ground environment (SAGE) sector run by a senior colonel, and my squadron. My ADC command channels ran through the SAGE commander, Colonel, soon to be General, Tom Hayes, a World War II P-51 ace. He and I developed a great relationship, with him helping when he could but allowing me maximum freedom to run my own show. The SAC base commander, Colonel Zeke Summers, had all the support responsibilities, from guarding the gates to fixing the plumbing, and Zeke and I also got along great.

Our squadron area was in the southwest corner of the base, and we were pretty well secured within a chain-link fence. All of our functions were within this area except for barracks and housing, which were on the main base. We had twenty-six F-106s and two T-33s and could store six of them in my one heated hangar. We always had four interceptors on hot five-minute alert in our alert barn, which also housed the alert pilots and crews, plus the best minichow hall imaginable. That meant that the rest of my birds roosted in the open on the ramp, but under galvanized roofing supported by metal posts sunk into the ramp. This arrangement was not bad in the summer, but not good in the winter, when the chill factor constantly lingered in the danger zone. Our coldest single day was forty-six below zero, with forty-knot winds, which dropped the chill factor off the charts. My basic maintenance shops, such as engine, hydraulics, and ground power, all had their own facilities. The avionics section had a new and modern building of its own, with extensive electronics test benches. Since one of the munitions we carried was the MB-1 nuclear rocket, known as the Genie, our weapons section was about a quarter of a mile away from the rest of the buildings, and it was very secure, spotlessly clean, and extremely efficient. And hardly anybody bothered us. Due to the harshness of the winter weather, we could usually plan on inspectors from higher headquarters at the end of July or the first of August.

It didn't take very long to take the pulse of the unit and observe some of the areas where improvement was needed. The point of our arrow was the alert barn and the four five-minute-alert birds. That function was in good shape, but there was plenty of slack in the rest of the squadron. Air Defense Command had a rating system that set minimum performance standards and assigned points for everything a squadron did. A recent major inspection by the ADC tactical evaluation team validated command concerns over shortcomings that had been showing up in the squadron's rating index for some time, and resulted in my being assigned as the new squadron commander.

The performance standards set goals for flying and weapons-delivery categories, aircraft-maintenance accomplishments, nuclear weapons inspection, and maintenance reports and the like. Timely and accurate reporting were also factored in, and at the end of each month the numbers were compared between squadrons. You either got an "attaboy" or a "gotcha," with no consideration of whether you were working out of Victorville, California, or Minot, North Dakota.

We had a great fighter interceptor aircraft to fly, a neat physical facility, and plenty of good people. But there was not enough intensity. It was too easy to find excuses for not getting the job done right and on time, and nobody seemed very concerned whether it got done right or not. That made it simple to determine my initial plan of attack. I needed to establish myself as their warrior leader. I got with Capt. Larry Huseman and Capt. Carl Osborne, and we started putting the details together.

Larry had more F-106 flying time than most anybody, and he was an expert in all phases of weapons delivery. Carl was a graduate of the U.S. Air Force Instrument Pilot School, which qualified him as an instrument instructor, and he was a good one. I reminded them that I had been around for awhile in the fighter business and said that from the initial flights in the F-106 that I had flown while at Hamilton, I felt confident that I would soon be a very capable "Six" driver. But that was not enough. I wanted to be the best, and I wanted them to teach me to be the best. We had two tandem-seat F-106s, and I wanted at least one flight a day with one of them as my instructor, with me flying in the back seat, under the hood at all times, or even better, in nasty weather when it was available. I wanted them to run me through every emergency procedure they could think of and make me a true instrument and weapons expert in the F-106.

I finished up by saying, "I want to be good enough in this machine so that you have to worry that with some additional flying time I might be better than you." They took me at my word, and our course of instruction was indeed demanding. I got sick of sweating like a cadet in that black-hole rear cockpit, but it wasn't long before I felt very proficient and could prove it.

SAGE was part of a sophisticated plan to standardize and automate our Cold War air defenses. Way, way up north there was a series of defense early warning radar facilities that formed the DEW line. They were up there to pick up the first indications of penetrations by Russian aircraft or missiles and relay threat information southward to and through Canada to our SAGE centers that stretched across the northern U.S. border. SAGE centers, such as ours at Minot, were large, windowless buildings stressed to withstand a nuke hit. Inside were myriad computers and display scopes operated by weapons controllers who could relay intercept information to our pilots and also to the automatic pilots in our F-106 cockpits.

The book said that once we got the aircraft to the end of the runway, the system could take over and fly the mission without a word of radio contact and with only a few minor pilot actions. It could perform all the necessary engine and airframe controls to intercept an enemy aircraft, launch our missiles, and take us back to landing roll on the runway. Sounds great, and during the entire time I was at Minot I got it to work that way one time.

The use, or nonuse, of automation available to us was one of the core problems within the 5th. I directed my guys to use the SAGE auto function anytime it was available, simply because we were supposed to be trying to validate the system for combat use. It was often not even available, and it almost never worked all the way, which would force us back to voice control, but we needed to try. I had to order my pilots to try, and over time we helped prove the system less than capable, thus allowing new technologies to take over and turn the original SAGE into a dinosaur.

The F-106 autopilot worked well when the pilot used it to chase that elusive dot and keep it in the shrinking circle between radar lock-on and firing. If you were just driving up the tail of a slow-moving target, where last-second steering was not a problem, it was easy to complete the interception manually. But we were working things like snap-up attacks up around fifty thousand feet, and high-angle off intercepts at high speed, and it was often beyond a pilot's capability to manually put the rabbit in the hole and keep it there during those last five seconds before firing. If the autopilot was properly tuned, and if the pilot used it properly, it could turn you upside down, halfway backwards, with your nose twitching up and down, and still get a successful launch when a guy could not react fast enough to do it. Not all pilots completely accepted the system's automatic capability, since pilots had been making manual intercepts forever. It was more fun to try to do it manually, and that was also the macho thing to do. Within the 5th, that had been the accepted thing to do, and if you missed, so be it.

Then, when it got to be the end of the month and the squadron had not accomplished the required training intercepts, well, ho-hum. That was not the only example, but it was a good example of why the 5th was last. I got the pilots together and said, "Starting today, each of you will use autopilot, on every intercept, from lock to fire signal."

I immediately got a, "But colonel, the autopilots don't work very well."

My answer was, "Yeah, you're right. And every time you get down from a flight where it doesn't work, I want you to write it up in detail. You guys have not demanded quality, and it shows. I'm demanding quality of you, and if you demand quality from our support troops, you'll get it. I will not accept less." I turned sharply and strode out the briefing room door as they all popped to attention. Big Ed would have been proud of me.

It worked to some extent, but progress was slow. We had a room in ops that housed a thing called a Nadar viewer. Each F-106 produced a videotape that recorded what the radarscope saw during the countdown to missile firing. All pilots were required to review their intercepts on the Nadar viewer after each training flight, but in the past, whether you hit or missed had not been of overwhelming importance to pilots or their supervisors. I gave my directive about a week to soak in, and then I started to be a regular viewer at the Nadar machine. The word was out that you could never tell when this sombitch would be watching what you had done. I waited until I knew that everyone knew the rules and knew that I would probably be watching. I didn't have to wait long to find what I was looking for. One of my senior captains came up with an obvious manual-control goof. He was right on his target until the five-second-to-go point, when the target bounced and he tried to correct but missed by a bunch.

Nobody said a word as the tape wound down and I asked, "Were you on automatic steering?"

He hesitated for a few seconds before answering, "No, sir."

I nodded and said, "C'mon out in the hall. I want to talk to you for a minute."

I told him he was off the flying schedule for the next two weeks and that I wanted him to run the Nadar room for those two weeks and personally analyze and critique each intercept. Additionally, he was to arrange a daily meeting with our chief of maintenance and our master sergeant who ran the avionics shop to see that they were all on the same course to maximize the performance of all of our systems. At the end of those two weeks, we were truly on our way from last to first in accomplishing our primary air defense mission.

One of the focal points of squadron activity was the alert barn. It was closer to the end of the runway than it was to the rest of the squadron, and it housed the four F-106s that were always on five-minute alert. It was a good-sized building, made mostly of metal. It did sort of look like an oversized barn, with four roll-up doors in front of four compartments, each containing not only a cocked aircraft, but all the support equipment required to quickly launch that fighter. Four pilots and the required support people would pull forty-eight–hour alert tours. When a pilot went on alert, he would strap into the cockpit, and he and his crew chief would go through all the procedures required in preparation for takeoff, right up to punching the start button.

The second floor of the barn was crew country, and we made things as comfortable as possible for the short-time lockups. When the alert Klaxon sounded, day or night, good weather or bad, you never knew if it was for an inbound Russian, a stray aircraft in the wrong place, or a headquarters evaluation. Thus, you always played it for real. You had five minutes to get airborne, but like any time trial, faster was always better. When the Klaxon sounded, it was just like the firehouse, and you could slide down the brass pole, or leap down the stairs, or sprint across the floor, whatever. With the war horn wailing and the tower radio blaring, it was indeed intense. The ballet had been well rehearsed many times, and as the doors were opening, one or more F-106 engines were coming up to power, parachute and seat harnesses were locked, helmets were donned, canopies were shut, chocks and power units were pulled, and wheels were rolling. The alert barn was angled twenty degrees off of the runway heading, with a taxiway leading to the runway, so you just shoved the throttle forward, steered her to the runway heading, and lit the burner as your nose pointed down the runway.

The most popular thing about the alert barn was the kitchen, which was the exclusive domain of Sergeant Matthews, a happy staff sergeant known to all our alert barn patrons simply as "Red." His one-man operation bore absolutely no resemblance to a GI mess hall. I never knew how he managed to do it, certainly not because of the small slush fund we maintained for him, but he constantly came up with steakhouse-type meals, three times a day, 365 days a year. I felt it was my duty to inspect the barn periodically around mealtime, and I was never disappointed.

The 5th Fighter patch featured a green-eyed Canadian lynx with razor-sharp teeth bared, which was the root of the Spitten Kitten label. The circular blue patch background was split by a pair of white lightning bolts and five white stars. the outer white ring identified the unit and included the Latin phrase *Isti Non Penetrabunt* (The Bastards Shall Not Pass). Our pilots wore bright orange flying suits, designed to enhance snow-survival recognition. Our silk scarves, which really do protect against neck chafing, were blue with white stars. The patch and the orange suits were a striking combination. Our flight boots were black and well shined. Additionally, the F-106 demanded that pilot's boots have a two-inch-high domed chrome fitting on each heel. That fitting locked us to a foot retractor on our ejection seats, and the fitting made a tinkling sound every time you put your foot down. Thus, they were known as jingle boots. You could see and hear a F-106 pilot when he entered a room, but that did little to identify our enlisted troops. I came across an advertisement for Russian Cossack-style headgear, and since winter was never far away, I ordered one. They were made of a synthetic material that looked like curly, black lamb's wool, which made them both dapper and practical for head and ear protection on a frigid flight line. I ordered them by the gross, passed them out to everyone, and they were an immediate morale-boosting hit.

One reason the 5th was not in better shape was the almost complete lack of a sound administrative section. The commander's office was a small room on the second floor of the operations building, and administrative things just sort of happened, but mostly they didn't happen. There was a moderate-sized building just outside our squadron area that SAC had abandoned when some of their new facilities were completed. I asked Colonel Zeke Summers if I could have it to transform into an office, and while he said I could have the building, he had no SAC funds to fix it up for us. He did agree to my proposal that we would fix it up on a self-help basis if his air-installations section would give me some lumber, drywall, paint, and the like. I turned the entire project over to Jim Gormley, one of my pilots, and soon we had another first-class addition to the squadron. I hired Senior Master Sgt. "Robbie" Robinson as my first sergeant, and a majority of the past problems with our enlisted folks immediately went away. Robbie and I worked well together, since I was anxious to delegate lots of authority to him, and he was delighted to have the authority to make the changes we both considered necessary. By the time I moved into my new office, I had a pilot as my adjutant, a sharp, old-school first sergeant, a functioning administrative crew, and a secretary. Squadron efficiency took a quantum leap forward.

Winter was setting in for real in our part of the world by the time the Cuban Missile Crisis captured the world's attention. We were already on an increased alert status as we watched the president's speech warning Russia to back off or face our use of military force. Thus, the call on the hot line from ADC shortly after was not a big surprise, but the details were sure a surprise. I was in our squadron operations center and watched the authentication procedure performed as the message came through. I read the message and told our ops chief to authenticate again for a retransmission of my instructions. It took less than a minute for the same message to arrive again. I was to dispatch my four five-minute alert birds to Fargo Municipal Airport immediately, with all armed with Falcon and Genie nuclear missiles, and replace them with four more hot, five-minute birds at Minot. Airlift for twenty ground-crew specialists and support equipment would arrive within three hours. No flight clearances were required, and flights were designated Priority One, which was the president's priority.

Buzz Sawyer, my senior captain, was on five-minute alert with three others from his flight, and I went to the alert barn and briefed them that they were part of history in the making. Fargo was only two hundred miles away, but none of us had ever had any reason to land there, let alone land there with hot nuke weapons. The weather was acceptable, but there was ice reported on the Fargo runway. I looked each one of them in the eyes and asked them individually, "Any questions?"

I got four replies of "No, sir."

"OK, go. And do good work." There is plenty of documentation as to how the Cuban missile crisis played out, but I wonder how many people know that four Spitten Kittens with four hot nukes flew into Fargo Municipal that night, landed on an icy runway they had never seen before, and set up to intercept the Russians should they decide to come at us over the North Pole.

By coincidence, the Spitten Kitten lynx logo was most appropriate to the squadron's current location along the Canadian border. There were plenty of lynx around, not as pets but as predators who specialized in chicken coops. We had given Carl Flagstad of the *Minot Daily News* a ride in our B model, and since he was a long-term friend and supporter, I asked him to run an article to the effect that I wanted a live lynx for a squadron mascot. Before long a gentleman from town offered us a stuffed lynx trophy from a past hunt, but at first that was the only response to the article.

Finally, shortly after our first mean cold snap and snow of the year, a call came in from a farmer who lived about a hundred miles out in the nothing area of North Dakota to say that he had just shot a female lynx who was raiding his chickens. She had survived just long enough to leave a short blood trail in the snow, and he tracked her to two newborn lynx cubs. He had scooped the tiny cubs, one male and one female, out of the snow and wanted to know if we wanted them. I said yes, thanked him profusely, and said we would pick them up as soon as we could get there. I cornered Capt. Dave "Diz" Disbrow, who already had the additional duty as squadron personal flying equipment officer, and said, "Diz, you are now the keeper of the cubs." The roads were not fit for driving, so Dave talked the SAC base operations helicopter guys into flying him out and bringing the cubs in to their new home. We hadn't seen them yet, but we had already named them Spitten and Kitten.

I never surprised Robbie much when I gave him some off-the-wall requirement, and I seldom asked him how he got some of those tasks accomplished, but he never failed to produce the desired results. I said, "Robbie, let's take a little walk around the area. We need a place for two live lynx to hang out." As we walked and wondered what would suit Spitten and Kitten, we passed the blank eastern wall of the ops building that was bordered by a twenty-foot-wide strip of grass that sloped gently down to the road. That was to be the site, and Robbie's only other question was, " How big you want it, boss?" About an hour later, Robbie and another master sergeant from the base were doing some sketching, and before it got dark, the jackhammers were busting up frozen dirt. Two days later, the side of the ops building sported a fancy cage that was fifteen feet deep, forty feet long, and twelve feet high in the front. The top inclined upward and back toward the wall to accommodate a goodly portion of the trunk and upper branches of a tree. Other décor included a large doghouse, rocks, and bushes, and that is where Spitten and Kitten thrived and grew.

Red insured that our supply of raw chicken breasts and thighs was adequate. Feeding the lynx was not difficult; you just tossed the chicken their way. The once–a–day feeding was a scheduled task for the operations duty sergeant, but caution was mandatory. When the lynx sensed food, nature took over and unhinged their jaws, much like a snake, and they rotated past vertical, revealing long and very sharp teeth that snapped shut with amazing force. Somehow, one of the duty sergeants forgot the rules one evening and tried to hand them their food, and if it had not been for some excellent work by our medics, he would have lost a large part of a hand.

I got to know Spitten and Kitten quite well. A good squadron commander could always find things that need to be done after hours and on weekends when the office was empty and quiet, and I often spent thinking time or break time with my lynx. Too much noise or confusion made them nervous, but when it was quiet, and as they got used to me, they would meet me when I walked up to the cage, and they would sit and cock their heads to listen to me. When they were a little older, I could bring them into the building on occasion, and as long as they were well fed and not close to feeding time, I could pet them and get Spitten to lie calmly on my shoulder. Kitten was more nervous, and I never could get her up on my shoulder. But their favorite time was playing catch with me. I had a red rubber ball for summer, and I used snowballs in the winter. I would call them to the front of the cage and show them the ball, then I would throw it up on the inclined slope of the chain-link roof over the tree branches, where it would hesitate, then roll back down the incline. Talk about interceptors: those cats were uncanny. They were lightning fast, and a ten-foot leap was routine. They never both chased along the same path. Sometimes they were there before the ball hit, and the winner was the one who got to the ball first. The instant one of them got to the ball, the other one backed off and headed back for the front of the cage. The perfect pass was when one of them would get to the impact point before or as the ball hit, stick a paw through an opening in the chain link, and knock or throw the ball back down the incline to me. The first time I saw that happen, I wasn't sure that I had really seen it, but the more often we played, the better they got. One winter Sunday afternoon, I got AJ to stand across the street and record a game with our home movie camera just to prove that it was real.

Things were changing in the 5th. The "who cares?" attitude among pilots was disappearing under kicks from me and from peer pressure. Baby steps completed, I still had gut problems to solve. Once a week we had a scheduling meeting, where the ops people said what they wanted to do for the next week and the maintenance people said what they could support for the next week. The result was a printed document forecasting the events of the week to come. ADC evaluated what a squadron scheduled versus what tasks it accomplished, and the 5th had taken it in the shorts month after month. Major Pat Green, as ops officer and thus number two in the squadron, was used to dominating those meetings and making unreasonable demands for more aircraft per day than maintenance could provide. Internal ill will was obvious. First Lt. Karl "Norsky" Norris was the maintenance officer when I came on board. Norsky, who regularly flew one of our T-33s as target on training missions, got along well with most everyone except Pat Green. They clashed at the weekly meetings, and though the lieutenant fought fiercely, the major prevailed, and the ratio of accomplished missions to scheduled missions continued to be subpar. I added a new dimension, because I attended those meetings and did not like what I saw. I had a long discussion with Pat and noticed a slight improvement, but suddenly Norsky got hurry-up orders to go to Panama. Panama's terror regime was in full swing at that time, and we could never get any details, but Norsky's body came back to the United States in a closed casket within a few months.

Chief Warrant Officer Dick Dalton, who had been Norsky's assistant, took over maintenance. As skilled and dedicated as Dick was, he was no match for Pat, who even embarrassed me in a scheduling meeting. That was not the place for me to lower the hammer, but I could feel the redness rising past my ears. I said, "Gentlemen, let's reschedule this meeting for tomorrow at the same time."

As the troops filed out, I beckoned Pat toward the front door, where the blue maintenance van was parked. I guess I must have noticed that Dick was sitting on a side-mounted bench in the rear of the van, shaking his head and making notes, but it failed to register. I broke a cardinal rule that says if you are going to ream someone out, do it in private. I sat sideways on the driver's seat and motioned Pat to sit on the side bench as I launched into my career-high ass-chewing. I outdid any West Point plebe-takedown lecture I had ever given, as I went through the list: "Who is in charge here?" "What do you think I've been trying to do all these months?" "Do you understand the gravity of ignoring my request for common sense and the don't-care attitude as regards being the duds of ADC?" I took a deep breath, squinted, and barked, "Dismissed." As a startled Pat Green popped to attention and saluted and left, I recognized that Dick was still there, shaking his head in the back of the van. My blood pressure was still too high for further conversation, so I just turned to Dick, said, "You too," and thumbed him toward the van door. You're not supposed to chew ass that way, but I imagine the word got to most of my maintainers that they had a CO who appreciated them. They served me well until the day I left.

But in a multifaceted operation on a base of that size, it would be tough to impossible not to run into individuals who don't see things your way. Unfortunately, with all the good guys on our SAGE Sector staff, they had a deputy for operations (DO) who was a colonel who wore wings but didn't fly airplanes, and did kibitz those who did. Since everything in the squadron had been upbeat and improving since I arrived, the DO and I had made only minimal contact, and thus had minimal conflicts. That changed abruptly when my people were involved in a dreadful fire in the enlisted housing area.

Frank was an extremely intelligent tech sergeant in our avionics section who could skim through highly technical literature and complicated schematic drawings with ease. The F-106 had the most complex computer-oriented radar, flight-control, and weapons systems in the U.S. inventory, and Frank's knowledge and dedication made him an outstanding troubleshooter and instructor. On top of that, he was a nice gentleman, mild-mannered and shy to the point that his many awards and commendations seemed to almost bother him. Frank was a bachelor, and on a Friday evening, after a long, strenuous work week, he offered to babysit the three infant sons (all under the age of three) of a fellow tech sergeant so the sergeant and his wife could enjoy dinner and an evening out at the noncommissioned officers' club. With the three infants asleep in three cribs in a common upstairs bedroom, Frank slumped into an overstuffed chair, lit a cigarette, and fell asleep.

Frank awoke with flames all around him. He rushed to the stairs to get the children, but the old wooden barracks-style structure was erupting, and the flames scorched him, beat him back, and choked him. The swift response of the fire crews from only a few blocks away was still too late, and the three infants were dead from smoke inhalation. The first firefighters on the scene found Frank slumped by the front door and weeping.

I was at home and heard the sirens, and then the phone rang with the emergency alert notification. It was a sickening scene, but I knew I had better take it all in for the inquiries that were bound to follow. The kids' room with the three white silhouettes on the black sheets did it to me, and I had to get some fresh air. Who should I see outside but the sector DO, making profound statements about punishment and the responsible party. I couldn't handle that and confronted him with, "Hey, colonel, let's not be making accusations about my troops until you get all the facts."

Yes, there were all sorts of investigations, and throughout them the sector DO was on one side and I was on the other. On the air force side, our air division in Kansas City and ADC investigated, and on the civilian side the city of Minot and the state of North Dakota investigated. The facts of the fire were quite clear, but there were many views on intent and what was to be done about Frank. My position was that it had been a tragic accident, and at each hearing I praised Frank's duty performance, personality, and dedication. On the other extreme were military cries, to my disgust, of court-martial on multiple charges up to manslaughter, and some civilian cries in the same tone.

After much hullabaloo, it was ruled an accident, and we hastened to keep a heartbroken Frank as busy as possible, which was easy. Getting him back up to his normal emotional level was tougher. When Christmas rolled around, the base chaplains held a nondenominational midnight mass, which usually drew a packed house. I had some seats blocked off up toward the front, and we waited to enter until the place was almost full. I walked the length of the aisle with AJ, Mark, and Sheila, and Frank carried our infant daughter Maureen. That worked out quite well.

Exercises and tactical evaluations were a recurring event for all ADC squadrons. They varied in length, but you could usually figure on being in a practice war for about a week. If it was a tactical evaluation, which we could expect yearly, a team of ADC full-time evaluators would descend on you and start with a day or two of inspecting every niche of the squadron as the simulated war scenario developed and the alert level went up. We also had more frequent exercises that were broader based, involving many units, and with less individual unit inspection. Your performance in either case was an important indicator of your readiness for the real thing, and though it had been awhile since the 5th had been highly regarded, we were changing that.

There was always a boost in adrenaline as the exercise built up to the first scramble, and some things were fun and some were not. Scrambling in the middle of a cold night is not always fun, but that was often the best time for the northern lights, and sky dancing with them was indeed a kick. Often, ADC would bring you up to a high state of alert then leave you sitting there. One early morning about 2 they had our entire squadron on cockpit alert for a possible flush. When the word came through to flush, that meant inbound nuke missiles were on the way, so get everything airborne as fast as you can. The first one to the end of the runway was the leader. I was in the number-one spot closest to the runway as we lined up along the ramp in the inky black night, with light, blowing snow. My crew chief had already helped to hoist me into the cockpit, clumsy in long johns; black sweater; light cotton flight suit; a lightweight, fur-trimmed parka whose hood was folded back behind my hardhat; and that huge, black, hand-knitted wool scarf that I had gotten from a Red Cross lady as I boarded the USS *Rushville Victory* for Europe in early 1946. The only things I could move were my arms, legs, and head. The canopy was open, and I noted that at 2:23 a.m. she was twenty-three below zero, with a twenty-seven-mile-an-hour breeze from the northwest blowing right at us. The falling snow was mixing with the stirred-up snow already on the ground, making everything from the ramp up to one hundred feet look like a white pillow fight, while the ramp itself was covered with constantly swirling circles of snow dust.

My maintenance guys had done what was almost impossible, and we had twenty-six of twenty-six F-106s ready to go. Happily, our cockpit radios barked, "Flush!" and twenty-five Spitten Kittens fired up. Back in the second row, one of the cold-soaked birds that had been sitting in an open-air parking shelter couldn't accept the thousands of pounds of air pressure on the starter mechanism, and that bird was silently spraying red hydraulic fluid in all directions. Canopies came down with minimum delay to cut off the wind, and I pulled my scarf down from my face to replace it with a frigid rubber oxygen mask. I was first off, and by the time I pulled my gear up, I was above the swirling snow, climbing in burner for twenty thousand feet, looking northwest toward the North Pole, with not a light or star in sight. Twenty-four burner blasts later, we were all airborne in ADC record-setting time, and I doubt that anyone in the local area slept through that.

In March the squadron passed a milestone of over twenty thousand flying hours in three years without a single aircraft accident. That achievement brought a visit from Maj. Gen. Webster, the number-two general in ADC, with a fancy plaque, pictures, and newspaper coverage. Since the general came and went early in the day, AJ and I, having been tightly tied to the squadron for almost a year, took off for a three-day break in Minneapolis. When we checked in at the hotel, I had a message waiting to call Capt. Tom McCarthy, my flying safety officer. Larry Huseman had flown a test hop in 014 and had bellied her in on the runway when the nose gear extended, but the main landing gear would not come down. The underside was severely damaged, and that was the end of that safety record. AJ and I shrugged and continued with our weekend.

The officers' club was our social hub, since there wasn't anything to compete with it for hundreds of miles. Once every month, one of the squadrons on base would be scheduled to host a Saturday night party, and when it was our turn we put on Gay Paree Night. We decked the lynx out with ribbons and rhinestone collars and put them in a small cage in the lobby of the club with a sign advertising it as the Parisian Cathouse. Six of our pilots had an amazingly good can-can line, and their falsie-laden costumes and their dancing were the hit of the night.

One of the fun things we did in the squadron was race go-carts. We had an improvised course set up on the roads and ramp in front of ops, and it got plenty of use for practice during off-duty hours and for races on Sunday afternoons. As more people bought carts, the ops course became less practical, and we got some plans for a real course. Since there was a mile of flat North Dakota nothing behind the orderly room, there was plenty of room for the course. There was even room for a rough par-three golf course that Maj. Bob Smith, my new number-one maintenance officer, wanted to put in. I turned Robbie loose on it. About the time we got the twisting five-eighths of a mile race track bladed out, a team for Peter Kewit, an engineering firm, was working on a large SAC project that included laying asphalt on several roads. Each day there would be partial truckloads of asphalt left over, and the contractor would take the excess to the dump. They agreed to not only dump it on our track, but to finish and trim it for us. We put a kids' playground in between the track and the golf course and opened it up to everyone on base, and it got plenty of action.

The next time ADC tried us on an alert and a flush exercise, it got a bit dicey. They blasted us off just as the sun was coming up, so we still got to be sure that nobody on base overslept, but there was a lot more lower-cloud cover than forecast, and there was more nasty-looking stuff blowing in from the west. By the time we got everyone airborne and identified so headquarters could verify that we had again done good work, the cloud-to-runway clearance (the "ceiling" in aircraft ter-minology) had deteriorated to two hundred feet or less in heavy rain. I told SAGE and the base tower to start recovering us while we still had plenty of fuel. I was the last one to check in with approach control, and by the time I got on approach it was less than two hundred feet in heavy rain. More importantly, I drew an approach controller who must have been tired or confused. I flew his pattern as directed, with no problems or unusual corrections as regarded headings or altitudes, but on final approach, as I descended through one hundred feet with noth-ing in sight but weather, I was already on the go-around before he almost screamed, "Go around! Abort! Go around!"

As I got the gear up again, I called him and said, "Hey, I'm get-ting a little skosh on fuel. Let's make this next one a good one." He tried too hard and cut corners on the pattern as he attempted to get me lined up on final faster than he should have. He didn't have me lined up with the runway and was still giving me heading corrections as I caught a glimpse of the runway through a hole at one hundred feet, but he had me about fifteen degrees off course. At least I knew that at that instant there was some cloud-to-runway clearance somewhere below one hundred feet. I called again, "Well, now we got a problem. I'm way below minimum fuel, so you got to make this one right, 'cause I can't hack another go-around. Just sit back, take a deep breath, and line me up right." I quit looking at the fuel indicator.

He steered me around a nice, smooth pattern, and we were locked on heading and altitude on final as I hit one hundred feet. I just kept going down until there was the runway up ahead, and I don't think I was more than twenty-five feet above it. I pushed the throttle forward, and she flamed out. Ever so gently I eased in a little back pressure, and she stalled as I crossed the overrun and fell to the runway. I coasted about halfway down the strip, and as I rolled to a stop my guys were there with a tug to pull me into our parking area. As we stopped and they put a ladder on the canopy rail, I looked past the nose of my aircraft and my blood pressure started to rise. Walking toward the ladder was the pilot-rated but nonflying sector DO, and to his left, one step back (perfect military etiquette), was his timid captain flying-safety officer, who had declined my offer to check out in the six. As my feet hit the concrete, the colonel was in my face with, "Why didn't you land the first time?"

I glanced past him and looked at Dick Dalton, and my crew chief, and the guys who had just tugged me in, and that glance saved the rest of my air force career. I was ready to deliver a knuckle sandwich to a ranking officer, in front of witnesses, and then I saw it in a flash. That bastard wanted my scalp because I had insulted him by defending Frank, and my guys knew it better than I did. I took a deep breath and replied, "The runway was not in sight at one hundred feet, sir."

The captain seemed to feel that he needed to speak and asked, "Well how about the second pass?"

I stretched my shoulders, looked down on him, and thought, hell, he wouldn't even be worth hitting. "You know, captain, it's tough to hit the runway if you're crossing it at fifteen degrees off course."

That's when my crew chief grew to about nine foot tall as he pushed up to me with the Form One, purposely distracting me, and said, "How about filling this out for me, colonel."

The DO was still strutting as he spun on his heel and said to the safety officer, "I'll expect a full investigative report of this on my desk without delay."

The safety officer waited an appropriate second, and as he spun into position, he replied with a hearty, "Yes, sir." They did indeed investigate all the details, including reviewing the tapes, reviewing the end-of-runway weather observations, and talking to the controllers. As a result, they proposed that I be nominated for an award. I told them to forget it; I would not accept it.

A few weeks later came the good news that ADC had decided that they had too many SAGE sector headquarters, and while the console operators at Minot would remain, the Minot sector staff was history. The 5th Fighter Interceptor Squadron was now the property of the Great Falls sector, located at Malmstrom Air Force Base in Montana. Some good friends moved out, but I would be privileged to never again see their DO. Once again, I was as close as you can get in the air force to being an independent operator, with first-class equipment and people. That's good duty.

CHAPTER 14

THE KILLER SEAT

Since we were now beating ADC's minimum requirements in all categories, I was able to sell a deal to our air division headquarters. We arranged for each squadron that had exceeded the performance requirements for the previous month to be excused from five-minute alert and all other headquarters-directed activities one day each week. One of the other squadrons would cover the free squadron's alert responsibilities, and in return we would have a double responsibility one day each week. Everyone looked forward to Thursday, our free day. It was a chance to catch up or even get ahead on your responsibilities, and for my pilots a chance to fly formation. All fighter pilots like to fly formation, because it is another chance to prove that you're the best. Because of the difference in missions, you fly a lot more formation in a tactical squadron than you do in an interceptor squadron. It was an even greater challenge to my guys, as they had an ex-Thunderbird leader to lead them. Maintenance could always use the free time to clear deferred discrepancies, so I took however many aircraft they could comfortably provide each Thursday, and we flew formation. Be it four, six, or eight ships, everyone wanted to be included, and I rotated pilots each week. We would go away from the field and practice for about thirty minutes, then come back and put on a mini air show over the flight line. One of the good things about Minot was the fact that you didn't have much competition for use of the airstrip.

A little formation flying practice turned out to be a good idea, as we were ordered to Colorado Springs to perform the flyover in conjunction with the Air Force Academy graduation presided over by President Kennedy. I did not get to lead that one, as I was tabbed to brief the president on ADC interceptor squadrons. I had to report to ADC headquarters two days early to dry-run the presentation for General Lee, the commander of ADC. The headquarters brought in people from all over the command and set up a large number of exhibits in a hangar-like building. The president and his entourage were to enter the building at one end and walk past the exhibits, with the president receiving a short briefing at each exhibit. I was the last exhibit in line, and after my turn a group of significant Canadian politicians were scheduled to meet with the president. My exhibit was limited to me, wearing my orange flying suit, blue starred silk scarf, Spitten Kitten patch, and shiny jingle boots.

General Lee was uptight from the moment we arrived, and he personally controlled the dry runs and monitored the stopwatch. At first, each briefer was to speak for two minutes. Someone revised how long the President wanted to spend there, and our time was cut down to one minute. With each dry run our time was cut further, until by the last dry run on the day before the show we were down to thirty-nine seconds each. How much can you cover about all the interceptor squadrons in the command in thirty-nine seconds?

The next day the president was late, which I guess was not unusual. When he turned the corner to head my way, there were some radar displays between us, and they obviously did not interest him, as he waved politely to the briefers and walked up to me.

The group behind the president included a one-star general and a nervous civilian, both with walkie-talkies, and they were frantically twirling their right index fingers aloft, signaling me to hurry up. I was told later that the Canadian dignitaries had a hissy about being kept waiting. I was standing at attention as the president approached me, and I realized that he was a larger man that I had imagined him to be. I also thought that the sharp black silk suit he was wearing probably cost at least two months' worth of my salary.

He stuck out his hand and said, "Hi, my name's Jack Kennedy."

As we exchanged a firm handshake, I replied, "Hi, my name's Jack Broughton." As I launched into my thirty-nine–second special, General Lee was positioned between and behind us, and his face was flushed. The president interrupted me with a question, and I quickly dumped my canned act and answered him. General Lee's face turned beet red, and his eyes narrowed. I had discarded his script. One question led to another, and I was surprised by how much the president knew about fighters and weapons systems. Pretty soon I was standing at ease and flying with my hands like I was talking to another pilot in a briefing room. As soon as General Lee saw that the president was enjoying the conversation, he was all smiles. Air force Secretary Eugene M. Zuckert was also in on our conversation, which was already over five minutes long. Pointing at my patch, he asked what the Latin meant, and when I said, "The bastards shall not pass," it brought a chuckle of approval. The secretary glanced at his watch and made a thinly-veiled reference to a very special and personal appointment that the president had in White Sands, New Mexico.

That also generated a chuckle as the President said, "Yeah, I guess we better get going." We shook hands again, and his group went behind the closed door to meet the Canadians.

I hustled back to Minot, because we were well aware of the fact that we were due for an ADC tactical evaluation, which we guessed might come any time after the Colorado Springs trip. They hit us almost immediately, and it was a tough, week-long shakedown. We did great, and set a few ADC performance records in the process, which was a dramatic change from their last visit.

In those days, the air force had a program called IRAN, which stood for inspect and repair as necessary. It was accomplished at the various large maintenance and supply depots, and the work consisted of major modifications that would not be practical at squadron level. While the depot technicians, who were almost exclusively career civil servants, were taking the aircraft apart, they were also supposed to correct any problems they found along the way. In the last half of 1963, we had to run our birds through an IRAN called Project Red Glow. We knew you needed to get the upgrades accomplished, but we also knew that when we got our birds back, we could count on a bunch of shakedown test hops and local maintenance to get our birds back into good shape. I became concerned when the birds we were getting back from Red Glow started to do more weird things than usual. With hindsight, project Red Glow probably should have been called Project Red Light.

The first red light went on during that unforgettable wild ride that interrupted my August flight to Malmstrom. Since we had found and fixed the depot oversight that had allowed an improperly installed heat exchanger to put me in a thirty thousand foot rudder exercise stall we didn't recognize it as an indicator of a deadly series of similar goofs that was to follow.

Captain Wayne Wendt was my flight-test maintenance officer, which meant that he was partly operationally oriented and partly maintenance oriented. The third of October was a very clear and comfortable day. Wayne had gone to the depot in Sacramento in the back seat of one of our T-33s, where he picked up one of our birds coming out of Red Glow and brought it back to Minot late that afternoon. Our maintenance folks had a local test hop waiting for him, and he needed a half-hour of nighttime to fill out his annual requirements. Therefore, he took off before sunset, went through the flight-test requirements, and stayed airborne for another thirty minutes after dark. As he came over the end of the runway at a thousand feet to break into his 360-degree landing pattern, the control tower advised him that his wing-tip running lights were not on. As he broke left, his nose dropped more than usual, and his angle of bank continued to increase until he was almost inverted. After 130 degrees of turn, the aircraft struck the ground, exploded and Wayne was killed.

There wasn't enough left to give us any clues of what might have happened, so Larry Huseman and I decided to pursue a "what if" drill so we could perhaps give the accident board some leads. We brain- stormed for all we were worth, and nothing made sense until we got to the tower's call about Wayne's red and green running lights. What if right after breaking left he looked down at his left cockpit console for two or three seconds to check the position of the running light switch? Where would he have been, and what would he have seen when he raised his head? Larry went to the crash site and stood at the point of impact while I cranked up an F-106, got airborne, and kept her in burner to take the fuel down to about what we figured Wayne would have had left. I entered traffic, broke left, and looked down at the light switch while counting thousand one, thousand two, thou- sand three. As I raised my head, I was frightened. I was going past ver- tical with my pitot boom pointing directly at Larry, who was waving his arms wildly, trying to signal, "Pull up, you idiot." It took a hefty pull on the stick to change direction, and I still gave Larry a pretty good buzz job.

We had not pinned down the cause of the accident, but in our minds we had only two questions: Did Wayne lose track of where he was? Did the depot modification gremlins that sent me straight up send Wayne straight down? The accident board didn't do any better, as they listed the primary cause as undetermined, with possible causes of malfunction of undetermined components of the flight-control system or pilot disorientation.

On the nineteenth of December, I had a late-morning meeting scheduled, so I had ops put me on the early-morning mission. At 6:00 a.m. in the pitch dark, at thirty below zero with blowing snow, it really did feel early. I was scheduled to fly 006, but as we were finishing our pre-flight briefing, maintenance called my bird out for radar problems. Bill Richardson, one of my flight leaders, was scheduled to fly 017 on the early shift. Thus, I explained my schedule conflict to him, saying I'd like to take his bird and move him to a later mission, which was fine with Bill. As we were suiting up in our winter survival gear, Sergeant Mansfield, my favorite avionics crew chief, came bounding by to say "balls six" was back in and ready to fly. I switched again, gave 017 back to Bill, and we all launched per the original schedule. I went north toward Winnipeg, and Bill went south toward Dennison, North Dakota, as we looked for our practice targets.

The F-106 had an internal weapons bay where we carried our four Falcon guided missiles and our single, fat, undependable Genie nuclear rocket. An instant before firing time, a door in the belly rolled internally to the open position, the rails extended, and the selected missiles fired. The system was activated by air pressure of four thousand pounds per square inch that was stored in an internally mounted fiberglass flask that looked like an oversize beach ball.

Bill was working against a T-33 target, which was moving through seventeen thousand feet, when he locked onto it for his first practice run. As the fire-control system counted down to the fire signal and the door sequence started, the high-pressure air bottle exploded and blew four thousand pounds of random force through the innards of 017. Everything quit—the engine, hydraulics, electrical, radio—and she started to spiral down. Bill undoubtedly pulled the ejection seat handles many times, but the seat did not fire; just like it had not fired for the previous twelve guys we had already killed, as the F-106 ejection system maintained its zero-percent success rate. Twelve tries, twelve dead guys, and my friend Bill Richardson, flying the F-106 I had planned to fly, was rolling the dice as number thirteen.

Bill undoubtedly tried the backup method of activating the seat, but he was attempting a physical impossibility. The backup was a triangular nylon strap loop that lay on the cockpit floor between the pilot's feet. The book said to reach down between your feet, grab the loop, and pull the loop and connected mechanism straight up to attempt foot-pan retraction and enable further seat sequencing. Try sitting in a straight-back chair that is high enough so that your thighs and knees are parallel to the floor. Next assume that there is a backpack parachute between you and the back of the chair and that you have a nylon strap over each shoulder and a broad nylon belt across your lap, which lock you in position. Now drop your hands to the floor between your legs, grab your toes and pull them up and back. You can't get there from here. Zero One Seven descended silently through two and a half circles before she impacted in the frozen, swirling snow and disintegrated.

The tow pilot notified the Minot tower on guard channel, so we were all alerted, as was some listening clod who hastened to call the local radio station so the word could go out immediately and frighten all the wives. I rode the burner back to Minot and put on my blues and overcoat, as Bob Smith rounded up a maintenance team to join the medics on the scene. The chaplain and flight surgeon joined me as I drove to the housing area. The radio was indeed full of the news, but they didn't know who was down. Joan Richardson and her two very young daughters had been making Christmas cookies, and as I parked and walked to the front door, she appeared with a little girl clinging to each side of her apron.

She pointed to her chest and mouthed, "Me?"

I just nodded and said, "Yes." I still have trouble handling even the memory of that one.

Later, the accident investigation would determine that another case of a hot-air leak had indeed been allowing high-temperature air to weaken the air flask in 017, in turn causing it to explode and tear the guts out of the aircraft. They also proved that Bill had attempted to eject, with complete failure of the ejection system.

The post-accident formalities mixed poorly with jingle bells. While parts and pieces were still being recovered and sorted, my chief egress sergeant and his helpers began cycling through all of our F-106s to disassemble the ejection seats to be sure that they were free of FOD and were rigged to specifications. On Christmas Eve at 10:30 p.m., we were all tired and concerned as we agreed that what we really needed was a new ejection seat for the F-106 before we killed more pilots. My egress guys would have just kept on working, but I shut them down, wished them Merry Christmas, and headed for the house to wash my face and head for the midnight service. As I stepped out into the cold night, the sky was crystal clear, cloudless, and very dark. I did a double take as I looked up and saw a single, very bright star directly overhead. I just stared at that star for a while, shook my head, and told myself I wasn't even going to think about the F-106 or ejection seats until after Christmas, but I lied.

Then on December 29, ten days after we lost Bill Richardson, one of our trusty machines, cruising at forty-two thousand feet at Mach 1.15, responded to a pilot thumb tap on the stick-mounted trim tab by rolling to inverted, nose down, and diving straight down for seven thousand feet before repenting and recovering to straight and level all by itself. I thought of that old wives' tale the U.S. Air Force Test Pilot's School guys used to relate that out-of-commission aircraft sulked in the hangar thinking of ways they could kill you.

The following day, Dewey Berg shot a practice low approach and at one hundred feet started to go around to reenter the traffic pattern for a full-stop landing. His bird started to porpoise and turned toward the housing area. I just happened to be walking between ops and maintenance in time to view what could have been a wipeout of the Minot housing area. I met a shaken Dewey as he climbed out. He told me he was just flying normally when the bird took over the controls, porpoised, and then gave the controls back to him. That was it for me.

I got on the phone to both my sector and division commanders, explained the situation, and said I sought their concurrence in grounding my squadron, except for my four hot, five-minute alert birds. Obviously, in case of an air-defense emergency alert, that plan would be dropped, and we would go back to max effort. They agreed, and my maintenance guys and I began to figure out how we were going to tear our aircraft apart to inspect them.

Bob Smith established a detailed inspection system to probe every facet of our birds. As we moved the first of them through the inspection cycle, the results were startling. The FOD situation was bad, and we collected and documented a sizeable rogue's gallery of objects capable of causing accidents. We found things ranging from nuts and bolts in flight-control systems to screwdrivers, clamps, and wrenches from nose to tail. We even came up with a depot-labeled rivet bucking bar and an unopened package of rivet-anchored fasteners under one ejection seat. Both of our two-seat F-106s had the same heat damage that shot Bill Richardson down, and multiple hot-air routing connectors were bad in other aircraft. In a short time, on four of our aircraft we identified major discrepancies that were basically catastrophic accidents waiting to happen. Despite the fact that I kept all my headquarters in the loop and apprised of our progress, ADC was extremely unhappy that my inspection was taking so much time and effort. They seemed to consider the inspection an embarrassment. That is when I was summoned to Colorado Springs to defend my actions before Gen. Herbert Thatcher, commander of ADC, and that is when my future in the air force was very much in doubt.

As I flew back to Minot after my abrupt dismissal by the general and his staff, my concentration was not the greatest. One of the goofy thoughts that floated by was that we had gone thirty-two days straight with the temperature never getting as high as zero. When I coasted into the parking area and popped my canopy open, my crew chief happily informed me that the temperature had momentarily peaked at one degree above zero. I gave everyone the afternoon off. With the squadron quiet, I did a bunch of thinking. I kept coming to the conclusion that a dedicated gent like General Thatcher could hardly have amassed those stars and risen to that level of command by simply ignoring problems—but. Then my confidence was quickly restored.

I got a message from ADC directing me to report to the Air Materiel Depot in Mobile for a conference on the F-106 ejection seat. I was scheduled to brief on my contention that we needed a new seat, so I rounded up Dave Disbrow with his winter flight gear, and my ejection seat noncom, and a complete seat minus the explosive charges, and we headed south to Alabama. Chairing the meeting was Maj. Gen. W. T. "Red" Hudnell, the depot commander, and attending it was a wide range of military and civilian experts, including a senior executive engineer from Hughes Aircraft, the maker of the seat. I briefed on the seat's fatality record and zero success rate. My audience was extremely attentive and very much into the problem, but all of them, including General Hudnell, were obviously disturbed by the repeated interruptions of the Hughes executive implying that I did not know what I was talking about. I finished up by addressing the general with, "General Hudnell, we need a new F-106 ejection seat. This one is a piece of junk that has never worked. It has killed the equivalent of over half of a squadron of F-106 pilots—everyone who has had to try and use it—and the emergency backup system is a farce that physically will not work."

Before the general could reply, the livid Hughes engineer was on his feet, talking way too loud and being way too pushy in trying to take over the general's meeting. I stepped away from my briefing spot, walked up to the general, and said, "General, if you'll give us a ten-minute break, I'll give you a demonstration of what I'm talking about."

He agreed, announced the break, and beckoned to two of his staff, who joined him as they left the room. Dave, dressed in flight gear, and our egress specialist were waiting in an adjacent room. We moved a rectangular GI table into the center of the conference room and placed the unarmed seat on the table. When the general reconvened the session, we had Dave don his winter parka, scarf, and gloves. We helped him up and into the seat, and strapped him into the shoulder restraints and seat belt as he put on his helmet and oxygen mask.

I looked around and said, "Gentlemen, here's a simulation of how Capt. Bill Richardson and twelve other F-106 pilots have been killed." Turning toward Dave, I said loudly, "You just had an explosion behind you, your engine has flamed out, and you've got a fire-warning light. Bail out! Bail out!" Dave dropped his hands to the base of the seat, pulled the ejection handles up and squeezed the triggers, and paused. Then he repeatedly squeezed the triggers.

Again, I barked loudly, "Dave, your engine is dead, the cockpit is hot and filling with smoke, and you're sinking like a rock. The ground is getting close. Go for the emergency bailout lanyard!" Dave reached for the floor between his legs and couldn't grasp the nylon lanyard. I continued, even louder, "Stretch, Dave, pull that lanyard up or you're dead." He was very honestly straining mightily against the harness and barely hooked the lanyard with his fingertips. "Pull, Dave, pull! Lift your toes up to your waist! You're falling through two thousand feet!" Again Dave gave it all he had, but it was a physical impossibility. "You're going through a thousand feet. Manually dump the canopy." He raised his right hand, pulled back on an imaginary jettison handle, and was pushed farther back against the seat by the rush of air. "Pull! Pull!" Dave strained, but his feet never came up.

I shrugged and said, "Forget it," as Dave released the lanyard and sat back motionless in the seat. I paused, turned, and said, "That's it, gentlemen. Any questions?" There was not a sound. I walked to where the Hughes executive was sitting and said, "You want to try it?" He simply shook his head no. The general excused us, saying we were clear to return to Minot, and told his staff to take an hour break and return ready for further discussion. From General Hudnell's smile and handshake, I got the feeling that we had done good work.

By March our inspection program was finally winding down, and we were flying our birds back into shape. It had taken a lot longer than we expected, but we had found and corrected a lot more problems than anyone thought we would, and we had saved aircraft and very probably lives in the process. We prepared a very detailed and revealing report on the project and launched it through channels, with some strong recommendations for change.

The snow had melted, and William Tell was on the horizon. William Tell was the competition to determine the worldwide top air-defense-weapons squadron. I flew an F-106 to division headquarters near Kansas City for a meeting where we went over all the details of the competition. It was late afternoon when we finished with the meeting, and it was just getting dark by the time I took off, heading north with an assigned altitude of thirty thousand feet. As I got airborne, I got a call from the tower requesting that I make the best possible time to my assigned altitude and directing that I report every five thousand feet. I left her in burner, accelerated, pulled up, and started calling five, ten, fifteen, and so on, with only a momentary pause between transmissions.

As I called thirty, an airline pilot came on and said, "That must be fun."

As I answered, "You bet it is," I was feeling like I was the hottest thing around. It was a relatively short flight to Minot, so traveling north I actually made up daylight before I started a high-speed descent. I entered the clouds about twenty thousand, and when I got down around twelve thousand I was treated to the world's greatest psychedelic light show. The clouds started alternately breaking and reforming as I descended, and some of them were white, some gray, and some black. The sun was still on the horizon near Minot, and clear of the clouds, the sky was a bright yellow. As I raced along at close to Mach 1.0, my entire field of vision was filled with an instantaneously changing panorama of darts and flashes of color combinations I had never seen before. It was like dancing up close with the northern lights, and the scene etched itself on my memory to last at least these forty years. I was almost sorry to break free of the bottom layers and see Minot straight ahead. It made me pause as I thought, "Well, maybe I'm not the hottest thing around."

I picked our team of pilots, ground-support personnel, and controllers for the meet, and we worked diligently to get ready. Things went smoothly until we got to what amounted to the F-106 semifinals, which were held at Richards-Gebaur Air Force Base outside of Kansas City. We were allowed to bring six pilots and six aircraft, which I had to cut to four and four before the bell rang. That should have been easy, but it wasn't.

Larry Huseman, my top dog regarding weapons systems, was having a radar problem that was supposedly minor, so my decision was whether to stick with Larry and his aircraft or to pick another aircraft and pilot combination. We all wanted to be the shooters but while he didn't talk about it, Larry had a special desire to compete. Larry had arthritis, the killer kind, and it was moving rapidly. His left knee looked like a basketball, and he had been grounded a couple of times for the most advanced treatments the air force had to offer, but he was getting worse, not better. My gut feeling was that he could well be on his last hurrah as a fighter pilot. At midday I declared Larry and his aircraft as part of our flight of four. By the time we went on five-minute alert for competition that night, giant thunderstorms ringed the base, and Larry's aircraft was boiling fire-control coolant and spewing froth onto the ramp while Larry and his crew sweated over it.

I was sitting number one on five-minute alert and was a bit surprised when they scrambled me at four minutes after midnight. The thunderstorms had let loose throughout the area, and with the ramp and taxiways awash, I could hardly see to taxi. My radar was functioning perfectly and looked exceptionally sharp and clear in my darkened cockpit. When your radar is looking at clouds or storm systems, you usually see a pale yellow/green/white presentation of the storm with a dark background representing the surrounding sky. When I rolled onto the runway at about three and a half minutes past scramble, my radar scope, just below my windscreen, was filled with the fiercest image of turbulence and electricity and water in action that I had ever seen. We were in the middle of a severe thunderstorm, and the leader of the Spitten Kittens was called on to perform. That was probably my best-ever instrument takeoff, as I lit the burner and launched right into the middle of that monster. Believe me, it was a rough ride. My ground controller set me up right on the money and, glued to my instruments and my radar scope, I splashed my target perfectly. The first time I saw anything other than the inside of my cockpit was a half hour later, when I picked up the flashing runway strobe lights as I passed through two hundred feet about a quarter mile out and squished onto the slick runway. We got three out of four, with Larry's F-106 still unable to answer the bell.

It was demanding competition over the next two and a half days, and even though Larry's bird never got airborne, and flying with only three of our four birds, we came to the last scramble needing only one splash from Larry to win. Larry took that last scramble in the middle of a clear afternoon in hopes of perhaps getting an eyeball shot, but it was not to be. He did get an eyeball, but the weapons system couldn't take the lock-on or process a fire command. Larry called splash on the radio, just to shake up the other team, but it was no go, and we lost by one intercept.

Back at Minot, Larry again turned himself into our flight surgeon and began a long road that led to a medical discharge from the air force. My strapping, good-looking friend was down to a withered ninety pounds when he died. I may have made the wrong call to win the William Tell shootoff, but that never bothered me, since I made a call that made Larry happy for a little while.

I became a short-timer at Minot as the annual personnel lists started coming out of Washington. One of them said I was on the list for promotion to colonel, and another one said I had been selected to attend the National War College (NWC), located at Fort McNair, Virginia, close to Washington, D.C. It was not a bad time to leave, as ADC had reviewed our detailed maintenance inspection report and directed a similar program for the entire F-106 fleet. On top of that, Air Force Logistics Command had dictated that all F-106s would be fitted with a new and entirely different ejection seat system. I got several "attaboys" from general officers in various commands thanking me for the good fight and wishing me well. While I appreciated what had been accomplished to date, the important thing was that almost thirty years later, when the last F-106 was retired, the new seat had a one hundred percent success rate, less two failures that were out of the envelope. One attempt was out of Minot at Mach 1.2, inverted at one hundred feet, and the other was two hundred fifty miles out over the North Atlantic in midwinter, and no ejection seat could be blamed for either of those. We saved a lot of fighter pilots' behinds, and the Spitten Kittens deserved to be proud.

The Saturday before we were scheduled to leave Minot, we had the annual squadron picnic, with the normal fun and games. I played a couple of innings in the ceremonial softball game before AJ, the kids, and I went home in the late afternoon to once again pack up and load the car. We were on the way at the crack of dawn, leaving my squadron full of tigers and my Spitten and Kitten behind. We spent a few days with my folks in Santa Barbara, and I pinned my colonel's eagles on my swimming trunks as we were warming up on the beach. As we drove back to Washington, I kept thinking about that funny war that seemed to be starting to expand in Vietnam.

CHAPTER 15

ROLLING THUNDER

About a week after we left Minot, bound for Washington, I began to realize how nice it would be to jump into my F-106 and go chase the clouds or the stars. But there were other things to do, like finding a house to rent for a year, getting Mark into a decent school, and all the other fun things a military move involved. Fortunately for me, some of my classmates at the National War College were old flying buddies, which made the return to student status a bit less traumatic. The college ranks at the top of the military academic ladder, and is often referred to as the stairway to the stars. The yearlong course is designed for a mixed student body, selected from all the military services, the State Department, and various other departments of the federal government.

I found good listening and learning available in the lecture sessions every morning, featuring presentations by top-level speakers from across the spectrum of national interest. Following each presentation, we were free to subject the high-level presenters to a no-holds-barred question-and-answer period, which was often the prime portion of the program. All comments of the speakers were, of course, on a nonattribution basis, which was faithfully honored by all concerned. Unfortunately, we had about a half-dozen students who were walking questionnaires. No matter what the subject was, or who the speaker was, they could be counted upon to have their hands raised when the bell sounded for questions. Their questions were never direct or about a specific point. They always had preconceived views, based upon their staff expertise, and the questions, which would last for at least a few minutes, were phrased to encourage the speaker to endorse their views. The other members of the class expected their regular performance, and we often audibly sighed when their hands went up. At the conclusion of particularly obnoxious questions for effect, I often wished that the speaker would simply say yes or no, but that never happened.

The war in Vietnam was definitely going on at that time. In fact, we had classmates who had already been over there in advisory positions with the Military Advisory Assistance Group (MAAG). Our direct involvement was increasing day by day, but Washington in general and the NWC in particular gave little evidence of a for-real wartime posture. I don't think I ever heard any discussions of Rolling Thunder, the interdiction campaign that was the prime thrust of the air war against Hanoi and North Vietnam. We had references to the domino theory, and to the inkblot theory, but there were certainly no discussions about the possibility that the North might not share President Lyndon Johnson and Secretary of Defense Robert McNamara's addiction to a new strategic approach called gradualism. In fact, if a speaker had told any of us who had ever been shot at in anger that we could make the North quit, and democratize and de-corrupt the South by firing a few rounds, then disengage and wait for the enemy to knock on the conference room door, the speaker would have been courteously laughed off the stage. We never considered the prospect that our nation would wind up retreating in national defeat and dishonor.

We were split into units consisting of about a dozen peers, representing all facets of government, plus a faculty leader, who was usually a military type. We met after each lecture to discus our individual thoughts on the day's topic, and it wasn't often that we all agreed on anything. The civilian students, mostly State Department people, seemed inclined to accept the gentlest approach to any problem. Generally speaking, they wanted to negotiate everything. No matter what we were talking about, if a military classmate suggested something like "go in there and blast them out," they usually, and sincerely, opposed such an approach. Most of our classmates were good guys, and we all realized that we were in an academic environment, but things often got hot and heavy. That was significant, since with our ranks and experience levels, we were only a matter of a few months away from returning to real-world situations requiring serious decisions.

The small groups were scrambled every few weeks, and by year's end I had met, debated, and socialized with each of my classmates. Those of us who were interested in an advanced degree took advantage of night courses offered by George Washington University. I managed to get a master's degree in political science, specializing in international relations. You can't help but get smarter after a year in that environment.

Getting some flying time and making some attempt to stay proficient was something else. Air force types with wings on their chests had to fly four hours a month for pay purposes. We needed one hundred hours of flying time for the year, including specifics like instrument time, night time, an instrument check, and so forth. Andrews Air Force Base was our designated flying yard, and it was understandably overcrowded with low-priority aviators from all over the D.C. area. We had two choices: the T-33 two-place jet trainer, or the light, twin-engine Cessna 210, which was more common as a civilian aircraft than as a military aircraft. Those with little previous jet time struggled through all the regulatory hoops to get a hundred jet hours. Those of us who already had appreciable hours of jet time choose the less complicated 210 program. The slower, lower-level 210s were painted a solid dark blue and were dubbed as Blue Canoes. John Roberts, my good buddy since 1946 in Germany, joined me in taking the Blue Canoe route with a simple checkout, minimum supervision, and an available aircraft about any time we wanted one.

John and I had two prime mission plans. If we just needed four hours for our monthly pay, we would pick a convenient afternoon, fly around for awhile, land at the civilian airport at Martinsburg, West Virginia, and hit the coffee shop for a sandwich. Then, we would get airborne again and float around the local area for a while before landing back at Andrews. If we needed some of our specific yearly minimums, we would set up a Friday-and-Saturday venture. There was a meat market in Montgomery, Alabama, well known to many air force people for excellent meat, reasonable prices, and delivery to your aircraft. We would get on the phone and order enough to fill our freezers, fly to Maxwell Air Force Base, enjoy the night at the officers' club, and return in the morning. Two people were a load for the Blue Canoe, and by the time the market delivered a goodly load of steaks, ribs, roasts, chops, chicken, and fish, we were usually pushing max gross weight for the machine. Luckily, the runway at Maxwell was pretty long. We always figured if we crashed and burned on takeoff, the accident investigators would have a tough time trying to determine what type monsters were flying the Blue Canoe.

The first of the two big events of the NWC year were the early spring, two-week, overseas trips, and the second was the posting of our next assignment after graduation. For me, it turned out that those two events were closely intertwined. Of the four route choices offered, I got on the Pacific trip. We were briefed, wined, and dined by high-level representatives from every government from the Philippines to Saigon and back. The Tokyo stop was the most important for me, since that was the location of Yokota Air Base and the fighter wing that was providing F-105 Thuds, pilots, and support to the air war in Southeast Asia. The wing was operated by two of my old compadres from Fritzlar and Neubiberg days, and they badly needed someone who understood combat and knew and flew fighters, to run their operations section. I, of course, said I wanted that job. They were woefully short of Southeast Asia–qualified fighter pilots, and promised to request me by name for the job and to press the assignment people through channels up to the Pentagon.

Our last visit of the trip was to Saigon and a few other spots in South Vietnam. We stayed in the swanky Caravel Hotel, which was certainly not on a war footing. Our alarm for the next morning was a gun battle in the street outside the hotel. I looked out the window just in time to see some uniformed people finishing off someone in civilian clothes, so the war was indeed for real in some quarters. Saigon traffic was insane at all hours, and there were more Oriental nightspots in sight than there were soldiers. After getting more than our fair share of briefings crammed into a few days, departure day arrived. We crowded onto a GI bus, with a Vietnamese driver, and plunged into that futile traffic mess en route to the U.S. Embassy for a mandated checkout stop. Part way there, the driver ran over a young child who was embroiled in that traffic. The bump was very audible. The driver looked in the mirror but never stopped.

Our midmorning stay at the embassy was relatively short, and with our passports and other required documents, we were on our way to the airport, our comfortable, plushed-up C-135, and a stopover in Hawaii. The Honolulu newspapers greeted us with headlines announcing that the U.S. Embassy in Saigon had been bombed, minutes after our bus left. Spooky.

Back at NWC, the air force colonels' assignment section at the Pentagon (known to us as the "Puzzle Palace") was grinding out our next assignments, and a lot of them were for jobs and stations that I wanted to avoid. The first lot I drew was for a personnel slot in general officers' assignments in the Pentagon. After I made appropriate wailing, moaning, and begging noises, they withdrew that and selected me for a less attractive one, in legislative liaison, still in the Pentagon. My protestations that I wanted to go and fly and fight the war in Southeast Asia failed to impress the personnel folks. I fought the assignment, without success, until graduation from the War College, and it looked like I was stuck. I even had to attend a legislative liaison welcome cocktail party, and I did not like what I saw.

As the college closed down for the year, the name request for me from the combat-oriented command folks in Southeast Asia finally made it to the top personnel levels in the Pentagon. The colonels' assignment chief, whom I had been jousting with, called me, not pleased that he had been overruled, and said, "God damn you, Broughton, you're going to Southeast Asia."

It didn't take us long to get out of Washington. AJ and I had lots of experience in bouncing around the world. We moved twenty-three times in the first twenty-one years we were married, and the three kids we had at that time had experience in packing up and moving along. We had to be a bit cautious as we loaded up and headed for Yokota Air Base outside Tokyo, since AJ was seven months pregnant and had to go easy on her normal routine of packing, crating, and hauling. The air force had some rules we had to battle on transporting pregnant wives, but AJ did her usual superb job, nobody questioned us, and military airlift delivered us to Yokota, no sweat.

There were only a few houses on base, but my job and rank qualified me for one of them, and my friends set us up in a small but adequate base house. It did take a while to get used to living there, since the main north and south railroad track in and out of Tokyo was twenty yards behind our back door. Another twenty yards behind that was the main north and south Tokyo highway.

We got somewhat used to it, but you always knew when the 3:00 a.m. express had passed the back door

Chester L. Van Etten, also a 1946 friend from Germany, was our fighter wing commander. To those of us who knew him well, he was still known by his World War II call sign of John Black. I was his deputy commander for operations (DCS/Ops), which meant the flying end of things. We had several facets to our primary mission. Our prewar mission of maintaining nuclear alert for our corner of the world was still very much in being. We were always cocked for nuke strikes from both our home base in Japan and our temporary duty (TDY) base in Korea. We also coordinated the program for rotational TDY Thud squadrons that flew back and forth through Yokota, bound for combat duty on the base we were building and supporting at Takhli, Thailand. We had three Thud squadrons in our Yokota wing, and we always had one of them on TDY down south. My operations staff and I had lots of irons in the fire.

At Yokota I got my first close-up look at the awkward and dysfunctional organizational structures within the United States Pacific Air Forces. Talk about togetherness: our wing headquarters building also housed our next-higher headquarters, the small and ineffectual function designated as the 6441st Air Division. The next one up the line, Fifth Air Force Headquarters, was located a few miles away in downtown Tokyo. I only stayed there about a year, so I never did understand what those two entities were supposed to be doing, or why they were in existence.

Swinging into the tempo at Yokota was smooth, and I constantly found things that we could do better and easier. Building a better mousetrap was not always easy, primarily because of the nonoperational staffing of the air division down the hall, but with John Black running interference for us, we did make some significant improvements over the year.

My number-one task on arrival was getting qualified in the F-105 Thud, simply because it is a farce to try to run a bunch of Thud jocks unless you fly and appreciate the Thud. I had flown everything Republic built, from the World War II P-47 to the swept-wing F-84F, and they all flew about the same, except for getting larger and faster. As far as larger, the Thud was sixty-five feet long, with a thirty-five foot wingspan. The first time you climbed the ladder to get into the cockpit, you realized it was twenty feet high. Like all Republic aircraft, the Thud was heavy, weighing thirty-six thousand pounds, and fuel and armament took her up to fifty-two thousand pounds. At low altitude, under the right conditions, you could get her up to Mach 1.2, but I never had the opportunity to get her up to the advertised high-altitude speed of Mach 2.0. The first time you strapped into the cockpit, you could easily feel the similarities to the P-47 and the various F-84 models, but the Thud cockpit had lots more goodies packed into it. Getting used to my new mount was no problem, and one ride made me comfortable as a Thud driver.

The Thuds were not built for the mission we hung on them. They were designed to go a long way, fast, on the deck, and put a nuke weapon in the center of the target. Once Vietnam reared its head, we found ourselves without fighters built for the required duties, so naturally we declared that we really had meant the Thud to be a conventional-weapons fighter-bomber. It also remained a nuke strike-fighter. One of the first things we did was convert the internal nuclear weapons bay to a large fuel tank, and then hang the nukes externally. Multiple hardware modifications helped as regarded a double-duty mission capability, and the Thud became the workhorse of Southeast Asia, delivering 75 percent of the ordnance that went to downtown Hanoi.

Despite the ever-increasing tempo down south, we never received any reduction in our nuke-alert posture. We were nuke-ready at Yokota, and we rotated our pilots and crews in and out of our nuclear operation at Osan, South Korea. One of my fascinating duties was participation in our nuke certification program. Before being certified for our nuclear mission, and periodically thereafter, pilots went through extensive flight and ground checks. I got to participate in graduation exams after pilots had successfully gone through all the other wickets. The pilot and I would meet in an isolated and highly classified room, just the two of us. I would be armed with the pilot's target folder, which contained the maps and assorted details of each pilot's primary or alternate targets. The pilot would be armed with nothing but his professional expertise and determination: no maps, no references of any type. With appropriate administrative and security formalities aside, I would call on the pilot to brief me on any and all aspects of his specific mission. From engine start to landing, he had to cover preflight checks, fuel quantities, fuel flow, and power settings. He had to cover navigational details, such as courses, duration in seconds on each leg, altitudes, and landmarks. The pilot would describe defenses, target descriptions, nuclear switch settings, approval code specifics, delivery, and recovery techniques. Finally, he would tell me how, if things went well, he was going to return to a recovery base. Many of the profiles made fuel consumption, weather, and battle damage as the yes-or-no factors that would determine the probability of recovery to friendly territory. These young stalwarts knew the odds, and it always made me proud when I could OK one of them as ready.

Takhli was a nothing spot in the Thai jungle, north of Bangkok, when the United States became actively engaged in military operations in Vietnam. There was a sort-of runway there, and the United States had given Thailand a few F-86s, which were the basis for their limited flying activities under the control of the Royal Thai Air Force. Korat Royal Thai Air Force Base (RTAFB), farther to the west, and Takhli RTAFB were designated as the two F-105 bases for the war effort, and both were rapidly becoming first-class bases. They remained Thai property, "controlled" by Thailand, but that was no more than a part of the diplomatic game.

We were tasked with supporting the development and construction of Takhli, and the facility that was literally chopped out of the jungle was host to F-105 squadrons and other miscellaneous aircraft and organizations participating in the Rolling Thunder air war against the North. Stateside F-105 squadrons would fly into Yokota and then continue to Takhli for sixty-day deployments. We took care of their broken aircraft and replaced them with our Thuds when necessary. The squadrons would accomplish their own routine maintenance while at Takhli, but when aircraft parts were a problem, or when major maintenance was required, we had that job. When their aircraft suffered severe battle damage, they would paste them back together as best they could, then we would fly in a healthy replacement and nurse the sick bird back to Yokota. Since such sick-bird recovery flights were over a big, deep ocean, we always made those flights with at least two birds at a time.

About the time everything came together on base construction at Takhli, the 355th Tactical Fighter Wing was activated and set up there. The wing had personnel strength of 5,500 people and lots of F-105s, and all the facilities and equipment that it took to support the mission of striking against downtown Hanoi. When I got orders to join the 355th as vice commander, I packed up the family and moved them to a neat house overlooking the beach and the Rabbit Islands in Lanikai on the windward side of Oahu, Hawaii. We hoped that I might get a break to return for a few days during the Southeast Asia tour, but I was to find there was little time for that.

Since I had already been involved with the Takhli operation, and being eager to get back into combat, I tried to avoid the jungle survival school in the Philippines, which was a mandatory requirement for aircrews before heading north in a Thud. I couldn't sell that, so I arranged my orders to fly directly from Hawaii to Clark Air Force Base, which was operated by Thirteenth Air Force and was located outside Manila, so I could get on with the ordeal. And an ordeal it was. Small groups of us surrendered everything except our flying suits and shoes, and were taken out into the wildest country I had ever experienced up close. Learning to nibble snakes and monkey bananas wasn't thrilling, but descending precipitous cliffs where the solid rock was covered with rain and mud, to dunk into a frigid, roaring, boulder-filled mountain river was plain dangerous. At the end of the week, we were led to a strange area of the jungle and given the task of surviving from dusk to dawn and avoiding capture by short, spear-carrying native Negritos. I evaded until shortly before dawn and stretched out for a few minutes under a giant bramble bush. As I was about to catch my breath, I was joined by a nasty-looking, aggressive, hissing subic cat that definitely did not want my company. As I crawled back out from under the bush, there were three unfriendly Negritos staring at me. They knew the area well, could not only track us but could smell us, and received, by their standards, a large reward for each capture. It had not been much of a contest from the start.

When we got back to Clark, I called my old squadron commander from Fritzlar, Germany, now Maj. Gen. Mike Ingelido, vice commander of Thirteenth Air Force. After a few remarks about old times and families, I told him of the dangerous aspects of the survival school operation. He was completely unimpressed with my warning, and he ended our conversation abruptly. That was an early indicator of the command attitude in the area. A couple of weeks later, another group of thirteen much-needed fighter pilots were headed our way. They were going through the same drill, in the same place, when the mountainside turned into a giant mudslide. The entire group of students was killed.

It didn't take me long to get into the swing of things at Takhli. Our construction of the jungle airstrip had already resulted in an efficient operating base with a thirteen-thousand-foot runway and all the basics we needed to carry the air war into North Vietnam. We needed that long runway, since on takeoff in full afterburner we rolled for

7,500 feet before rotating the nose to lift off at 250 miles per hour. If you had to abort at speeds like that, you could easily use the rest of the runway to stop. On landing our final approach speed was 200 miles per hour with touchdown at 175 miles per hour, and even when you deployed your twenty-foot-diameter drag chute, you could still roll quite a way.

There was still a lot of construction going on, and we were constantly pushing the jungle farther and farther back. The wing-command duties were often complex, and always very time-consuming, but the important task was getting a local-area flight check so I could head north. Despite what Washington was putting out to the press, we were woefully short of combat fighter pilots and leaders. We were hurting to the point that having arrived on base in late afternoon, I was airborne in a Thud the next day.

We had three Thud squadrons. Initially, I flew with all three of them for a few missions while I learned the wing's combat routine. There was also the normal feeling out of who was who, while the troops figured out how well this FNG could fly and how well his balls held up when the guns, surface-to-air missiles (SAMs), and MiGs lit up. The plan was for me to get a few missions with each squadron and then settle into flying with the 354th Tactical Fighter Squadron.

One reason I flew with the 354th was that they had really taken their lumps on recent strikes around Hanoi. They had not lost their fighting spirit, but we thought having Mr. Vice, the number two guy around, who was also ex-Thunderbird Leader, mixing it up in the North with them might buck them up a bit. All the Thud squadrons were getting hammered, but the 354th had absorbed a lot of punishment over a short time period. Somewhere across the spectrum of Thud squadrons, someone came up with the song of the moment, which was "There Ain't No Way." It referred to the fact that a primary-duty Thud pilot needed one hundred missions north to earn a ticket home. However, statistics proved that the average mission expectancy of a Thud driver was sixty-five. Thus, there ain't no way. Their definition of a supreme optimist was a Thud driver who quit smoking because he was afraid of dying from lung cancer.

Each of our squadrons was originally authorized and staffed with twenty-five primary-duty pilots, plus an operations officer and a squadron commander, both of whom were regularly flying combat pilots. Combat shootdowns had reduced the 354th to a total of thirteen pilots on board.

Our pilots were not junior-birdmen, and they were well educated. Almost all of them had bachelor's degrees, many had master's degrees, and the 354th had a squadron commander who was killed in combat while on my wing in the Hanoi area, who had an engineering PhD. The average age of our pilots was thirty-eight, and they had thousands of hours of air force flying time, with previous combat experience. Republic built 610 single-seat F-105Ds, and we lost 344 of them. Republic also built 143 two-place F models, of which 75 were converted to the anti-SAM Wild Weasel configuration. In the F models the pilot was in the front seat, and he had all the controls that D-model pilots had. His backseater was surrounded by electrical and radar equipment that allowed him to pinpoint the location of SAM sites, and to monitor their prelaunch activity. When the backseater had locked on to a SAM site, the pilot could initiate an attack on the site with their anti-SAM munitions. They were a very close-coupled and efficient pair. We lost sixty-eight F models. On a more personal note, we lost 326 experienced, well-educated people to either killed in action (KIA), prisoner of war (POW), or missing in action (MIA) status.

The reason for the high loss rate was that we were poorly utilized, we were hopelessly misdirected and restricted, and we were woefully misused by a chain of stagnant high-level civilian and military leadership that didn't have the balls to fight the war that they ineptly micromanaged. We were forced to operate within what had to be the most awkward organizational structure in military history. Even the president and the secretary of defense, in Washington, were involved in picking out our targets and our munitions loads and giving the go/no-go decision on each of our daily missions that went north to the Hanoi area. Next on the pecking list were the Joint Chiefs of Staff, including the air force chief of staff, then came the commander in chief, Pacific Forces, who was located in Hawaii. Our next specific link, also located in Hawaii, was the commander in chief, Pacific Air Forces. Moving on across the Pacific, we had the ultimate in clumsy and wasteful dual headquarters. Our operational command came from Seventh Air Force in Saigon, South Vietnam, while our material, personnel, aircraft maintenance, and other administrative support supposedly came from Thirteenth Air Force at Clark Air Force base in the Philiippines. All the Thirteenth ever did was physically and administratively haze us. For good measure we had the 32nd Air Division, in Udorn, Thailand, which was an almost make-believe liaison tool for the U.S. ambassador in Bangkok, Thailand. None of these monsters coordinated to any degree with each other. Confusion and friction were rampant, and we had more generals, none of whom were very combat or fighter oriented, than we had combat-oriented fighter squadrons. This resulted in what was probably the most inefficient and self-destructive set of rules of engagement (ROE) that a fighting force ever tried to take into battle.

The absolute number-one priority forced on us was genuflecting to the ROE. If you looked at our schematic map of Vietnam, you would find it divided into six segments, called route packages, or pacs. Pac one, the farthest south, was technically the easiest place to work, but we still lost many good guys there. The route packages got more difficult as you moved north, but we still called them the easy pacs, until you got to pac six, where the Thuds went. Pac six included Hanoi, Haiphong, and the Chinese border, and was the location of the ninety-four targets identified as true priority targets that we needed to hit if we were to humble the North and thus diminish their capabilities in the South. It was also the location of the fiercest air-defense environment in the history of aerial warfare. That's were the Thuds went, day after day, and we called it going downtown.

The ROE consisted of a one-inch-thick stack of legal-length paper, hung vertically in a manila folder. The clasp at the top allowed for the constant changes that could be recommended by anyone up the chain of command who made more than forty cents an hour. We were required to sign off that we had read and understood all of them before we were allowed to head north for the first time. Recertification was a periodic requirement.

The second priority we had to struggle with was being nice and correct as we responded to the never-ending flow of visitors to our base. It is important to note that nobody in public life was anybody unless they had visited the boys in the field. Sometimes they came as individuals, sometimes as groups, but we had them to entertain almost every day, and almost all of them were from Washington. We got senators; congressmen; Department of State people; arrogant, wise, young owls from the DOD; military gears; reporters; and celebrities. There were a few sincere visitors, but most of them just wanted to get their ticket punched, so they could leave still holding whatever predetermined views they held before visiting the troops. We gave them all the same briefing, took them on the same base tour, and saluted all of them smartly as they departed, in air force aircraft, for the next stop on their tour, which was almost always the bright lights and cheap junk of Bangkok.

There was also a constant flow of inspection teams from every headquarters between Takhli and Washington. Those teams usually garbaged-up all of our people for days at a time, but each afternoon they were on their personal air force aircraft, well on their way to Bangkok in time for cocktail hour. Then it was a posh hotel, an evening on the town, and shopping for local mementos. Then they were back on base, usually by late morning, to clutter up another day for us. Incidentally, these trips to the war zone, which often covered the last of one month and the first of the next month, qualified them for two months of combat pay.

But the war in the North was more important to us than all of that fluff. From the very start, we were Hanoi Hanna's Dirty American Air Pirates. We took our Thuds downtown every chance our national leaders allowed it. We were fearfully accurate with our loads of bombs, and we never hesitated to hurl our little pink bodies against the fiercest air defenses in the history of aerial warfare. We hurt them, but we could have hurt them a lot more if our national objective had been to win that war.

Hanoi's air-defense system had not been much to talk about in late 1964 when hostilities started. By 1966, with Rolling Thunder in high gear, the Russians had supplied the North with MiG interceptor aircraft and provided and trained pilots for them. Russia also provided SAMs, along with the technicians capable of installing, calibrating, and operating them. China established and trained a sophisticated and well-coordinated air-defense system, with efficient radar and communications interfaces. Various communist nations had supplied a multitude of antiaircraft artillery (AAA) pieces of various calibers and lots of ammo to go with them. They were good.

Johnson-McNamara & Co. gave them their first advantage by forcing us to launch our strikes at the exact same times every day, while dictating the same courses and altitudes, and defining where we could enter and exit the North. On takeoff you could see the "peasants" in the rice paddies off the ends of the runway, lying on their backs, counting the aircraft and checking their watches, and undoubtedly forwarding the information northward. After the war I participated in a seminar at the University of West Virginia, where another participant was a very sophisticated, pro-American Vietnamese woman from Hanoi. She told me how they faithfully scheduled their shopping, naptime, and teatime around our predictable schedule, and then hustled to shelters in advance of our arrival.

When we were inbound to the target, the first line of defense we encountered was the SAMs reaching out and up for us. As we continued letting down, the SAMs would decrease, and the MiGs would take center stage. The MiGs were very agile and had a definite turning advantage over our Thuds at higher altitudes.

We had the advantage down on the deck at higher speeds, and we approached our targets nibbling at Mach 1.0. The MiGs couldn't hurt us down there unless they got dead astern, unnoticed by anyone in the strike force. Thus, the Thuds and the MiGs would often fly parallel courses toward the target, thrusting and parrying at high speed. If they got us in a position where any of our flights had to jettison their bombs, they won and we lost. If all of our flights out-dueled the MiGs, followed our game plan, and blew away our target, which we almost always did, then we won and the MiGs lost.

We approached targets at 3,500 feet and at least 620 miles per hour, which is nine miles per minute, and descending to a few hundred feet as required. A ride on the deck carrying three tons of armament at close to Mach 1.0, with everyone in sight trying to kill you, was a unique experience. That put us in the AAA arena. We went fullburner and popped up eight miles from the target, and tried to climb to 14,000 feet but accepted 12,000 feet. We could expect the big 85mm to 100mm guns to reach for us at those altitudes. They hurled ugly, black bursts with bright orange centers that, if they got close enough, you could feel, hear, and smell. We rolled over the top when our air speed got down to about 450 miles per hour. We stayed in burner until the nose fell through the horizon in a forty-five–degree dive. Then we came out of burner but stayed at full throttle and opened the speed brakes as the blue-gray puffs from the 57mm guns picked us up. We punched our bombs off at 5,000 feet at about 575 miles per hour and recovered at 3,500 feet, with the white cotton balls of the 37mm guns all over us. Then it was the same thing again, in reverse order, until you were well clear of that part of the world.

It wasn't all that easy to get cleared to attack a really good target and also get the OK to hit it the way you wanted to, so you could cross it off the target list. We were perfectly capable of getting the physical job done with the equipment and the people we had. The intelligence people of that day and the military planners were able to identify the good targets, and it was established that there were ninety-four significant targets in North Vietnam. I have never met anyone within the military establishment who envisioned that there could be such an intense gap between target identification and mission accomplishment as our own leaders hung around our necks in the war in Southeast Asia. Admiral U. S. Grant Sharp, the joint commander for the entire Pacific, repeatedly approached and begged Secretary McNamara for permission to exercise our plans to destroy those ninety-four targets. McNamara never granted that permission. President Johnson's five-man Tuesday Lunch Bunch determined specific targets and mission tactics, and they paid little or no attention to the recommendations of military commanders. President Johnson was quoted as bragging that "Them boys cain't hit a outhouse lest I say so." Gradualism was a farce.

But when you did get the OK to go after a good target, all the political foolishness was forgotten. If you were the strike leader, the number-one guy for both Thud wings, the responsibility was very real. You had decision-making authority for about seventy-two bombed-up Thuds; a dozen or so anti-SAM, two-place F-105 Wild Weasels; and several B-66 electronic aircraft. And of course there was the indispensable KC-135 aerial tanker and countless rescue forces.

We could not have accomplished anything up north without the tankers and their dedicated crews. We could not even make it as far as the North without them. Our Pratt & Whitney J-75 engine could put out 24,500 pounds of thrust in afterburner, and when we used our thirty-gallon water-injection tank, which only lasted for thirty-five seconds, we were pumping out 26,500 pounds of thrust. Great, but we were burning 150 gallons of fuel per minute. Cruising north with a load of bombs, we would fall out of the sky at much less than 95 percent power, and that configuration cost us 600 gallons per hour. If every cubic inch of our tanks were crammed full of fuel, we had 2,365 gallons on board when we started our engines. To accomplish our normal mission profile, we started looking for the tankers soon after takeoff, and we had to hit the tankers and refuel no later than takeoff plus forty-five minutes. We were also fighting performance-compatibility. Loaded, we could not go above twenty-five thousand feet, and with their fuel load the tankers could not go above twenty thousand feet, nor could they go faster than 250 miles per hour in level flight at that altitude. Even under ideal conditions, with our leading-edge flaps out for extra lift, by the time we had refueled, we could not keep from stalling and falling off the tanker if our speed fell below 285 miles per hour when we were stuffed with fuel. Throw in a little bad weather, excessive radio chatter, and some occasional confusion, and you could easily get into some dicey situations.

I distinctly remember one particular hot, sticky day when I had that entire fleet behind me. Taxiing out for takeoff, I ran my seat all the way up, my head above the open canopy, relishing the breeze my motion was creating. I was pumped up and so was everybody else. I felt like I had a large American flag stuck in my belly button. It is an indescribably great sensation. It's even better when you do good work, blow the target away, and get all your troops out in one piece. We almost always did good work.

I have been asked how we did it when we were losing brave, young pilots so often; sometimes a couple in the morning and a couple more in the afternoon. The answer is simple: we used fighter pilots. For one thing, the sooner a buck pilot got a hundred missions, the sooner he was on his way out of there. Also, any Thud mission over there was dangerous, so why sit around and worry about what you might have waiting for you? But the main thing was that almost without exception, fighter pilots were super-dedicated, and they were egotistic to the point that they prided themselves in the belief that they could handle anything you threw at them. When the next day's targets clicked in on the teletype machines, you could bet that there would be a mission that was almost certain to be an ass-buster. That was the mission most everybody wanted to be on. Each one of them knew that he was fully qualified to do the toughest job and beat the odds. If you were designated to lead, you knew that you were the best one to get in there, bust the target, and get your guys back out. If you were primarily a wingman, even if you went on the schedule as Tail End Charlie, you wanted to fly the tough ones, and if you were in the toughest leader's flight, so much the better. In many ways we were like racecar drivers: we knew the odds, but while bad things could happen, it happened to the other guy, not to us. When you made it through the roughest of missions, it was customary and fun to say, "Aww, that was a piece of cake."

There is no doubt that Secretary McNamara's rules were the most dangerous thing we faced. They were assembled to make sure we did not win the air war over the North. They killed lots of our pilots. They put hundreds of our aircrews in the dreadful Hanoi Hilton for seven long years. If, from ten thousand miles away, you draw a box or a circle around all the major meaningful targets, then tell those doing the actual combat work that they can't even enter those prohibited areas without your express permission, then no matter the on-scene capabilities, your troops will be operating at a distinct disadvantage. It is tough to fly combat with one hand tied behind your back. Unfortunately, the North knew our ROE, and they got the changes and updates about as fast as we did. If you spread those circles and boxes all over the North, stamp them PROHIBITED, and then assign targets so that your fighters will have to weave through that maze of imaginary lines at six hundred miles per hour, you have tied a large can on the pilots' tails. The North was not stupid. They concentrated their guns and SAMs just inside areas where we were forbidden to enter, allowing them free fire on us. If they didn't have a convenient off-limits area, they just put the SAMs and guns in the middle of villages, or on dikes, both of which were off-limits to us under all circumstances.

My friend and Congressional Medal of Honor winner Leo Thorsness and I found a fun way to beat the ROE. Leo was the boss of our Wild Weasels, the two-place crews whose proud motto was First In And Last Out. They entered the target area early and stayed around until the strike flights were clear, silencing lots of SAM sites and saving the strike flights a bunch of grief. One of their weapons was the Shrike antiradar missile, which could go fast and far as it homed in on a radar signal and destroyed the surrounding real estate. One day, before a clear-weather, midafternoon mission, Leo and I agreed to rendezvous after the strike, assuming everything else was going OK. I got on his wing to provide MiG cover as he headed us toward downtown Hanoi. There were all sorts of radar signals up that way, but some of the strongest came from SAM training units in nonmilitary buildings in the center of the thirty-mile-diameter Hanoi prohibited circle.

We leveled at thirty-five thousand feet, plugged in the afterburners, and quickly went supersonic. As we reached max speed, Leo pulled the nose up, and we climbed until we were at max altitude. That's when Leo launched a Shrike on the strongest SAM radar signal coming out of Hanoi. We were to learn later, from Hanoi Hanna, that the strong signal was emanating from the Romanian Embassy, where a school for SAM radar controllers was in session. One can envision the many bewildered sighs of "Ah-so" as the students stared at the supersonic radar blip that headed their way then suddenly came straight down.

We broke south, pulled the power back, and coasted down toward our friendly tankers, which, as always, we needed to get home. It didn't take long before our tactic was labeled as a no-no. All the diplomats in Hanoi had screamed, and by the next morning there was a "Personal To All Addresses" from no less than LBJ, that such tactics were expressly forbidden.

Despite the ROE, the Tuesday Lunch Bunch, the many pauses and cease-fires, and all the noncombatants milling around, we and our navy compadres off the coast operating from carriers did super-good work during the spring and summer of 1967. We knew it, but there was no note of praise, no hint of encouragement in print or on TV screens back in the States. The only evaluation I considered valid appeared much later in an article in *Atlantic Monthly* by John Colvin, the British consul on duty in Hanoi during that time frame. He had witnessed us in action and admired our precision and pinpoint bombing accuracy. He said that "you almost had them . . . there was malnutrition in the streets and the people's eyes showed a fear of defeat . . . they no longer reacted with enthusiasm to the recorded martial music that blared day and night from loudspeakers on every corner . . . military supplies and equipment was stacked all over town and was not moving south as intended." His estimate was that had we maintained that pace for two more weeks, the North would have been pleading to come to the negotiating table. But of course we didn't. Lyndon Johnson cancelled Rolling Thunder, and the rest of our involvement over there is ugly history.

The time was approaching for me to leave Takhli and head back to the States. About that time, I became involved in a situation that, at best, diverted my attention. Once again, the colonels' assignment section in Washington had me headed to what I considered to be a nothing job in Washington. However, it looked like the wing commander's spot in the photo reconnaissance wing at Udorn would be coming open very soon. I was checking the possibilities of taking that job, and the chances looked pretty good. My old squadron commander, now Maj.

Gen. Mike Ingelido from Thirteenth Air Force, made what would probably be his last inspection visit to Takhli while I was there, and I squired him around for the day. As I took him out to his little T-39 to head back to the Philippines, we stood by the tail of his aircraft for a moment while his pilot completed his preflight preparations.

He patted me on the back, right between my shoulder blades, and said, "Jack, we know who's doing the good work over here. You're doing great running the wing and the base, and your combat leadership is just outstanding. And we're going to take care of you." There was a general officer promotion board scheduled for Washington, and my time as a colonel made me barely eligible for the first time.

I saluted as he taxied out for takeoff, and pondered, "How about that."

I didn't have much time to be concerned about that statement. Two of my majors, who had often flown my wing up North, were suddenly covered with flak of all sizes from the guns surrounding Cam Pha Harbor. At that time, a Russian freighter we had given them under the Lend-Lease program approached the docks to unload war supplies for the North. The North's gunners surrounding the harbor covered our guys with flak, and the major leading the Thuds fired his Vulcan cannon in hopes of getting the gunners' heads down, so they could get out of there. That was a big no-no. The Russians screamed and the North Viets screamed, and I was ordered to court-martial my majors. I refused, and they charged all three of us with four counts of conspiracy against the United States. Remember that spot between my shoulders where General Ingelido had patted me so firmly? That's exactly where the knife went in. The trial and everything connected with it was classified Top Secret, which made sure that nobody outside of those trying to hang us could find out what was happening. The trial was a farce. I took personal responsibility for those under my command, and both of the majors were found not guilty. I beat three of the conspiracy charges, but was found guilty of some lesser charges under the fourth conspiracy charge. I was found guilty of processing gun-camera film in an unauthorized manner and destroying $42.50 worth of government property. I had a nasty letter inserted into my previously outstanding personnel records and was fined $600. The four-star general commanding Pacific Air Forces had personally orchestrated and directed the entire show. It was common knowledge that he was about to become the next commander in chief of the entire air force, and nothing like supporting his combat pilots was going to stand in his way. A while after he got me, he even shot down a four-star general who worked for him. Any time you get top brass and the government lined up against you, it is like fighting a steamroller barehanded.

The four-star who had called the shots against us had wanted all three of us convicted, and he viewed the verdict against me as not nearly harsh enough. He made everything concerning my transfer back to the United States as nasty as possible. I knew that the trial and associated venom meant that I would never again have a command position in the air force, and that was absolutely unacceptable to me. But I was not quite ready to resign my commission. I packed up my third and fourth Distinguished Flying Crosses that I had earned over there, plus my two Silver Stars for unusual heroism in combat, and my presidentially awarded Air Force Cross, which is the air force's highest award for individual heroism in combat and is second only to the Congressional Medal Of Honor, and left Takhli and the air war over Southeast Asia behind me.

The Military Air Transport Service (MATS) was overloaded with logistic duties in support of the Southeast Asia operation. To relieve the pressure on MATS, the air force had established contracts with several civilian airlines to provide air service between Bangkok and the United States for individuals and small groups. Usually, pilots who had finished their combat tour would catch a ride on a base Gooney Bird for the ninety-mile, thirty-minute trip to Bangkok, and then head home on one of the contract airlines. In the spirit of the previously mentioned nastiness, word came from higher headquarters that I would not be authorized to utilize that relatively convenient service, and I was ordered to board the next Seventh Air Force Gooney Bird that came through Takhli on a regular schedule on an arduous trek through all the intermediate bases to Saigon. That was a hot and sweaty ride that took nine hours on an aluminum bucket seat in the back of the non-air conditioned goon. I was further ordered to report directly to the MATS terminal and remain there until space opened up for my departure. I got there at about 8 p.m. and found the terminal sparsely occupied except for a few enlisted troops lounging around in their jungle bunny suits. I was quite conspicuous in my Class A blue uniform with my silver wings and combat medals on my chest and nobody seemed to know what to do with me. I knew that this was going to be a tough one.

Sitting there in the huge, darkened room on a wooden bench, I looked down at the silver command pilot wings and the seven rows of brightly colored cloth medals on my chest, and shook my head. For a minute I felt like the Wings, the Distinguished Flying Crosses, the Silver Stars, and the Air Force Cross were about as valuable as the Little Orphan Annie secret decoder pin that you could get by sending in the label from a jar of Ovaltine, back in grammar school. But then I said to myself, "No, I'm proud of my wings and what I've been able to do." Then I said a little prayer for the souls of those I'd seen vaporized in a red ball as they flew on my wing. I prayed for those shackled in chains, in solitary confinement, in rodent-infested three-by-eight cells in the Hanoi Hilton; and for those missing God knows where. Then I thanked God that I was going home to my family in one piece with everything working. It was about 4 a.m. when they called my flight, and I popped my chest up, picked up my B4 bag, and strode briskly to the back end of a C-141 cargo aircraft that was loaded with who knows what. I strapped in, this time into a canvas bucket seat, and headed for Hawaii.

With many hours of sitting ahead of me, I drifted into a little bit of "what if" thinking. At the time we got involved in Vietnam, the North Vietnamese had by far the most advanced nation in the area. The ninety-four targets we had sought represented significant industrial and security advancement, and, in that respect, they were the envy of their neighbors, and were all symbols of intense North Vietnamese national pride. What if our leaders had assumed a warlike attitude rather than pussyfooting around with gradualism and the like?

We had two air force F-105 wings in the Pacific, plus readily available rotational fighter wings spread around the world, but ready for immediate deployment. The navy had significant carrier forces in the Pacific off the Vietnamese coast, with more strength quickly available. Strategic Air Command had their bomber forces on either airborne or ground alert. With even a part of those forces, we could have destroyed the ninety-four targets in a few weeks.

Would such action have involved us in the China card scenario that LBJ and the secretary of defense seemed to fear? It was doubtful, since China was embroiled in severe internal conflict, and its relations with Russia were strained. The closest U.S. foot soldier was four hundred miles from China, and the prospect of direct, large-scale jungle combat with the Americans, who had not even begun to display their overall might, had to be less than interesting to either China or Russia.

Would decisive American air action to destroy those ninety-four targets have eliminated the North's ground forces and the Viet Cong in the South? Of course not. But would it have caused Ho Chi Minh to reevaluate the situation? I believe it would have. Seeing his proud accomplishments quickly destroyed could have made him think that we Americans were for real. He could have been expected to consider the communist principles that time was on their side, and that half a loaf was better than none. If he had reacted along those lines, the scenario in Southeast Asia might have been completely different. I wondered how many of the fifty-eight thousand brave young Americans we lost over there would have lived to return to the United States.

When I got back to Washington, the assignment I had not looked forward to was waiting for me. I was assigned to the Weapons Systems Evaluation Group (WSEG), which reported to the Defense Advanced Research Projects Agency (DARPA), within the Department of Defense (DOD). I was the senior air force project officer for the Vertical Takeoff and Landing Aircraft Study. Sound impressive? Read on.

The first thing I did was to look up the air force legal officer at Bolling Air Force Base and start the complex chain of actions necessary to eventually get a hearing with the congressionally appointed Board for the Correction of Military Records. It took a year, but they were the only group I could appeal to in order to get the railroad job of a court-martial reversed. Meanwhile, I had to hurry to work in my new assignment.

The head of my study group was a PhD employed as a very senior government civil servant. He was a nice guy, and we got along great, except that, at first, I didn't understand the definition of work in that league. The first task he gave me was a research project, and he wanted it back in one month. I retreated to the unfamiliar surroundings of my cubicle and attacked the project. It went together easily, and I had it neatly prepared in final form when I went back to his office three days later. When I presented it to him, he thought it was great, but said I had apparently not understood my instructions: it was not due for a month. Amazed, I asked what my next duty might be, and was told to take the project back, return it in a month, and then I could pick up my next task. I started asking around and learned that what I had experienced was the way the place was run. it seemed like everyone had their own things to do. My PhD, for instance, was building a place on the New Jersey shore, and was in his WSEG office only occasionally. Another colonel on the military side of the group was selling real estate full time, and so it went. I decided that was the time to write a book. So in my government cubicle, on government time, using government supplies and typist service, I wrote and sold *Thud Ridge*, and after all these years, it is in print and pushing the five hundred thousand sales mark. Even with that diversion of effort, I was still known as one of the most efficient and eager members of WSEG. Thank you, fellow taxpayers.

I was fortunate to be granted a review by the corrections board within a year. The review was like a compact version of the trial, but involving only me, my friend the Boeing legal officer, and six civilians from way up topside in Washington acting as judges. It was a tough workout, and they were very thorough and impersonal, but for the first time since the day of the *Turkestan* incident, I sensed an air of honesty and some hope of an unbiased outcome. The waiting for months on end was torturous, but I finally got the verdict. They threw the court-martial out and expunged it from my records. One of their comments was that the court martial had been the grossest miscarriage of military justice they had ever seen. Thus, I joined air force founder Billy Mitchell in our two-man club of the only officers of any service in the history of the United States to have had a general court-martial verdict reversed.

Then it was really time to move on. I had worked with the Pentagon personnel folks and had my retirement papers all filled out, except for the signature and the date. The protocol officer at WSEG had been aware of my retirement plans for some time and had asked me what kind of a retirement ceremony I wanted him to arrange for me. He was surprised when I told him, "Nothing, I've had all the formal government ceremonies I can stand."

I was advised of the verdict at 10:00 a.m. on a Friday. By 11:00 a.m., I had signed my retirement papers. By noon, twenty-six years after raising my right hand to take the oath on the plain at West Point, I was out of there.

CHAPTER 16

AND THEN . . .

There was little doubt in my mind that I was heading into a completely different branch of my life. After all, I was launching a new career that turned into several careers, and I looked to new ventures with confidence. I can't deny that I was just plain mad at several of my old fellow airmen and supervisors, and I recognized the fact that they had been both powerful and clever in steering the fickle finger of fate my way. It took until 1988, when I wrote *Going Downtown,* to finally get over that syndrome—well, almost over it. I also realized that sitting around and pouting was a waste of time, as was any expectation that my wife and I, plus our four growing kids could live decently on the few bucks the government would send my way for "retirement." Besides, I was only forty-three, in good health, full of piss and vinegar, and anxious to get on with life.

Through the tribulations of the year of appealing the courts-martial and waiting around in Washington, I had been getting ready to shift gears. I had agreed to go to work with my friend Charlie Blair, who owned Antilles Airboats. That meant flying seaplanes, in the Caribbean, out of St. Thomas, U.S. Virgin Islands. Obviously, I needed to learn something about flying seaplanes, so I located a gentleman named George Lambros, who had an amphibious training and check-out program at his base in New Jersey. He gave his training in the twin-engine Grumman Widgeon, which was a smaller version of the Grumman Goose I would be flying for Charlie. The Widgeon was responsive, light and comfortable on the controls, and fun to fly. We did most of our training above the Hudson River, and I even looked forward to George repeating his teaching drill of pulling one or both of the throttles to idle and declaring, "Forced landing!" Then I could maneuver in graceful, sweeping, descending turns, and tickle the smooth river surface with the underside of the tail before easing the nose down into the water. When he was satisfied with my flying, George signed me off as seaplane-qualified, took care of the certification paperwork, and wished me well. As I drove happily back to Washington, I thought, "Man, that was a piece of cake. I'll bet Antilles Airboats is going to be a fun job."

The day of my departure from Washington had some surprises in store for me. My best connection was a red-eye flight out of D.C. to Miami, then a change for the flight to San Juan, Puerto Rico, and a mini-commuter flight to St. Thomas. That was the day the radio and TV were blaring about some racial disturbances in downtown Washington. That evening, by the time I caught a bus to the main downtown bus station, it was easy to see that we were headed into a flaming mess. It was a completely anarchistic scene of crumbling structures and out-of-control people, with fires and looting erupting everywhere. I was more than a little frightened as I checked my bag through to San Juan and watched it tossed into the baggage compartment of the airline bus. The fires were coming closer as I got into the bus, hoping for a speedy departure for the airport. I remember thinking of the brand-new, champagne-colored sports jacket I had just bought, and wondering if the jacket and I were going to get out of there. It was a very long night, and when I got to San Juan the next day, guess what: no B4 bag. I don't think it ever got out of the bus station. I was concerned that I didn't even have a toothbrush, but I was more concerned about the prospect that some lawless rioter was wearing my new sport coat as he helped the attempt to burn Washington down.

I had first met Charlie Blair when I was at Takhli, and we became close friends during the *Turkestan* court-martial. He was a reserve air force brigadier general, and among his accomplishments was being the first man to fly a single-engine P-51 from the States over the North Pole and back, to demonstrate a new piece of navigational gear. He was also the second pilot in seniority for all of Pan American Airways, and had seaplane experience dating back to Pan Am's China Clipper days. One of his seniority perks was that he satisfied all his monthly flying requirements with a one-week-long flight around the world. One of his stops was in Bangkok, followed by a day's rest, and that's when he would regularly visit us at Takhli. He was incensed by the obvious deviations from the code of military justice and the obvious examples of unlawful command influence in our courts-martial case. Charlie and I had a mutual friend in Senator Barry Goldwater, and both Charlie and Barry did all they could to help us. It was to no avail. Charlie arranged for a personal appointment with Pacific Air Forces commander General Ryan in Hawaii, but he was rudely snubbed, and Ryan barely recognized his presence before curtly dismissing him. Barry's appointment with the air force chief of staff in Washington was also a complete rebuff, and he contacted both of us to dejectedly report that there was nothing he could do to assist us.

When Charlie wasn't flying around the world, he was either accomplishing Antilles money business in New York, or flying the Goose or the Antilles four-engine China Clipper in the Caribbean, or courting Maureen O'Hara in Los Angeles. When AJ and I first met

Maureen, we were amazed at her real-life beauty, which was even more striking than her screen presence. It was even more impressive to see her down-to-earth sincerity, her affection for Charlie, and her interest in Antilles.

As soon as Charlie had finished his huge stone castle overlooking St. Croix harbor, he and Maureen were married, and she took over the castle. Charlie had quite a romantic history, and Maureen was his seventh wife. The first six, mostly stewardess types, were all very friendly with each other. The only time I saw Maureen upset was during Charlie's annual vacation week, when all of his ex-wives and kids would descend on the St. Croix castle and share a week together, which was not exactly to Maureen's liking.

Charlie had built Antilles from scratch. When I came on board, St. Thomas was the hub, and we served St. Croix, St. Johns, St. Martin, Fajardo in Puerto Rico, and Tortola in the British Virgins. Our plan was that when I brought AJ and the kids down, we would live in Fajardo, and make it a second hub. We would then expand the route structure to include the island of Vieques, San Juan, and several other spots around the coast of Puerto Rico. We were looking into purchasing several Mallards, which were a larger, more sophisticated member of the Grumman airboat family. It all sounded promising.

It was not surprising that I experienced some culture shock. The first major surprise was when I checked out in the Goose. If the Widgeon I had flown to get my seaplane rating was light, maneuverable, responsive, and fun, the Goose was underpowered, heavy, sluggish, and a bunch of effort to haul around. We had very used, tired aircraft that were mostly devoid of operable flight instruments, radios, and navigation aids. It was different, very different from what I was used to.

On a hot afternoon, with no warning, Bill Soren, our operations manager, provided another surprise as he announced that it was time for my checkout ride for certification as a people-hauling amphibious captain. It was indeed a ride, as opposed to a flight. As I climbed in and headed for the cockpit, I found all ten passenger seats occupied by jovial members of our administrative and maintenance staffs. Bill took the right seat in the cockpit and told me to take her into the water of St. Thomas harbor. He then gave me the odd order to take her to full throttle on both engines, but to hold her on the water and not get airborne. That got me up on the step, ready to fly, but in the water, like a racing hydroplane. The Goose wanted to lift out of the water as I rolled in full nose-down trim, to little avail. I locked my elbows and pushed forward on the control yoke as those in back yelled and tried to peek past me and out the windscreen, acting like thrill-riders on a roller coaster. I was fortunate enough to be in good physical condition, since the next sweat-filled minutes were as tough as anything I have ever experienced. It was tough to steer among pleasure boats, fishermen, and sunning tourists. Bill would pull one throttle all the way back, and I would jam in full opposite rudder to maintain some semblance of staying straight, while the crowd roared and he reversed the procedure. I guess one of the goals was to get me to pull the throttles back and ask for mercy. However, despite the sweat half-blinding me and soaking me from head to toe, and the aching muscles, I didn't capitulate. Twenty minutes later he said, "OK, Captain Broughton, take us back to the ramp." We never did get airborne, and thinking back, I don't recall ever having seen Bill fly one of our aircraft. The exercise he put me through was a stupid and completely unsafe drill.

Flying the line in a Goose was not simple or easy. The islands were scenic, and the coloring of the water plus the visible underwater mountains and valleys were something to see. But sometimes the weather could give you some concerns, and it would have been nice to have even an operable radio and some navigation aids for reassurance. We made eighteen water takeoffs and landings per day, which was a bunch.

Of all our stops, St. Croix was our busiest and most unique. The picturesque harbor was always jammed with water traffic, bright colored sails, and people. When we taxied in to the ramp, we were guided in and serviced by a nice gent we called "the Hook." He had lost the lower part of his right arm in an electrical accident and now worked most efficiently with a shiny hook replacing his arm and hand. There was very little space in and around our docking spot, and I was always extra alert as he stood on the wet, wooden surface, guiding us forward and waving us on until the hook was only inches from the whirling prop on the left engine.

When AJ and the kids arrived, we got a house in Fajardo and got Mark into a very good Catholic boys' school in Humacao, where he boarded during the week and commuted on weekends. Our older girls, Sheila and Maureen, got some of their best schooling ever from an astute Englishman who ran an exceptionally good academy in Fajardo. The town was sort of jumbled and junky, but a large, Las Vegas-type hotel operation, complete with gambling and show girls, was being built on the hills overlooking the harbor, so you knew the place would blossom.

When I started looking objectively at our aircraft maintenance procedures, I got my first clue that we needed some changes in what we were doing before we got serious about expanding the route structure. Our concept was sort of like waiting until something was so badly broken that you couldn't get airborne, then writing it up in the aircraft flight records, and hoping that somebody could and would fix it. With practically no qualified maintenance supervision, write-ups were often cleared by entries like, "Could not duplicate—ground checked OK." A large percentage of our ground crews were closer to being reservicing crews than maintenance crews. We had some of the tallest, dark-skinned gents, with the whitest teeth I ever saw, from Trinidad, who were involved in maintenance. Among other things, they took care of the propellers after each day's flights. Bouncing on and off the salt water put tiny dents in the props, which decreased their air-biting efficiency. The Trinidad troops were tall enough to stand on a stool and reach the top of the props and file them smooth again. The props soon looked like sickles as opposed to full-bladed propellers. I voiced my concerns to Charlie and proposed some maintenance changes. He acknowledged my comments, but allowed that cash flow was the problem of the moment and that all else must wait.

On a nice, sunny day, with the sea and the sky looking just like the postcards, I went down to the Fajardo harbor to catch a ride on one of our flights to St. Thomas and pick up my Goose and fly my daily circuits of the islands. The flight was full, and we had sold the copilot's seat to a passenger. She was a middle-aged native who spoke little or no English, and was carrying a crate of avocados that she refused to surrender to the baggage compartment. No sweat, there was plenty of clearance between her and the crate and the copilot's control column. With the seats full, I sat on a shallow metal protrusion at the rear of the aircraft in front of the open area we used for baggage. The engines roared as we bounced along the open water, climbed to about two hundred feet—then we were in trouble. The gent flying the Goose suddenly hunched forward, leaned over his shoulder and let out a terrified, "Jack!" I didn't know what was wrong, but it only took about three giant, running strides to bound up the aisle to the rear of the cockpit.

I could hardly believe what I saw. The half-wheel-shaped top of the pilot's metal control yoke was lying on the floor, having broken off the control column, and for the moment, our Goose was out of control. The pilot was leaning full forward, straining at his seat belt, with both arms wrapped around the stub of the control column. He was barely keeping the nose up, but with the nose gyrating freely, it was a matter of seconds before we stalled out and fell into the ocean, or dove straight in.

I reached across the avocado crate and grabbed the top of the copilot's control yoke and was able to momentarily slow down the vertical gyrations. The lady in the copilot's seat, of course, had no idea what was going on, but twisting my head to look under my right arm, I saw an alert but absolutely terrified face. Utilizing my best Spanish, I commanded, "Vamoose!" In no time she was out of her seatbelt, had writhed under and past me into the aisle and, still clutching her avocados, was out of the way so I could plop into the copilot seat and adjust things for a normal climb. I gave my companion a few moments to catch his breath before turning the flight back to him.

It wasn't long after that when we put on a show in St. Croix harbor. After being sent off by the Hook, one of our guys worked his way through the recreational and commercial traffic for takeoff. Finally finding a clear lane, he popped the coal to her and accelerated with both engines at full throttle. Approaching liftoff speed, the right engine quit cold. He tried to retard the throttle on the left engine, but it was stuck in full throttle, and it would not respond to any attempts to back it off. His first thought was to cut the fuel flow to the engine to shut it down. The Goose had a main fuel-flow rotary selector that would do the trick, but it was mounted behind, above, and full outboard from the pilot. If he could let go of the controls and twist in his seat, he could reach it, but by then he was dashing around the harbor, avoiding lots of traffic, with a sick machine that wanted to turn right into the dead engine. He found a clear spot and let her wind up like a centrifuge in a constant, tight right circle. He was able to reach back and twist the left shutoff valve, and after a little more circling, the engine coughed and quit. The Hook towed him back in with his outboard rowboat, and called for maintenance people from St. Thomas to fly over and fix it. After changing the right engine, they moved to the left engine throttle problem and, guess what: "Could not duplicate. Ground checked OK."

Then it was my turn. My friend Tom, who had checked me out in the Goose, was deadheading in the right seat as we made an intermittent stop at Tortola, in the British Virgins, on our way to St. Thomas. Tortola harbor is long and narrow, with a stone breakwater separating it from the ocean, and we normally took off toward the ocean. I was barely airborne when the right engine quit. By the time Tom had reached back and shut off the right fuel valve, the left engine had quit. I didn't have much air speed, but there was not enough room to put her back down in what was left of the harbor, so my best bet was to try to clear the breakwater and get her into the ocean. I held her at absolute bare-minimum speed as we coasted and sank through the few feet of altitude under us. But the tail started to wash out on me, indicating the Goose was only seconds from stalling. Rather than crash head-on into that pile of stones, which looked huge at the moment, I opted for the jungle. I managed to skid about twenty degrees left as I ran out of everything. I locked my elbows and held her as steady as I could as we went into the trees, with nothing to steer with but a little bit of effective rudder. It sure is dark when going through the jungle at 120 miles per hour. We didn't travel very far once we hit the ground, and didn't hit any trees. One of the passengers had banged and cut his elbow, and one young girl was hysterical, but other than that, the passengers were all OK. I had given my left ankle a rap when it caught between the rudder pedal and the side of the cockpit, but we were very fortunate.

One of our people who wanted to see what Tortola was like, flew a Goose in from St. Thomas with maintenance people and parts, and I flew his aircraft back to St. Thomas so we could fill the morning schedule. By the time I got airborne, darkness had moved in, but I had no problem dead-reckoning back to the lights of St. Thomas. Getting her down on the water in the pitch black was something else. Landing on the water at anytime could play tricks on your depth perception, but on a completely black night, approaching completely black water, you simply had no depth perception. Thus, we never did it under normal conditions. I buzzed our ramp just to let them know I was there, and then went way out on the far end of the harbor. I let down to one hundred feet on my altimeter and headed inbound. We didn't have any lights on the aircraft, but they wouldn't have done much good anyway. It sure seemed to take an eternity to inch down, holding landing speed and trying to find the water. I finally felt my tail barely touching the water, which was my signal to gently lower the nose into the water. I was down. Bill putt-putted out in an outboard, chewed me out for landing at night, thanked me for getting the Goose back, and towed me in to the ramp.

I had one-quarter of a full fuel load when I took off, so it had to be an aircraft problem that caused the engine failures at Tortola. Seems some of our people knew that the wing tanks on that particular Goose were one-quarter full of many years worth of accumulated corrosion, metal flakes, and slime. Therefore, a full load on the cockpit indicator really meant three-quarters of a full load, and when you got to a quarter of a tank, you were right at empty. They didn't bother to share that knowledge with the pilots. The only significant visual damage on the Goose was that all the props were bent back from ground contact. The folks at Fajardo borrowed a Jeep and dragged her back to the water's edge, where they took sledgehammers and beat the props straight. They poured in a drum of gas, which brought the tanks back above the one-quarter level. When the tide came in to float her a bit, the holes in the bottom didn't leak badly enough to sink her before one takeoff and landing, and Tom flew her back to St. Thomas in the morning. They hung two different props on her, and after a bit of patching and paint, she was back flying the line, carrying passengers. Charlie made one of his trips to San Juan, reportedly came back five thousand dollars lighter, and, as usual, we never heard anything from the FAA.

I expected that we might have some sort of an internal investigation and maybe thoroughly check all of our aircraft, and get a decent maintenance plan going after those three fiascos. Forget all that. I made one more stab at trying to sell a new maintenance approach, but it was not to be. Charlie said any excess funds were going for insurance against the

"Great Disaster." I told him that I could no longer in good conscience continue flying passengers around while knowing the dangerous condition of the aircraft. He said he was sorry I didn't accept the fact that they operated differently than what I was used to. I didn't respond to that. We parted, still good friends, and wished each other well.

I was back in the States on other projects when I heard that, with Charlie flying, the four-engine clipper had gone down between St. Thomas and St. Croix. The result killed a few and injured a few. Charlie was among the few who were rescued. Some time after that, Charlie was flying a Goose, carrying passengers from St. Croix to St. Thomas. They were only five miles off the shoreline that defined St. Thomas harbor when they lost one engine, and making the harbor should have been a snap. The book says that the Goose can maintain altitude and even climb a bit on one engine, but the book doesn't consider tired engines and sickle-shaped propellers. They fell out of the sky, and Charlie, as good an amphibious pilot as there was, couldn't translate five thousand feet of altitude into five miles of distance to the protected water of the inlet and harbor. He had to ditch in the open ocean. The impact rolled the Goose on its side, a wing dug in, the aircraft was destroyed, and all aboard were killed. He was flying the same Goose that I was forced to land in the jungle.

The "Great Disaster" had hit Antilles Airboats. There was no covering up that crash, and the FAA came forth, viciously citing all the maintenance discrepancies they happened to have missed over the years. Valiant Maureen assumed command, and carried the management load until it was beyond carrying. Antilles Airboats was sold and that chapter closed.

When I got back to the States, one of my self-imposed prime duties was giving speeches and interviews about the deplorable conditions our POWs were stuck in at the Hanoi Hilton and other prison facilities in the Hanoi area. I was always amazed at the number of people who had no knowledge of that dreadful situation. Our government seemed reluctant to make too much out of the situation. In fact, they were often noncooperative with family members and formal survivors' groups. I got more than my share of chicken, peas, and mashed potatoes as I spoke at every community group, veterans group, or educational group that would listen to me.

You never knew how much you did on efforts like that, but I know I scored big on two occasions. Before he became a congressman, Bob Dornan was a California Air National Guard fighter pilot and a television talk show host in Los Angeles. After my first book, *Thud Ridge*, got some good national recognition, Bob invited me on his show for a book review. Bob was not aware of many facets of the POW abuse and our government's apparent indifference, and what was supposed to be a few minutes' book interview turned into a pretty good condensed speech. Bob dove right into the situation and became an outstanding supporter of the POW wives and families, including participation in their trip to Paris to confront the Vietnamese hierarchy face-to-face. The other bigtime hit came during a round-the-country book interview that J. B. Lippincott Publishers set up for me. They had interviews arranged at every stop, and in Dallas my radio host was the well-known Murphy Martin. He was completely amazed at my account of the POW situation, and did something about it. Murphy was a friend of the Texas industrial tycoon and later presidential contestant H. Ross Perot. Murphy's account turned on Perot and galvanized his massive financial personal support of the POWs and their families.

Back in Santa Barbara, I went to work for Conroy Aircraft. Conroy's business was arranging and accomplishing anything anybody wanted done in connection with flying, like buying, selling, leasing, completing contract jobs, you name it. I came on board to manage the operations aspects of a contract with Mobil Oil for moving supplies from Anchorage to Mobil's drilling site at Kuparuk, on the North Slope of Alaska. We leased a big, Canadian-made CL-44 cargo machine with a large back door that allowed us to pack in lots of sacks of drilling mud and long lengths of pipe. We hired a retired airline captain to fly it and gave him a regular copilot. I commuted between Santa Barbara and Anchorage and was the liaison with Mobil, which gave me a peek at how a giant oil company attacked a difficult task.

One look at the North Slope would make all the challenges of ice and cold worthwhile. I also got to travel with the Mobil people in their classy, twin-engine King Air as we hit multiple stops relating to the pipeline and associated logistic functions.

Flying into Kuparuk, Mobil's site at the top of the world, next to the North Pole, was all under our own control as far as air traffic clearance, weather, and time were concerned. On approach it looked like you were just flying into a little pierced-plank landing strip in the middle of nowhere, with the major landmark being giant herds of caribou, which ignored us completely. When we opened the cargo door, the cold was like a visible thing coming after you. The Mobil unloading crews worked very rapidly and efficiently, as it was to the benefit of all concerned to get their supplies and get us out of there. Everything was impressively silent, unless you were nose-to-nose talking with someone. Standing next to the aircraft nose, with nothing in front of you, and looking north was awesome. Above the white surface there were shades of blue, purple, and orange, all underlined by a semicircle that was truly the top of the world. Even at 64 degrees below, you could stand silently, transfixed.

After the few minutes it took to unload, it was back into the CL-44, shut the back door, and get out of there. After takeoff, low and still at full throttle, we again failed to get any show of interest from the caribou. If you dropped your nose and gave them a good buzz job, those directly underneath would jump and bounce momentarily before returning to their nose-down grubbing for food.

Visiting the drilling sites was also a kick. The living areas were typical of the overall project's efficiency. Everything was clean, neat, and compact, and the fresh-cooked, hearty food was good. Looking at a new drilling hole as it was being started was impressive. I saw one hole that was only about ten feet deep, whose sides showed multiple stratified layers hard as steel and multicolored. The walls of the hole were shiny and glass-smooth, and the entire thing reminded me of a magnified precision machine shop product.

A far-north whiteout is also something to behold. If you run into one while you are airborne, you are immediately on solid instruments, and even navigation-aid assisted approaches and landings are to be avoided. I was on the ground at one site, looking around not far from the main building, when things went whiteout instantaneously. All sense of orientation was gone, and even on the short walk back to the building, I was unsure of my position and balance and quite happy to get back to a reference point.

The fascination of the North Slope project wore off rather quickly, and I was ready for something new. I had some friends across the runway in the Super Guppy project, and we talked about possible employment, but that huge, slow-moving, four-engine balloon of an aircraft that had cargo space for an entire missile just didn't turn me on. They had a lot of internal conflict within their organization and were hurting for development capital, and anyway we never got to a firm offer point, which was OK with me. A short time later, I was extra glad we hadn't clicked, as my test pilot friend Van Johnson and all on board were killed in a stupid disaster. They were on a certification flight to gain government blessing, with Van flying and an FAA inspector in the right seat, when it happened. The Guppy's four relatively small engines and its bulbous bulk made every takeoff a critical event. On takeoff, the FAA inspector pulled two throttles back on the same side, and that was all she wrote.

I decided that it was time to take a crack at something I had wanted to do ever since Ike Isaacson and I went crop-dusting in North Dakota many years before. My initial thoughts were of an air-cushion vehicle (ACV), hovercraft if you will, that would replace currently used spray aircraft. Further, how about a truck- or bus-sized ACV to satisfy the requirements that outfits like Antilles Airboats were struggling to satisfy? I even thought about large hovercraft, like the British were using to cross the English Channel, but decided that concept was not for me. Our size of vehicle would be great for Red Cross flood rescue work, and could be a ground-water taxi in remote areas. It could traverse the north of Alaska, summer or winter, without damaging the sensitive tundra. Oil prospecting tasks were attractive, especially in places like the Indonesian Archipelago islands-and-sea mix. Crop control was still of interest, and the military possibilities were numerous. The list went on and on. There was no shortage of potential uses for a practical, truck- or bus-sized amphibious vehicle, and I had no trouble generating interest and encouragement, "when you get it into production."

I formed a California corporation and began beating the bushes for development capital. That was a tough task that never got any easier. Over a ten-year span, along with the small crews I hired, I designed, built, and tested seven air-cushion vehicles. Each one grew in size and power, but I never changed from a concept in the truck-bus range. I was awarded a U.S. patent with twenty-seven individual claims. I had to move the project to wherever the money and support were available. Thus, numbers one and two went together in Santa Barbara, while three and four moved to Dallas. Five was a flop, but six flew and showed well in Moses Lake, Washington. Then it was back to California and the San Diego area for a reliable and quite sophisticated number-seven prototype. For public relations purposes I called her *Whistler 007*. She had three Lycoming IO-360 aircraft engines and a ten thousand–pound payload that could move at fifty miles per hour over land and sixty over the water.

There were laughs along the way, like leaving number six out in a North Dakota wheat field overnight for an early morning photo shoot and, in the morning, finding the cows had fallen in love with it and did not want to leave. And thrills, like one early morning demonstration run for some potential investors. As we set up in pea-soup fog on the edge of the Tijuana Slough, an estuary south of San Diego, my crew chief failed to adequately secure four water-filled fifty-five–gallon barrels on the cargo deck that we had placed there for demo purposes. After I disappeared into the fog, I made a sharp left turn, and the heavy barrels broke loose and slid outboard to the right and off the deck into the slew. Without warning, that force threw me into a violent, nose-high snap roll to the right, which stopped when I was inverted above the slew, and drove me straight down into the murky water. Fortunately, it was about twelve feet down to the mud, where I stopped rather abruptly. Man, it was dark and quiet down there. Pushing the cabin door open against the weight of the water was tough, but you sure have a lot of strength at a time like that. I was about out of breath when I popped up out of the slimy water and swam to shore. Those potential investors declined the opportunity of placing funds with me.

Probably our best shot at goodly development funds came when the Marine Corps expressed interest in the machine. I had briefed it as having good beach-assault potential, with water-to-beach transition in the forty miles-per-hour range. Number seven was capable of easily transporting twenty armed troops, and there was room for nose armament if required. Alternatively, it could have been used as an amphibious, high-speed, command-and-control jeep. We set up on the beach at Camp Pendleton, and in addition to the evaluator, we had a group of enlisted troops looking on. They had been through beach transitions in a navy vehicle known as the Duck. In that vehicle, they sat below the waterline in groups of six, huddled around a diesel turbine and trying not to throw up from the fumes, as they hurtled toward the beach at a maximum speed of six knots. I cranked up for the evaluator, and after a short run down the beach, I skimmed around in the surf, hit the beach, then turned and crossed a deep ocean inlet before reversing course and returning to the evaluator. He was very busy with his notes, and the troops on the shoreline loved us. The Marine Corps eventually opted for a many times larger, and much more expensive and complex Bell Aerospace amphibian. I didn't consider that a defeat, since we were talking different sizes and different operating concepts.

Things were getting mighty skinny on the development cash front when I got a shot across the bow from an unexpected source. A gentleman walked into the office, flashed his identification, and announced himself as a Security and Exchange Commission inspector. I knew that my corporation and I were squeaky-clean, but I also knew his presence meant trouble. Every piece of paper that represented ten years of company history got looked at and questioned, but after many weeks of my being completely on the defense, the results were clear. I was indeed clean, but a member of my board of directors was a crook. He had previously enthusiastically steered development funds our way, but it turned out that he had a record of security violations and fraud wherein he would hit, get caught, con money from someone else to satisfy the Commission's judgments, then run to hit again. At that time we were not yet authorized to sell our stock, and our directors' shares were not saleable. The board member in question had previously brought a nice, retired Asian gentleman and his wife to visit our operation as potential investors. After he left, he doctored up the documents and took all of that gentleman's savings in return for fraudulent stock, leaving the gentleman and his wife destitute. The SEC got him, but as usual, he paid up and moved on to his next target. Not much later a slickly-dressed gent, who looked like he had just left Al Capone's office, showed up looking for our ex-director, and referring to past-due obligations. I often wondered if he found him.

That was all our prime backer and investor could handle, and his financial inputs ceased, despite the fact that we had received two pending orders from the Taiwanese military. It would have taken five million dollars to take that next step, and in the venture capital market of the late 1970s, that cash was not available. I still had a bunch of good ideas, but I couldn't fund them, and I couldn't beat up my family any more. I looked around and there was nobody there but me and $268,000 worth of bills, which took me many years to clear, but I did.

As I was finishing up the ACV battle, incoming President Ronald Reagan was reversing many of outgoing President Jimmy Carter's decisions, and the formerly cancelled B-1 bomber was reemerging as a Rockwell Aircraft development. Rockwell wanted me as a member of their expanding flight test and development program, and I couldn't get on board fast enough. For the first eighteen months, I worked out of the Rockwell facility at Los Angeles International Airport. Then I went back to the desert to be manager of flight-test support at Edwards Air Force Base.

One thing struck me immediately: the basic concept of military aircraft flight-testing had changed dramatically. In earlier years the manufacturer would develop a program and build a prototype to respond to the general requirements set forth by a service such as the air force. If the air force bought the project, the company would build and flight-test additional aircraft, with air force pilots involved in that phase, and offer the finished project to the service. If the service signed on, the company built and delivered the aircraft in the specified quantity.

Things were a lot different by the time I joined the B-1 project. The air force and Rockwell were in it together from the start, with the air force in charge. From a practical standpoint, that worked quite poorly. Air Force Logistics Command, in Dayton, Ohio, put a brigadier general in charge of the project, who then appointed a colonel to be the direct project manager. The colonel running the entire B-1 test program was a nonrated ground-pounder, who had never flown any type of aircraft, but who had an advanced degree in nuclear physics. He was not an advisor: he called the shots, and Rockwell Aircraft and the U.S. Air Force at Edwards danced to his tune. Typical air force assistants calling the shots for individual portions of the program were nonflying lieutenants, with a few captains, who had graduated from college with an ROTC commission and gone through a year of academics at the Air Force Institute of Technology. Try that combination on a Rockwell design engineer with thirty years of practical experience building aircraft and see what happens.

The test-pilot configuration was rigged the same way. The small contingent of air force test pilots were graduates of the Air Force Test Pilot School, and for most of the time I was in the program, their commander was a nonflying colonel, and the Rockwell pilots were subservient to the air force pilots. You didn't have to look far or wait long for a tragic demonstration of the weakness of that system.

One of the air force pilots was a young major who seemed to enjoy infuriating almost anyone who was forced to associate with him. Even though we knew we should avoid him, many of us had been drawn into shouting matches with him, and naturally he always won. The bitterest conflict was between the major and our senior company test pilot. They hated each other. One morning the schedule called for them to fly a test mission together, with the major as pilot and the company man as copilot. They went through a long series of runs at medium altitude with the onboard flight engineer and the ground monitors logging the required numbers. The pilot sat looking out the left cockpit window, repeatedly clicking the nose-trim button to push the nose down, and the copilot sat looking out the right cockpit window. Finished with those runs, they added power to climb to a higher altitude for the next set of test events. Something was wrong: the nose wanted to come up too high. Out of nose-down trim, due to the pilot's previous constant trimming, and with forward control pressure ineffective, they noticed an item on their mission-event cards, strapped to their upper legs. That item had long since directed them to transfer fuel from the rear tanks to the front tanks, which had been steadily going toward empty. Proper switch action could not pump the fuel forward fast enough. They were completely out of balance, and the nose was going up until the aircraft departed control. They punched out just before she went.

The ejection capsule housing the three of them cleared the stricken aircraft as programmed, and the smaller drogue chute deployed to stabilize the capsule and start the slowing process. Small, bullet-shaped explosive squibs were then to fire, separating the drogue chute and allowing the main chute to deploy for descent. The right-hand squib failed to fire, leaving them with a still attached, streaming drogue chute that rolled them to the right. They hit the ground hard, still cocked to the right. The copilot in the right seat was killed, and the other two were severely injured. Cause of the accident: pilot error compounded by material failure (not to mention personal hatred).

When the B-1 production runs had started, I found the flight-test program was no longer of interest. To compound a dull program, several company personnel were now after each other's throats over minute details. After eight years of Rockwell, I was ready to move on, but I was still two years from taking their short retirement plan. I requested and received a transfer to the space program at Palmdale, California, where I was a technical planning advisor involved in the test and checkout program for the Space Shuttle *Endeavor* That was the most detailed work I was ever exposed to, and about as far away from flying your own fighter as you can get and still be involved in aerospace. I put in my two years with all the dedication I could muster, and signed out of Rockwell right on time. I continue to look for new, fun projects.